**OFFICIALLY
DISCARDED**

How to Prosper During the Hard Times Ahead

How to Prosper During the Hard Times Ahead

A Crash Course for the American Family in the Troubled New Millennium

Howard Ruff

Since 1947
**REGNERY
PUBLISHING, INC.**
An Eagle Publishing Company • Washington, DC

Library of Congress Cataloging-in-Publication Data

Ruff, Howard J.
    How to prosper during the hard times ahead : a crash course for the American family in the troubled new millennium / Howard J. Ruff.
        p.   cm.
    Includes index.
    ISBN 0-89526-313-0 (alk. paper)
    1. Finance, Personal. 2. Investments. 3. United States—Economic conditions—1993–   I. Title.
HG179.R784 1998
332.024'01—dc21   98-50851
                                                                                              CIP

Published in the United States by
Regnery Publishing, Inc.
An Eagle Publishing Company
One Massachusetts Avenue, NW
Washington, DC 20001

Distributed to the trade by
National Book Network
4720-A Boston Way
Lanham, MD 20706

Printed on acid-free paper
Manufactured in the United States of America

10 9 8 7 6 5 4 3 2 1

Books are available in quantity for promotional or premium use. Write to Director of Special Sales, Regnery Publishing, Inc., One Massachusetts Avenue, NW, Washington, DC 20001, for information on discounts and terms or call (202) 216-0600.

Contents

Part One:
The Cleansing—Diagnosis and Prognosis

Chapter One   3
The Minefield Ahead

Chapter Two   19
On Little Cat's Feet

Chapter Three   35
Y2k: We Turned Our Lives Over to HAL

Chapter Four   73
Power to the President

Chapter Five   83
When You Have a Hammer in Your Hand,
Everything Looks Like a Nail

Chapter Six   103
Social Security: The Ponzi Chain Letter

Chapter Seven   115
Sin Tax: The Decline and Fall of Western Civilization

Part Two:
Prescription

Chapter Eight   135
Panic Proof

Chapter Nine   161
Gold: $2,000 in 2000?

Chapter Ten   179
Opportunity: Investing for the Year 2000

Part Three:
Making a Brave New World

Chapter Eleven   205
Rebuilding the Shattered American Family

Chapter Twelve   217
Renewing America

Chapter Thirteen   227
Do Thy Patient No Harm

Appendix   239

About the Author   249

Acknowledgments   257

Index   259

Part One

The Cleansing—
Diagnosis and Prognosis

Chapter One

The Minefield Ahead

After almost two decades of unprecedented prosperity, we are now at the intersection of several deadly serious threats to social peace, financial stability, and political continuity.

One of them will hit us on a nonnegotiable schedule, on January 1, 2000. It's the Year 2000 computer crisis, or Y2k. After years of being virtually ignored, Y2k started to get publicity late in the game, finally attracting some of the attention it deserves. Even so, it is now much too late to entirely head off the problem. Y2k will play havoc with our lives, although it is not yet clear how much. Prognosticators disagree over how great the short-term disruptions will be and how long it will take to repair damage to the banks, the power and water companies, and essential government services.

Unfortunately, Y2k is only part of the crisis we face.

Despite the brilliant performance of the economy over the past fifteen years, America is dangerously vulnerable to internal weaknesses just waiting for some precipitating event like Y2k. In fact, Y2k will expose some big, unstable fault lines.

When Rome fell to the barbarians, it came as a surprise to most Romans, who believed Rome was so strong, so stable, so dominant, that it would live forever. But in truth, its social and political

3

foundations had been so weakened—by unrestrained sex and the resulting disintegration of family structures, profligate public spending to buy the political support of the masses with "bread and circuses," a crumbling military, and soft, self-centered upper and middle classes who believed "it can't happen here"—that Rome fell to the barbarians like a ripe plum.

The Romans had conquered and subjugated entire nations of barbarians for almost a thousand years, but when they undermined their fundamental institutions they no longer had the inner strength to weather their crises.

When Y2k hits on January 1, 2000—or even before—the odds are it will slam into the banking and monetary house of cards we have built out of funny cybermoney like Hurricane Hugo hitting the house of the first little pig. In the resulting economic and systemic confusion, what will happen to our fraud of a Social Security system, which depends on earnings from current workers and current low-unemployment to stay afloat? After decades of disintegration some sociologists are finally noticing what some of us have been pointing out for years: the family is the fundamental building block of society, and it has all but collapsed for millions of Americans. We have never weathered a crisis as great as the one we now face with the family in such a weakened condition. All these factors plus the creeping loss of freedom to an ever more powerful government have so weakened us that Y2k could be a fatal blow to the way of life we now take for granted.

Could it really be that bad? The Y2k collision is inevitable, and no American family can entirely avoid the consequences. But there is room for hope on three accounts.

First, we don't really know how badly Y2k itself will hit us. And though I believe we are headed for hard times regardless of Y2k, the size of the Y2k crisis could spell the difference between some rough sledding and real catastrophe.

Second, there are things you can do to protect your family and your finances.

Third, if Y2k does hit us hard, it could turn out to be a cleansing, as it topples some institutions that have defied reform efforts. Wiping the slate clean, Y2k could provide a glorious opportunity to renew America.

There is more than one possible economic scenario, but the most likely one includes a monumental crash of the grossly overinflated stock market. If it hasn't already crashed by the time you read this, a bear market will be precipitated by the Asian economic crisis and assorted related crises, and, if all else fails, it will be precipitated and/or intensified by Y2k. There will be at least a deep worldwide recession, most likely a depression.

Even if the other destructive trends could be slowed or postponed indefinitely, Y2k cannot. It is set in stone. It happens at midnight on New Year's Eve 1999. I believe it will be the single most life-changing economic event of our lifetimes, with the possible exception of World War II, affecting everything from banking to government checks to electric power to the social order.

Because of several destructive trends, the good years we now reflexively assume will continue forever do not have long to live.

The recession or depression will be followed by worldwide inflation that will most likely result from the 747s full of currency the Federal Reserve will be forced to ship to banks. It will be a desperate gamble to stave off the bank runs that are likely to occur due to the Year 2000 computer problem, when depositors become concerned over whether their bank will run out of money or the bank's computers will accurately report and credit their account balances. The Fed has already announced that it has $200 billion in printed currency to meet the expected increased demand for cash from Y2k-spooked depositors, hoping such announcements will preempt a national banking panic.

But even if events don't play out just that way, remember that there is one thing governments know how to do—which is inflate the currency on purpose. I'm not just talking about rising prices.

Throughout history, general price inflation has always been the natural consequence of monetary inflation—creating too much purchasing power in whatever form our money is denominated. When the world is wracked with a recession, stimulating the economy by inflating the currency to create more purchasing power will seem—once again—like the only possible cure, so the currency *will* inflate, and consumer prices will rise. Not inflating and letting the economy slide inexorably by default into the pit of a depression will be politically unthinkable.

History tells us that all paper currencies eventually die. Since Gutenberg invented the printing press, the world has many times been awash in dead paper money. Nations rise and fall—all of them. Nothing made by man is permanent or indestructible, least of all a paper currency pumped out by a corrupt government.

If the government's computers are still able to grind out government benefits, which is not a sure bet in light of Y2k, some of the inflation will be created automatically by the "entitlement programs," the social-spending programs that are on automatic pilot. As more and more people become distressed by the economy and unemployment, tax collections will fall at the same time that government spending soars, creating huge deficits that will have to be papered over by printing money.

In short, it is very likely that the good years we now reflexively assume will continue forever do not have long to live. Powerful economic and social forces are gathering momentum that will come together in the most unpleasant ways.

Because euphoria and optimism have been the order of the day throughout the 1990s, I almost feel like a skunk at a picnic, or the guy who yells "the cops are coming" at the peak of a great party. Well I'm sorry about that because there is even more bad news to tell.

An Old-Fashioned Perspective

You see, I look at the coming crisis from the perspective of an old-fashioned, middle-class, religious, political, and social conservative/libertarian in the Jeffersonian mold. I have always written for the purpose of teaching my family, which at publication includes thirteen children—nine homemade and four adopted as teenagers—and forty-eight grandchildren. My wife, Kay, and I have also raised eighteen foster children, mostly teenagers, for varying lengths of time.

I make no secret of my old-fashioned values. And though some people may think that such values have no place in a discussion of economics or investments, I disagree. The economic crisis of the 1970s, which I predicted and guided people through with my book *How to Prosper During the Coming Bad Years* and my newsletter the *Ruff Times*, was a crisis of values.

I believe passionately in freedom—especially free markets—because history tells us that without free markets, there is no free anything. I believe that the Constitution was a divinely inspired document. I believe that America is being slowly strangled to death by regulation and taxation, and the tax code has made Uncle Sam the biggest shareholder in our businesses, even though he has invested no capital, taken no risks, done no work, and lost no sleep.

I also agree with the old adage that "America is great because America is good. If America ever ceases to be good, America will cease to be great." John Adams said, "Our Constitution was made only for a moral and religious people. It is wholly inadequate to the government of any other." He wasn't talking as much about "church" as about the unique American social contract—the assumption that we Americans would honor our shared values, and that we would be "good" without having to be *forced* to be good by ever more complex and detailed laws and regulations. The Constitution, in fact, was not a body of laws to regulate our lives; it was a blueprint designed to constrain government so we could regulate our own lives.

The foundation of our democratic republic was laid on the bedrock of two unique assumptions: (1) Americans would take care of their own needs and not expect government to take care of them and minutely regulate their lives; and (2) the nuclear family, a stable two-parent structure, would nurture, educate, and prepare each new generation for responsible, independent adulthood. The social purpose of the family is to nurture and protect the young, and to pass on to each generation the wealth, knowledge, traditions, and values of the previous generation. A society that is collectively unable or unwilling to meet those responsibilities is only one generation away from dissolution.

The sexual revolution and the welfare state it enables and exacerbates are direct assaults on that bedrock institution. Unfortunately, it seems that the revolutionaries are winning, as a soaring government-dependent population, unwed couples living together, out-of-wedlock births, babies turned over to marginally educated, minimum-wage day-care providers, and all the associated ills, are rending the fabric of our hitherto stable society. In the wake of the Clinton sex scandals, it seemed terrifying that 64 percent of all Americans polled said that, even after he had confessed his sins—sort of—it didn't really matter. They didn't even care if he had lied about it under oath because it was "only about sex." Syndicated columnist Mona Charen summed it up aptly when she said we had in effect made a pact with the devil: "If Clinton will just keep us prosperous, we won't hold him to any particular moral or ethical standards."

The biggest social problem of our strange times is the illegitimacy rate: 70 percent of all black babies, 40 percent of all Hispanic babies, and 22 percent of all white babies are born without a legal father. Those numbers are double what they were in 1980, and rising. Those single-parent families are the breeding ground for the biggest crime wave in history.

Some 50 percent of all American children will spend at least part of their time in a broken home and grow up believing that what fathers do is abandon their children.

I am no critic of those brave souls who have had to raise children on their own through no fault of their own. My mother was one of them. But as great as she was, I had a hard time learning how to relate to my wife and guide my children because I had no example in my early life. Were it not for Kay, the extraordinary woman I married, and the family-support programs of my church, I would have probably failed as a father and husband.

These social trends have devastating economic consequences. When America survived the Great Depression the American family was strong, with divorce and illegitimacy at historically low levels. We can't say that today.

In the amazing two decades since I published my best-selling book *How to Prosper During the Coming Bad Years*, which sold more than three million copies, I have been an involved and fascinated observer, commenting, advising, and picking investments through a lot of historic events and towering (and not-so-towering) figures on the world stage. Among these have been Ronald Reagan and George Bush; Jimmy Carter (our born-again Christian president) and Bill Clinton (our morally challenged president); the collapse of Soviet-directed international communism; Desert Storm; the personal-computer revolution; 401(k)s and IRAs; hundreds of new and innovative investment and speculative instruments; the rise to political and economic power of the 1960s campus rebels; Democrats becoming born-again deficit hawks; the longest, most profitable bull market in history; soaring divorce and abortion rates; disintegrating schools; the court-sanctioned explosion of pornography; violence, nudity, and explicit sex in the media; an all-out assault on traditional western culture by "intellectuals" from the protected havens of our most prestigious universities; and the voracious appetite of the federal, state, and local governments for more and more of the fruits of your labors.

It is against this soaring social instability and erosion of freedom that we all have to make long-term financial and investment decisions. It's like trying to paint a masterpiece on a vibrating and deteriorating canvas.

In two-and-a-half decades of hard-earned experience, I have learned a great deal. But the bedrock principles I believed in twenty years ago, when I wrote *How to Prosper During the Coming Bad Years*, have been tested by fire, and have proven to be sound.

I still believe we cannot isolate current and future social and political trends from investment decisions, as government and personal ethics and morality affect every corner of our lives, and government spending at all levels is equal to nearly half of the Gross Domestic Product.

The erosion of family endangers the very existence of the institutions we invest in and depend on, especially if we fall for seductive ideas like "it takes a village to raise a child," with "village" really meaning "bureaucrats" and minimum-wage day-care workers.

We do have some room for hope: There are things you can do to protect your family and your finances.

Character and morality still matter in our public officials, even though that seems to have less and less influence on our political choices. Witness Bill Clinton, who has exploited our reflexive reverence for the office of the president to erect a poll- and PR-driven shield against the consequences of his detestable and perverted behavior.

But, despite Bill Clinton, sound principles die hard. There are still eternal, God-given absolute rules for which we will be held accountable in a heavenly judgment—and, if we violate these rules, we will reap a bitter harvest here on earth. God has given man the gift of free agency, but whole civilizations that have abused that gift have fallen because of the collective immoral decisions made by the majority of their citizens. When agency and freedom become license for too many people, the collective society is in deep trouble. When a society so weakened faces a major crisis—the modern equivalent of the barbarians—you cannot bet your life that things will go along as they have before. You must have a plan. You must be prepared. And if you are, you may find that even barbarians offer opportunities.

Forewarned is forearmed. This book has dual objectives, expressed in the title. We face some bad times of indeterminate duration, but they don't have to be bad times for everyone; there are ways to protect yourself and your family, and, indeed, to prosper in spite of the hard times ahead—even *because* of them. And although it is still true that money does not buy happiness, it can buy a lot of physical security in a world where the gap between the haves and the have-nots will widen. Depending on the choices you make right now, the coming years will be either wonderful or terrible. And if Y2k does serve as a cleansing, we will have a great opportunity for renewing America.

Overview

The book is divided into three parts: The Cleansing—Diagnosis and Prognosis; Prescription; and Making a Brave New World.

Part One: The Cleansing—Diagnosis and Prognosis

This chapter and the rest of the chapters in this section offer a sober look at the very real threats we face.

Chapter 2 describes the structural weakness of our banking and money system and the threats to it that may cause a depression or, at the least, a deep recession followed by inflation. We could see a worldwide bear market, a possible banking and monetary crisis, the collapse of foreign economies, a devastating plague of personal and corporate bankruptcies, and the Y2k crisis—the failure on or before January 1, 2000, of unknown numbers of critical computer systems in government, industry, and foreign countries on which we have become totally dependent.

Chapter 3 lays out the Y2k crisis and its consequences. Though we know *when* this will hit, we still don't know *which* systems will be affected and exactly *how* it will affect each of us personally. I have relied on the most respected Y2k experts for guidance on this one.

In Chapter 4 we will examine the extensive powers at the president's disposal to take control in the event of a serious Y2k-caused economic and social crisis, and we will explore their potential threat to constitutional government.

Chapter 5 explains why the very existence of federal regulatory agencies is an all-out assault on your personal freedom and an end-run around the Constitution. You will see how Y2k will affect them and possibly create a silver lining for us, the regulated.

Chapter 6 addresses history's biggest Ponzi scheme—Social Security—and explains just why it is a fraud that would send any CEO to jail if he tried the same trick and why Y2k could be its death knell.

Chapter 7 explores the bitter fruit of the sexual revolution, which is probably the worst and most dangerous long-term trend we will have to cope with. This family-destroying is not a single event like Y2k, but a deeply embedded secular trend that has been undermining America for decades and that will exacerbate the social impact of Y2k.

Collectively, these chapters reveal a superficially healthy nation with deep, hidden fault lines—with an earthquake just waiting to happen.

Part Two: Prescription

Chapter 8 describes in detail how some of the Y2k-created problems in the infrastructure may endanger the delivery of vital supplies, such as food. Just the threat of food shortages in your local supermarket may cause panic and hoarding. You must panic-proof your family; you can't assume the government will bail you out because of your own lack of foresight since an unknown number of its mission-critical computer programs will crash. In fact, the government probably won't be able to cut you a check for your Social Security, pension, tax refund, or welfare payment, or issue food stamps. For a while at least, the government may not be able to maintain safe, efficient airways, or dependably deliver electric power or mail. Vital supplies and services, such as food, electricity, and a host of government services we take for granted may not be delivered as promised. I will show you how to make sure it doesn't hurt you.

Chapter 9 explains how gold and silver will be keys to your economic security—and how and when you should buy them. In Chapter 10 we will examine the terrific business and investment opportunities in both the pre- and post-Y2k years. Some companies will have great advantages over their competitors because they anticipated the Year 2000 computer problem and started preparing for it, and their stocks will reflect their wisdom. Other companies are leading the pack in Y2k remediation services; they will have all the business they can handle and will be terrific investments in 1999 and beyond.

Chapter 10 also lays out ways to enrich yourself from falling stock markets. Many investments will be on the bargain counter, while some of today's most popular ones will be as dangerous as coiled rattlesnakes.

Part Three: Making a Brave New World

My keys to remaining prosperous are rooted in some old-fashioned ideas, all centered around universal spiritual principles and the family. Because you probably won't be able to depend on the government and other support structures, the family will be your main source of financial, emotional, and spiritual support, and Chapter 11 offers a plan to help organize, strengthen, and nurture that family-support unit. Like the little boy who found a pile of manure under the Christmas tree and was convinced there was a pony in there somewhere, I am an optimist, but a realistic one. I believe we can prepare for tough times, and even prosper from them, and the family is the key.

Unlike some of the real head-for-the-hills-because-all-is-lost prophets of doom, I am *not* predicting that the worst case is an absolute certainty, but I believe I can make a case that the coming years will be watershed years, with lifestyle-changing events that will affect everyone, even though their exact dimensions are impossible to predict at this point in time. In light of the tumultuous nature of the years ahead—and the potent threats to our stability—Chapter 12 offers a politically doable plan to renew America.

I take no pleasure in some of these forecasts. If I am wrong, and life continues as before, I will lead the cheering. Remember my forty-eight (and still counting) grandchildren? I want the best for them. That's why I am politically active, not as a candidate but as an opinion-maker through the *Ruff Times*, this book, and my full-time political offices in Washington. Although I am political, I am not particularly partisan; I care about principles, not parties. I want a freer world that goes back to America's constitutional roots.

Jonah is one of my heroes, the prototype prophet of doom. If you remember your Sunday school lessons, you may recall that God told Jonah to go to Ninevah and tell the people they would be destroyed because of their wickedness. Jonah didn't want to go to Ninevah, so he tried to go elsewhere and had some interesting adventures. After being literally thrown up onto the beach, he got the message and told Ninevah of its impending destruction. To his amazement, everyone from the king on down believed Jonah and repented in "sackcloth and ashes" (whatever that is), so the Lord did not destroy Ninevah. This offended Jonah, who felt his credibility was at stake, so he told God, "Destroy them!" When God refused, Jonah was never heard from again.

I conclude from this story that the function of a prophet of doom is to help prevent the doom he prophesies. It is an honorable profession.

A Real Adult

I am different from most other financial advisors, in several respects.

First, I am seasoned, both in respect to the markets and to life. I can identify with you. I do not live in or prognosticate from an ivory tower.

My wife Kay and I are in our sixties, and have raised a close-knit, loving family of successful, happy offspring. Because of the wide age span between the oldest (forty-three) and the youngest (sixteen) we have raised children during five of the most socially volatile decades in American history, and until our youngest, Terri, leaves the nest in three or four years to marry some brave and intrepid (and perhaps unsuspecting) young man, we aren't through yet.

Second, professionally I've been an interested commentator on our times for almost a quarter of a century, through inflation, disinflation, bull and bear markets, panic, and euphoria. I've been right often enough throughout to have a hard core of thousands of subscribers who have been loyal readers for years.

Third, as a businessman, I've started several companies. Some did well, and some of them bombed. I know what it is like to succeed and to fail. Those failures were an important part of the education of a financial advisor.

Not only can you avoid trouble, but you can even prosper in the volatile years ahead.

A dear friend of mine, Art Linkletter, is one of the shrewdest, most successful entertainers and investors to come out of Hollywood. He told me, "Howard, I've been in a lot of business deals, some of which were fabulously successful, and some of which failed. I honestly can't even remember what some of the successes did, but I can tell you everything about the ones that failed! I learned very little from the successes. Most of what I know, I learned from the failures."

Exactly.

Early on in my learning curve, back in 1968, I was forced into bankruptcy with business debts in excess of $500,000. Because of my old-fashioned religious heritage, I chose to devote the rest of my life, if necessary, to paying them off as an example to my children and for my own peace of mind. Although it took me twelve years (with interest), it was the best business decision I ever made. After such a traumatic failure, I was tempted to settle for a J-O-B. But then I would have never been able to earn enough money to pay off those debts. I had to remain an entrepreneur and get rich. It was shortly afterward that I decided to publish a financial newsletter to share my hard-earned and painful knowledge, which led to greater prosperity than we had ever experienced, as well as a clear conscience and new depths of tenacity.

As a practicing Christian (and I intend to keep practicing until I get it right), I have a deep and functional faith in the God who manages the universe while being acutely aware of the falling sparrow. I believe we are His children, created in His image, and He has a keen interest in people and nations. I have had miraculous spiritual experiences in my personal life that leave me no room for doubt. I also know from painful personal experience that when we, individually or collectively, reject His counsel and break His commandments, misery is the inevitable long-run result, since sin (an out-of-fashion but still valid word) has never brought happiness. Today when sinners get caught, they call it a "mistake." Sinful practices are called "sicknesses," which too often is just a way to dodge responsibility for our behavior. When age-old sin becomes the socially accepted norm, rather than the detestable aberration of a comparative few, the whole society is in jeopardy.

Sometimes when I leave my haven in peaceful, stodgy Utah to visit New York or San Francisco or Hong Kong or Bangkok or Los Angeles, I am reminded of the statement by Gary North, a newsletter-editor colleague. After taking a night-life bus tour of San Francisco on his first visit there, he said, "If God doesn't destroy this city, He owes Sodom and Gomorrah an apology."

To my sorrow, I have sometimes failed to live up to my own professed standards, but I try. I am an experienced repenter.

I have never lost my enthusiasm and zest for life, or my sense of humor (although my offspring have serious reservations about the quality of the jokes). There will be moments of off-the-wall humor in these pages, usually to illustrate a point, sometimes just to see if you are awake. This may be a serious book, but I can promise you it won't be grim.

A Word of Caution

Any book can only be a snapshot of the world as it was when the book was turned over to the publisher. This book won't hit the stores for at least three months after I finish writing it, and it could be years before you discover and read it. Because forecasting the climate is easier than forecasting the weather, I expect the principles to stay valid for years, but circumstances and details can and will change.

Some of the investments recommended in these pages may have been rendered obsolete by time. They may have risen too far to be good buys, or I may have found better places for your money. The markets are not a snapshot, but a passing parade, and things do change. Nothing is always a good buy, regardless of price.

To help keep current you can get a one-time-only current report on the status of the book's recommendations (updated monthly) by sending in the postage-paid card enclosed in this book, or by writing to me at P.O. Box 887, Springville, Utah 84663. You can also e-mail me at howard@rufftimes.com or check out my web site at <www.rufftimes.com>. Or you can subscribe to my newsletter, the *Ruff Times*, which will update you every three weeks.

Self-Interest

From time to time, I have recommended a company's stock or services when I have a personal financial or other interest in the company. Liberty Mint, a company founded by my oldest son, Larry, falls into that category. I am a shareholder and have been able to influence the company to develop products or services I feel can help my readers. But my self-interest is always fully disclosed so you can decide how much weight to place on my enthusiasm.

Also, for personal financial reasons unrelated to the outlook of the companies, I may from time to time trade the other investments I recommend in the book, although, for the most part, I am a buy-and-hold investor in companies I believe in.

We once analyzed my recommendations over a period of three years, assumed we had invested $1,000 in each of them, and measured the results. We found that I had been right about two-thirds of the time. The average gain was 23 percent, while the average loss was only 9 percent. The average holding period was six months. This compares favorably with the best records in the investment industry. My record has been remarkably consistent over the years.

I use a "stop-loss" system to protect you against big losses, based on the principle that "he who refuses to take small losses will take big losses." I will teach you how to do this in Chapter 10.

To get the best results from my advice, you need to get those odds on your side by setting up a *Ruff Times* portfolio that includes *all* of my recommendations. If you do, the odds are two out of three that you will make good money in the aggregate. If you just pick and choose the ones that meet your fancy, your results will be totally unpredictable.

So much for the preliminaries; let's get down to business. There is no time to waste!

As the title suggests, this book is written not just to warn you of trouble but to help you to prosper in the volatile years ahead. It is also written to teach you some real-world facts of life about how the world really works in terms any high-school graduate can understand. If you take it to heart, it can be the starting point of an education on money, technology, economics, investment, and having a sound and successful family life as a bulwark against the troubled new millennium.

Chapter Two

On Little Cat's Feet

B ack in 1977, shortly after I started my newsletter, the *Ruff Times*, we moved to Modesto, California. To draw attention to my new publishing business, I was willing to address any group, anywhere, no matter how few in number.

Invited to speak to a group of doctors in Grass Valley, California, I headed up I-80 into the Sierra Nevada mountains on a beautiful fall day. But as I got past the foothills and started up the steeper incline toward Donner Pass, the freeway narrowed to one lane due to construction, and I was caught behind a big diesel rig that slowed down to a crawl as we started up a steep hill. Finally, the truck struggled off the road at a turnoff.

Wanting to be a good samaritan, I pulled off the road behind him and climbed out of my car to offer assistance. But the driver—a huge man, about three feet thick—began walking back toward me, taking what looked like practice swings with a baseball bat.

Discretion being the better part of valor, I dove back into my car, ready to take off, but, paying no attention to me, the driver went to the back of his truck and started pounding on the big double-doors with his bat. Apparently this had happened before because there were dents all over the doors and the paint had mostly chipped off.

After a moment or two of furious pounding, he suddenly turned around and sprinted back to the cab with amazing agility for a man his size, jumped in, and took off up the hill like a scalded cat.

Overcome with curiosity, I followed him, and sure enough, on the next hill, the truck ground to a near halt and pulled off to the side of the road, and while I watched from a safe distance, the driver did it again.

This strange rite was repeated twice more before he pulled off near my turnoff to Grass Valley. This time, however, I pulled up next to the cab. As he jumped out, I yelled at him from the safety of my car, "What are you doing? I've seen you do this three times now."

"It's none of your business, buddy."

"I don't care! I've got to know!"

"Do you promise not to tell anyone?"

"Sure!"

"Well, you see, I'm on my way to Reno with a truckload of chickens. This is a ten-ton truck, and I've got fifteen tons of chickens. If I can't keep a third of them flying, I'm not going to make it up this hill."

This somewhat silly fable illustrates a very serious point: If what everyone else is doing isn't working, try something else, and don't worry what anybody thinks. Sometimes the unorthodox is just the conventional wisdom a bit early. All that matters is results.

We are rapidly approaching times unlike anything we have seen in our lifetimes. If you adapt to these strange times in advance before everyone else gets the message, and do the strange things that someday will be mainstream behavior but now look and feel like oddball stuff, you will not only get through the transition years without difficulty, but you can prosper—and may even get very rich.

Social and market volatility are the entrepreneur's friends. They're also the investor's friends if he understands what's happening and has the temperament to adapt to it. And we will see volatility in spades.

Until it's too late, however, most people on Wall Street and Main Street will assume that the world will roll on forever as before, and that the things they've always done with their lives and their money will continue to work as well as or better than they did before, and every downturn in the market will be perceived as really an opportunity to double their bet.

The coming changes will be painful for you if you are unprepared and inflexible.

These people will be sucked in and clobbered. Their families may be devastated and bewildered by a world whose changes may not be fully apparent for months and may last for years, or even decades.

Dramatic changes don't always come preceded by trumpets like earthquakes, avalanches, and tornadoes. Sometimes they sneak up on us on little cat's feet.

I have two kitties in my home, one of whom owns me and insists on sharing my computer keyboard. But because she approaches so quietly, I never know she's there until she has pounced on my keyboard, creatively adding to my writing or just deleting my last two paragraphs. She does it every day, so you'd think I would be ready for it, wouldn't you? Not so. She always surprises me.

The coming events that will change your life are like my kitty. They are sneaking up on little cat's feet on all those who have ignored reality, don't have the knowledge base to recognize the signs, are not paying attention, or assume people like me are merely crying wolf. Of course we are, but there are real wolves out there. Most people, especially if they reside on Wall Street, don't believe in wolves or believe they've got more than enough time to prepare for an attack.

A lot of Romans probably thought the barbarians were a minor and temporary inconvenience.

I have been called a Cassandra. That is an honorable title. Cassandra was the mythical Greek oracle who was never believed but whose unpleasant prophecies always came true.

The Vulnerable Society

The coming changes will be painful for you if you are unprepared and inflexible. Some of them will seem sudden and surprising, though their roots were planted decades ago. But for those who are informed and ready, it will be a chance to cleanse the errors of the past and to write new lives on a clean slate. And there will be mouth-watering opportunities.

Because of the complexity of these issues, we can't predict exactly what will happen down to the last detail or date; there are still too many unknowns. Some of the problems are a 100 percent certainty, and others are high probabilities that are already written in America's appointment book.

Give me a chance to make my case, then you decide.

Ruffonomics 101:
The Real Truth About Money

Before I can do a credible job of explaining why the scenarios I predict are so likely to hurt us, I need to explain the true nature of money because it is the most vulnerable link in the chain of your everyday life. It is the key card in our economic and social house of cards. It is also the most vulnerable to Y2k.

Money is something you take for granted, like air and water. It just *is*.

One philosopher has said that money is an idea backed by confidence. He's right. And that's *all* it is. And although that's certainly true of paper currency, it is doubly true of the computer "cyber-money" I will describe in a moment—the money that now is an inseparable part of your life. Once that confidence is shattered, money could, and just might, disappear like smoke in a high wind. Its stability, availability, and acceptability depend totally on the stability of the banking system, because the banks create it, keep track of it for you, and store it until you ask for it.

The so-called "money supply" is just computer-generated numbers on your bank statement. If the banks' computers are unable to account for it or give you cash on demand or the ATM doesn't work, shattering our confidence in the banks, the psychology of money that sustains the system is destroyed, and much of your money will become worthless as a means of exchange or a store of value.

As we shall see, the odds are that by the turn of the century—and the millennium—our money as we know it will be breathing its last. This problem isn't just America's, but rather it affects all paper- and computer-based currencies because a large number of the world's bank computers are headed for big-time trouble due to the Year 2000 computer crisis, the so-called Millennium Bug.

To complicate the issue, even if your bank swats its Millennium Bugs before the drop-dead failure date on January 1, 2000, the computers in the system that aren't repaired and aren't known to be Y2k compliant will have to be isolated from interfacing with other banks, and the monetary system will be severely crippled. Chapter 3 will explain why and how.

What Is Money?

I'll bet you thought you knew what money is. You probably don't.

Money makes it possible for people in a society to specialize in doing whatever their talents or inclinations lead them to do.

Long before money, we conducted commerce by barter. If you made shoes and I raised corn, and I wanted shoes and you wanted corn, we would exchange the fruits of our labors to our mutual satisfaction. However, if I wanted shoes but you didn't want or need any corn, we had a problem. Of course, if you wanted a hat, maybe I knew someone who made hats who wanted corn, so we would do a three-cornered trade.

It doesn't take a lot of imagination to realize that as society became more and more specialized the barter system became so complicated and cumbersome that it broke down. We needed some universally accepted means of exchange that would also serve as a store of value. This was especially important to those who produced perishable or seasonal commodities.

Alchemy Part One: Turning Gold into Paper

Gold and, to a lesser extent, silver were a natural solution. Gold was rare enough that the supply was relatively limited (even today, all the gold ever mined would fit into a cube less than fifty feet square). It was inherently beautiful. It was soft and malleable enough that you could pound it into a sheet so thin that light would pass through it, or stretch it into a thread so thin it was invisible to the naked eye. Because of those qualities, society after society throughout history has settled on gold as its real money. The first time I hefted a one-ounce gold Krugerrand in my hand, I understood why people had killed for it.

Now the shoemaker could sell his shoes to those who didn't have something he needed right then, because he could keep the gold until he needed something, confident that it would hold its value. Once it became a medium of exchange, gold became a store of value.

So how did we end up with green ink on paper?

The world monetary system that evolved out of gold is now a fragile edifice built on a shaky foundation of debt and trust— remember, it's "an idea backed by confidence."

Only 4 percent of the U.S. currency is minted, printed, or coined. The rest is merely computer entries in banks. The economists call this "fiat money." "Fiat" is Latin for "command," and fiat money is money with no intrinsic value, which is money only because the government says it is money. But even if the government says it is money, its value depends on people's confidence in it, and that depends on the health of the banks that create it.

Yes, that's right. Banks create money. Most people think the government creates our money. It is true that it prints our currency and mints our coins, but remember, that's only 4 percent of the currency in circulation. Banks, regulated by the Federal Reserve, create the rest of the money on their computers.

The Banking System's Shady Past: Money Out of Nothing

When money was gold and silver, minted into coins to measure its weight and value conveniently, the purchasing power of money was stable, and everyone knew precisely what that value was. But money eventually turned into something else, and the story is instructive. I will probably oversimplify a very complicated story to make my point clear.

Gold and silver were quickly controlled by the governments that issued the money, created the coins, stamped the head of their emperors or gods on them, and used them to buy goods and services from citizens, thus putting them into circulation.

But those who accumulated wealth had to do something with their money, and storing it in a cabinet in the castle was relatively inconvenient and not too secure. Keeping it in large gold or silver bars was a more efficient method of storage, but it was hard to bite off just the right-sized piece when you wanted to spend it.

Eventually a class of merchants arose that offered to store people's money in a secure warehouse for a fee. The owner of the gold in the warehouse was then given a receipt, testifying that "Julius Nausea has two hundred ounces of gold on deposit, which can be withdrawn on demand by the bearer of this receipt."

It was inevitable that, rather than having to go down to the warehouse to show their receipt and draw out gold or silver to buy something, the gold-owners would simply exchange the receipts for the goods they wanted. Once the printing press was invented, it was a natural evolution to issue, rather than one big "bearer" receipt, a bunch of smaller receipts to use for smaller purchases. This greatly increased the flexibility and usability of the receipts. Eventually, people became so accustomed to using the receipts in lieu of real money that they began to think of the receipts as money, and the modern paper-money system was created, basically as warehouse receipts for gold or silver in storage.

Then some warehouse merchant got a bright idea about how to become richer. He knew that at no one time did all depositors ask for all their gold, so he began issuing more receipts than there was gold in the warehouse in the form of loans, always keeping enough "in reserve" to meet expected demands for withdrawals. This was the first "fractional-reserve" banking system.

At first, the warehouse owners were cheating when they did it, but eventually it became common knowledge and a universal practice. Of course, whereas depositors used to have to pay the warehouse owners a fee to store their gold, the depositors now said, "If you're going to make money on my gold, I want you to pay me to store my gold in your warehouse." If the warehouse owner—now we can call him a banker—issued too many receipts, word got out, and people got nervous and started asking for their gold by presenting their receipts to be redeemed in gold, creating "a run on the bank" that could cause the bank to fail.

Our monetary system is a house of cards that depends entirely on confidence in the banking system, and we could well see a crisis in confidence.

After the invention of the printing press, all modern-era money was issued by banks. The warehouse receipts were called "bank notes," and were redeemable in gold or silver. But when bank panics occurred and runs on the bank became epidemic, we had widespread bank failures. There was a rash of them in the 1830s and the 1930s.

Sooner or later, using the excuse of "preventing panics," governments turned the issuance of currency into government monopolies. Eventually people completely lost sight of the connection between gold in the warehouse and the paper they were using. Today, rather than being a note redeemable in anything, our paper money is exchangeable only for goods and services.

Pull a bill out of your wallet. What does it say? "This note is legal tender for all debts, public and private." Even though it says on the bill it is a Federal Reserve "note," it is redeemable in nothing tangible. Try going to the bank and saying, "I want to call my note." Big laugh!

The final two steps in detaching money from gold occurred when (1) President Franklin D. Roosevelt called in all the gold in the 1930s and prohibited U.S. citizens from owning gold, and (2) Richard Nixon "closed the gold window" so that even foreign countries would not be able to exchange their greenbacks for gold at the Federal Reserve.

Money had evolved from gold, to paper warehouse receipts for gold, to paper with no gold in the warehouse—and the common denominator that made all this work was public confidence.

Alchemy Part Two: Turning Paper into Cybermoney

Computers then made possible the final leap; money became just a computer entry with little relationship to the paper currency—and that's where we are today. And therein lies the reason why mass computer failures that will result from the Year 2000 computer crisis could strike a fatal blow at the whole monetary system—because bank computers *are* the monetary system.

Let's back up for a moment.

At the present time, banks maintain no gold reserves, and they print no currency. They have to maintain only about a 20 percent cash reserve against withdrawals. The monetary reserves at the Fed are the receipts themselves—plus debt. The bank reserve requirement is set by the Fed, and the banks literally create money at will, within the parameters set by the Fed, without printing anything other than your bank statements.

Grossly oversimplified, here's how it works. Let's say you put $1,000 in the bank. You can now say, "I have $1,000 in the bank." But the bank doesn't just put your money in the vault and keep it safe for you. It is paying you interest, so it has to put your money to work making money. Under the present reserve requirements, it can lend out $800 of your money.

If your neighbor goes into the bank to borrow some money, the bank would say, "We can loan you $800. We'll deposit the $800 into your account."

At that moment, you have $1,000 in the bank, and your neighbor has $800, so your $1,000 has grown into $1,800, and no one has minted or printed any new currency.

Your neighbor then spends his $800, and it ends up in other people's checking accounts, which those banks can also use as reserves to lend money—up to 80 cents on the dollar—and this continues on until only about 4 percent of the money supply is actually minted, printed, or coined. The other 96 percent is phantom money, consisting of computer bookkeeping entries backed by debt.

Michael S. Hyatt, in his fine book, *The Millennium Bug* (Regnery, 888-219-4747), points out that this works just fine as long as the money never leaves the banking system, at least permanently. Even if you get it from your neighborhood ATM, it goes back into the system when you spend it because it gets redeposited in someone else's bank account. When you deposit your paycheck, Hyatt says, "A computer debits your employer's account and credits yours. The same thing happens when you write a check to the telephone company. Credits and debits flow back and forth within the banking system, but nothing ever leaves it. Therefore the fraud, the inverted pyramid, remains hidden from view."

Hyatt explains how the government prints just enough money to support the usual demands for cash. The system is completely unprepared for widespread excessive demands for cash. I know it sounds like something is wrong with all that, but that's exactly how it works.

Hold that thought—the 4 percent actually printed. It will become relevant later in the chapter.

Despite the oversimplification, the principles are correct, and this is why our monetary system is a house of cards. It depends entirely on confidence in the banking system. As long as everyone believes his money is safe in the bank, and he can get it whenever he wants, *your* money *is* safe.

But what if a catastrophic event casts serious doubts on the safety and solvency of the banks and too many people want their money? Could that happen, and if so, what would it be?

A lot of things will happen to change your life between now and January 1, 2000, and although the timing of these other events is difficult to forecast, the Year 2000 Millennium Bug problem will arrive exactly on schedule. That's the day when all the old, uncorrected, date-sensitive software programs that run the world choke on the two zeros that represent the year 2000, since most of their software is programmed to recognize two-digit years in lieu of four-digit years. Computers will then either quit operating (crash), or simply assume it's 1900, and start canceling your Social Security payment because you haven't even been born yet, or will mess up your bank interest or account balance, or not send you your tax refund, or cancel your flight or insurance policies, or....

We face several life-changing events that could lead to big-time trouble, rooted in systemic weaknesses.

Thousands of those computer programs are date-sensitive, and no one magic bullet will fix them. Worldwide, it will take more than 750,000 qualified programmers and systems engineers trained in obsolete programming languages three years to do the job, line-of-code by line-of-code, but there are only about 250,000 such technicians.

Despite huge expenditures and crash efforts, many banks, especially small- and medium-sized banks, will not be ready simply because they started with too little too late. Unfortunately, we don't know which banks will not be ready.

Sometime before the deadline, Y2k awareness will percolate down into the consciousness of enough Americans that large numbers of them will decide they want to turn their computer entries into what they consider real money, and the lines will begin to form at the tellers' windows.

When the cash is gone (just 4 percent of the money supply, remember), the bank will shut its doors, and the real banking panic will begin. The cybermoney, being inaccessible, has effectively disappeared.

I will expand on this in Chapter 3 and explain why the Y2k problem is set in stone and why thousands of the computer programs you depend on will not be repaired in time.

Wolves

Y2k isn't my only concern. I believe several life-changing events are potential precipitants leading to big-time trouble, rooted in systemic weaknesses.

1) The stock-market bubble: The grossly overvalued Clinton stock-market bubble will burst, possibly even before you read this book.

In the 1990s the stock market has gone way beyond every traditional measurement of value, sending us into totally uncharted waters. In the past, whenever the market reached even much less extreme levels of price-earning ratios and the other assorted measures of value, it retreated dramatically, but this time it sailed right on, like a hot knife through butter. Then in the late summer of 1998 the market began to dip, but it soared again in November and into December. The yo-yoing was just a sign of the stock market's volatility.

And who is making the crucial buy/sell decisions? Most of those who manage America's money are so young that they have never been through a bear market before, and they think they never will. Eighty percent of them weren't even brokers yet during the last bear market in 1987. They have known only prosperity, and they believe their only job is to find clients, put them into stocks, and buy on every dip in the market. They are a panic just waiting to happen.

History tells us that such market excesses result in bigger and bigger bubbles with thinner skins and more vulnerability to popping. The bigger the bubble, the louder the pop, and the overreaction on the downside is proportionate to the excessive overvaluation on the upside. The Dow Jones Industrials would have to fall 40 to

70 percent from the 9,000 level, at which it stands as this is written, just to return to *average* levels of valuation.

So the first great potential tear in the fabric of your life that should concern you is the collapse of the simple gross overvaluation of the American stock market.

There has been huge price inflation in the equity markets. All excessive price inflations end in collapse. They usually fall of their own weight, and the precipitating event is totally unpredictable.

2) Recession: One precipitating event could be the inevitable downturn of the economy. As this is written, we are near the end of an eight-year boom. And if you discount the minor recession in 1989, the economy has been in a continual boom since the Reagan tax cuts pulled us out of an incipient depression in the early 1980s. That's almost sixteen years! This is so unprecedented that it took the collapse of the Soviet Union and the end of the Cold War— also the handiwork of Ronald Reagan—to keep it rolling.

Like bull markets, economic booms can and do die of old age, and so will this one.

Will a dying bull market cause a recession, or will a recession cause a bear market? I don't know, and I don't think anyone else does either. But history tells us they both will end sooner or later. And the older they are, the closer the end.

3) The Asian economic crisis: Asian countries created huge overvaluations of their stocks, their real estate, and their businesses, as well as huge manufacturing overcapacity to satisfy what they thought would be insatiable, ever-growing worldwide demand for their products, especially in the United States.

Japan is a classic example. If it hasn't broken down by the time you read this, it will soon, for it is a national game of dominos, with all of its elements interconnected and interdependent in a unique way.

Traditionally, Japanese banks own stocks of the companies they do business with, and those companies own stocks of the banks that service them. Major companies own stocks of their suppliers, who own stocks of the companies they supply. The Japanese have a high cultural tolerance for insider trading, stock manipulation, and other things that would send an American CEO to jail, precisely because it has worked for them so far, and they see no reason to rock that boat.

But as this is written, some of Japan's biggest banks and broker-age houses are in desperate shape, and its once grossly overvalued real estate market has imploded. If a couple of big ones go down, they *all* go down.

China, despite the huge growth of its free-market sector, is still rotten to the core because of the incompatible marriage of a repres-sive communist regime and a wild-west, gun-slinging, entrepre-neurial circus, often run by criminals with no body of established commercial law to restrain them.

China also faces serious shortages of electricity, water, and food, and a younger generation that cares less and less about the opinions of its communist masters. In the long run this is good, but in the short run it will send out ripples, then waves that will hurt everyone in the world.

The breakdown of other Asian economies and markets will also send out economic tsunamis that will crash against our shores. World economies have become dangerously interdependent in the last two decades. The stocks of many of our biggest companies trade on foreign markets and are owned by foreign investors. We also trade the stocks of many of the biggest foreign companies on our exchanges. Our biggest corporations, moreover, depend more and more heavily on foreign sales, buy commodities overseas, or actually do their manufacturing abroad. Most of our biggest banks are now truly citizens of the world, deriving more than half of their profits abroad.

Ready for Y2k?

The biggest complication for the foreign markets is that their governments and major corporations will not be ready for Y2k. Some 20 to 30 percent of American corporations will not be ready, which is bad enough, but Europe, because it has devoted almost all its programming resources to be ready for the Euro (the new European currency), is way behind the United States in readiness. And Asia is way behind Europe.

This means that stock markets in Japan, Taiwan, Hong Kong, Singapore, Indonesia, and so on—which are huge and collectively have almost overtaken the U.S. stock market in volume and importance—will effectively be shut out of the international market and monetary system. One of the biggest problems with Y2k is that even if you are Y2k compliant but the other computers with which your mainframe interfaces are not, their bad data will corrupt yours. Y2k-compliant companies will be forced to refuse to let their computers have an electronic handshake with their foreign counterparts; this is especially true of their stock and commodity exchanges.

After January 1, 2000, it is nearly certain that most foreign stock markets will no longer be able to be accessed with a keystroke. International equity trading and money management will simply be unable to occur at the speed of light.

In August 1998 I watched Alan Greenspan on C-Span as he told the Senate Finance Committee that because of Y2k the whole interdependent system of international payments is "at risk."

In our computerized world, billions of dollars can and do move around the world from computer to computer in a nanosecond with a keystroke on a keyboard. But after January 1, 2000, this seemingly simple transaction will be impossible if the sending computer and the receiving computer are not both Y2k compliant.

Disappearing Wealth

What if, as a result of Y2k, the breakdown of the Asian markets, the popping of the stock-market balloon, or some other catastrophe, wealth as defined by personal balance sheets disappears by the billions—or trillions?

What if it finally dawns on the American people that their banks' computers may not be able to report their account balances accurately, and start asking for their money back?

What if their demands for currency exceed the amount of currency on hand at the bank?

What if tens of millions of people start to see Y2k coming? And as the fateful day draws near, you can bet there will be a rising tide of Y2k publicity.

I have personally seen the mountains of printed money at the Bureau of Engraving and Printing that can be shipped all over the country to meet the demands for liquid cash. The Federal Reserve announced in August 1998 that it was printing $200 billion in currency (up from the previous $150 billion) to meet Y2k-inspired demands for cash at the tellers' windows. The Fed is betting on three things: (1) People will get nervous and want to withdraw their money "just in case"; (2) such announcements will be oil on troubled waters, preventing panic and forestalling bank runs; and (3) $200 billion is enough.

But $200 billion is no more than a fig leaf to persuade the American people that it is not necessary for them to go withdraw their money. In a real panic, that fig leaf could be gone in a few hours.

Personally, I intend to be out of all paper assets and heavy into gold at that time, since I believe that some of the scared money coming out of banks and paper assets will go into gold, driving the price out of sight.

Money is an idea backed by confidence? Sure, and I believe a crisis of confidence is a high probability.

Chapter Three

Y2k: We Turned Our Lives Over to HAL

In the classic science-fiction movie *2001: A Space Odyssey*, HAL, the computer on a Jupiter-bound spaceship ("HAL" is just one letter off from "IBM"), had a cybernetic nervous breakdown. The crew members had to disable him to save themselves because they were totally dependent on HAL. He ran everything on the ship, including life support, and if he malfunctioned, they were doomed.

Incredibly, life is imitating art, and the real-world 2001 HAL crisis may arrive a year ahead of schedule, on January 1, 2000. And we will see the early signs of HAL's neurosis in the last half of 1999. It's called the Year 2000 computer crisis, or Y2k for short.

Starting in July 1999 and climaxing on January 1, 2000—with financial aftershocks that may rock the civilized world for years, maybe for more than a decade—we will experience what might be the most unthinkable, amazing problem faced by civilization in our lifetimes, and we did it to ourselves. And that schedule is fixed and nonnegotiable.

It will attack us where we are weakest, exposing the hidden fault lines in civilization's infrastructure, endangering government finances and services, private businesses, your personal life, your job, and the peace and tranquility of the American way of life.

Over the last several decades, we have allowed ourselves to become totally dependent on computer programs, including some that most of us hardly even know exist. Because of a silly little glitch that grew into a ticking time bomb over the years, many of these computers will fail. They might just crash, freeze up, or start spouting gibberish. Many will be repaired on time, but as many as half of them are so far behind schedule that they probably won't. The problem is that we don't yet know exactly which ones will not be ready.

Y2k will attack us where we are weakest, exposing the hidden fault lines in civilization's infrastructure.

Y2k is the precipitating event that will attack us at our weakest points—the banking and monetary system and government regulatory and revenue-collecting agencies—and will especially hurt those without secure family support systems.

In the best-case scenario, Y2k will cause a worldwide recession; a grisly bear market in U.S. stocks; unpredictable, sporadic disruptions of government services and benefits; a rash of corporate and personal bankruptcies; and a collapse of the foreign stock and bond markets.

In an intermediate case, the result will be a worldwide depression for some unknown period of time, while much of the cybernetic superstructure that supports our modern lives either grinds to a halt or limps lamely into the next millennium.

And if the real pessimists are right, we will be back in the horse-and-buggy days for years, only without horses or buggies.

This is not just a doom-and-gloom fantasy. It's serious stuff—so serious that when I first heard about it from some of my newsletter-publisher competitors, I thought that it wasn't HAL who had gone bonkers, but my colleagues.

The problem, as you may well know by now, is that, when these computer programs were designed twenty or thirty years ago, a flaw was built into them that seemed eminently reasonable at the time, and the programmers thought it would never cause problems because in their wildest dreams they never thought we would be using these same programs when the year 2000 rolled around. Over time, these faulty programming techniques became the accepted practice and are, incredibly, still in use today by some short-sighted programmers.

The June 8, 1998, issue of *U.S. News and World Report* explained why:

> Ironically, one reason the Y2k bug has survived is the concept of "backward compatibility," which was introduced in the 1960s to bring order to computer development. IBM and other computer companies, realizing they couldn't expect clients to buy new software every model year, made sure each new model was largely compatible with earlier programs. That, however, created an environment in which the old Y2k bugs have been able to worm their way—program by program—into the most modern equipment.

Hundreds of billions of dollars are now being spent in a race against time to root out and repair the glitches, but many institutions will lose the race. If they weren't well along on their repairs by the end of 1998, they will *not* be ready when the clock rolls over into the new millennium.

"But," I hear you say, "I don't even have a computer in my home. This doesn't affect me."

Wrong—fatally wrong—for two reasons.

First, you probably have dozens—maybe hundreds—of microcomputers in your home or office. Almost every electrical device in your home is controlled by these miraculous microchips—and they may not be Y2k compliant.

Second, the infrastructure that delivers your electricity, your telephone calls, your water, the food to your market, your Social Security check, your Medicare benefits, your tax refund, the parts and components needed by the plant where you work, your medical care, your airline trips—all these are run by what in many cases are flawed and vulnerable computer programs.

Given time and personnel, all of them could be fixed, but we have acute shortages of both time and personnel. Based on the best estimates, it is logistically impossible to fix even half of them before the inexorable, nonnegotiable deadline, because there are tens of thousands of programs to be checked, with trillions of lines of code. Worse, there are more than 50 billion embedded chips, and 1 percent to 2 percent of those chips—500 million to 1 billion of them—are date-sensitive and must be examined laboriously one at a time and replaced or reprogrammed.

"Malfunction" will be the operative word on that fateful day.

Have you ever been frustrated by calling a merchant or an institution and hearing an operator or a recording saying, "Sorry, our computers are down. Please call back later"? On January 1, 2000, millions of callers will hear that message—that is, if the phone company's computer isn't down and you get a dial tone.

And what about those microcomputers you didn't even know you had? They run your digital watch, your microwave, your TV, your VCR, your telephone, your desktop computer, your laptop, and your still and video cameras. Tens of thousands of modern, computerized office-building management systems that control the elevators, security systems and cameras, lighting, safes and vaults, and air conditioning may have date-sensitive chips and may fail if the chips and/or programs are not replaced or repaired in time. Some sprinkler systems will go off; some elevators will be stuck on the ground floor—maybe permanently. Some bank vaults will swing open on the weekend, and others will refuse to open on Monday morning.

Remember, even though 99 percent of these 50 billion chips are probably okay, non–date-sensitive, or harmless even if they do fail, between 500 million and 1 billion chips could still malfunction in ways that matter.

Embedded chips are probably the most controversial Y2k issue. Some experts with impeccable credentials say this is the most serious and intractable Y2k problem, while others with equally impressive credentials say the problem of embedded chips is exaggerated.

Among the latter is my son, David. He has a degree in electronic engineering, and until about ten years ago was programming those chips. I can only hope he is right.

Municipal traffic-light systems could fail or freeze, creating the mother of all traffic jams. Can you even conceive of being in a New York City taxi when the traffic lights fail? Hell hath no fury like a New York cabbie caught in traffic forever.

Fire engines and ambulances may not run if the communication systems that dispatch them fail because of Y2k. The airlines may not fly—as early as October 1998, KLM, Lufthansa, Delta, and American Airlines had already announced they probably wouldn't fly on December 31, 1999, and would probably have to restrict flights for some indeterminate time thereafter. Communications and global-positioning satellites may not fail, but their ground links will if they are not repaired.

Even in a best-case scenario, Y2k will cause a worldwide recession, a bear market, and disruptions of government services and benefits.

Many stores won't open on January 1. Loraine Gornik, senior Y2k project manager at Sears, has said: "We will *not* be open on Saturday, January 1, I'll tell you that!"

Your bank may not be able to credit your interest correctly or confirm your balance. Food stamps may not be delivered, and your insurance company's computer may think it's 1900 and you haven't even been born yet—or paid a penny of premiums. And the government, which mails out fifty million computer-generated checks every month, probably won't be able to.

The Year 2000 computer problem pervades all aspects of our lives. On June 2, 1997, *Newsweek* ran a much ignored cover story entitled "The Day the World Shuts Down: Can We Fix the Year 2000 Computer Bug Before It's Too Late?", which captured the extent of the threat:

> Drink deep from your champagne glasses as the ball drops in Times Square to usher in the year 2000.

Whether you imbibe or not, the hangover may begin immediately. The power may go out. Or the credit card you pull out to pay for dinner may no longer be valid. If you try an ATM to get cash, that may not work, either. Or the elevator that took you up to the party room may be stuck on the ground floor. Or the parking garage you drove into earlier in the evening may try to charge you more than your yearly salary. Or your car may not start. Or the traffic lights might be on the blink. Or when you get home, the phones may not work. The mail may show up, but your magazine subscriptions will have stopped, your government check may not arrive, your insurance policies may have expired.

Or you may be out of a job. When you show up for work after the holiday, the factory or office building might be locked up, with a handwritten sign taped to the wall: OUT OF BUSINESS DUE TO COMPUTER ERROR.

Could it really happen? Could the most anticipated New Year's Eve party in our lifetimes really usher in a digital nightmare when our wired-up-the-wazoo civilization grinds to a halt? Incredibly, according to computer experts, corporate information officers, congressional leaders, and basically anyone who's given the matter a fair hearing, the answer is yes, yes, a thousand times yes! Yes—unless we successfully complete the most ambitious and costly technology project in history, one where the payoff comes not in amassing riches or extending Web access, but securing raw survival.

Even though your local paper may not yet be headlining Y2k, it is anything but a closely held secret. A few brave souls have been sounding the tocsin for years, trying to arouse us from our ignorance or denial. I have clipped hundreds of newspaper and magazine articles on the subject. Major computer magazines have featured the problem. President Clinton finally appointed a commission supposedly to deal with it, and, after six years of silence, addressed the National Academy of Sciences on the subject, confirming what I'm about to tell you. Congressional hearings have been held, and there are literally thousands of Y2k web sites and discussion groups on the Internet.

I am really a Johnny-come-lately to the problem. Starting in 1996, a *Ruff Times* subscriber named Jim Lord started writing me letters to alert me to the problem and enlist me in his cause of helping people recognize the problem and prepare for it. I was unresponsive, partly because I was so computer ignorant at the time that I found it unthinkable that all the brain power in this amazingly high-tech world would have ignored the problem, allowing it to become so serious that these "techies" could not fix it in time. Surely Bill Gates would save us!

But gradually I evolved from a Y2k atheist to an agnostic, then a passive believer, then a deeply concerned believer. The more I looked, the worse it got. As I spent hours on the Internet, I found that the people who were the most scared were the experts who were responsible for repairing it.

So, what is the Y2k problem? How did it happen? How did we let it get to this point? Why isn't there time to fix it? What will it do to us? How can you prepare for it? How bad will it be? Who is most likely to be affected? What will government be able to do about it? Am I just a Chicken Little, or is the sky really falling?

And last of all, where are the *opportunities* for savvy investors? There are always great opportunities in volatility, and this time, that is true in spades. One unaware man's tragedy is another far-sighted man's opportunity. In the land of the blind, the one-eyed man is king!

How We Got into This Mess

Although the Y2k problem is receiving a fair amount of exposure in the media and will get more attention in the coming months, I cannot assume you understand exactly how the Y2k problem came about, so be patient as I explain it to the not-as-yet converted.

A few decades ago, many companies and government agencies found that they could no longer keep track manually of the sheer volume of data and transactions, so they turned to computers to manage the data and do the everyday grunt work of running the world's institutions. But the first computers were clunky, expensive giants that filled entire rooms, and their data-storage capacity was infinitesimal, even compared with today's mass-produced, garden-variety desktops.

Most critical, much of the work the computers were assigned was date-sensitive. Clocks and calendars were built into them, and, to save some of that scarce and expensive memory, programmers decided to drop the first two digits of the year, so that 1962 became "62," 1971 became "71," and so forth. Programmers never dreamed that those programs and computers would still be in use by the year 2000, so they never considered what would happen when the programs tried to read the year "00." The problem, we now know, is that many computers will choke when they read "00" as 1900 rather than 2000.

Federal Reserve Board Chairman Alan Greenspan was a lowly computer programmer way back then. Testifying before Congress, he expressed the difficulty of undoing the old programming:

> It never entered our minds that these programs would have lasted more than a few years. And as a consequence, they are very poorly documented. If I were to go back and look at some of the programs I wrote thirty years ago, I mean, I would have one terribly difficult time working my way through step by step…. It, therefore, is a very—it's a very difficult problem to get your hands around.

Who would have thought that the computers might conclude one day that you hadn't even been born, or that you were one hundred years late with your loan payment?

Rather than junking those aging mainframes, programmers just kept modifying and upgrading them and the programs that ran on them, and we kept making them more important to our lives. We didn't know they were setting up billions of little time bombs. All we cared about was whether our telephone or TV or microwave or central heating or local ATM worked, or our Social Security checks arrived, or our airplanes came and went reasonably on time.

The problem became far worse when programmers began putting whole computers with millions of microscopic circuits on tiny silicon chips, some of them the size of a match head. This was potentially even more dangerous than the obsolete mainframe programs, because there were so many of them—fifty billion "embedded chips" with whole computers etched on them. We put them in our household appliances and heating and cooling systems, in our communication and global-positioning satellites and oil-drilling rigs (often three thousand feet below the ocean floor). We put more than two thousand of them in every airliner to run all the complex systems that operate, navigate, and monitor the plane.

To make the solution infinitely harder for the mainframe programmers, these programs were written in more than five hundred different programming languages, most of which are now obsolete and long forgotten—and were written by programmers who are dead, retired, or otherwise employed. As each new generation of programmers added onto the work of those who had gone before, the new programmers often failed to provide the documentation necessary to diagnose and fix the problems easily and quickly, and in a high percentage of cases the crucial source codes have been lost, making evaluation and repairs far more difficult, expensive, and time-consuming.

When the programmers tried to wake up their bosses to the problem, CEOs and heads of government agencies went into denial. "Surely this can't be *that* bad. Are you telling me we will have to spend all of the next three years' profits fixing this thing, and put all our other critical programming jobs on the shelf? Our board will have my head for that."

And the general public, secure in their technical ignorance and their comfortable lives that went on much as before, never realized that their everyday existence was now being managed and facilitated by computers that were about to have a nervous breakdown. They simply refused to take the problem seriously. As my newsletter colleague Gary North has said, people who read those "extreme" scenarios would react as if it were just a scary amusement-park ride. "Whee!"

Embedded Processors and Dates

It's easy to see how banks and insurance companies might have problems with the two-digit year, "00," because they have to keep track of time and dates in order to calculate interest, loan payments, maturities, and so forth. But why do traffic lights, elevators, medical devices, electrical and other utility plants, satellites, and similar systems use dates?

One of the leading experts in this area is Jim Lord, the man who first brought Y2k to my attention. He is the author of *Survival Guide for the Year 2000 Problem* and publisher of a bimonthly newsletter, *Jim Lord's Year 2000 Survival Newsletter* (J. Marion Publishing, 888-Y2k-2555; $129 annually, plus $4.50 shipping and handling). I asked Jim to explain this problem:

> To simplify it, let's define embedded processors as "all computers that are not mainframe or desktop systems." An embedded processor usually has a *single*, rather than a *generic*, purpose. It can be a simple, single-purpose chip the size of a match head, as in a wristwatch or pacemaker. It might be a full-blown computer chip the size of a matchbook. It could be an entire computer-on-a-board installed in a much larger system, such as a missile or a patient-monitoring system. It could even be many chips, boards, and systems controlled by a central computer. Embedded processors are customized, rather than general-purpose.
>
> So why might some of them fail at the year 2000?

This is a bit complicated, but it's worth the trouble to digest it.

1) Hidden date capability: Some embedded processors have date functionality but are not programmed to use it. A fancy lathe might use an embedded computer to precisely control the machine. No dates are processed, but the computer chip contains a complete date routine that uses two-digit years. The problem arises when, like a time bomb, its calendar rolls over to "00," and the software may freeze or malfunction and disable the lathe until the chip is replaced. The extent of this problem is unknown, but testing has revealed instances of this sort of computerized hand grenade.

2) Time/duration: Many computerized control systems calculate time/duration. Suppose, for example, a manufacturing process or a municipal water system requires a valve to be turned on for ten minutes every hour, and the system uses an embedded processor with full time/date capability (a common configuration). A simple computer program might: (1) turn on the valve; (2) count ten minutes; (3) turn off the valve; (4) count fifty minutes; then (5) return to the first step.

There are two ways to count the required minutes. The first uses the computer's "clock," which, like a metronome, simply ticks regularly (once per second, let's say). To count ten minutes, the software counts six hundred ticks of the clock.

The second method uses the computer's date/time function, which behaves like a robot. When you ask, it tells you the complete time *and* date—and there's the rub. Time durations are calculated by continuously subtracting *two* time/dates until the result equals the time duration needed. While this is more complex for the computer (which doesn't care), it might actually be easier to use for the programmer (who does care), depending on the operative computer language.

At the year 2000 turnover, many processors will revert back to the year 1980 or 1984 instead of advancing. This throws the time/duration calculation out of whack, possibly causing equipment errors and shutdowns.

3) Data recording: Many automated systems collect and store data from sensors which continuously monitor physical conditions, such as voltage, temperature, pressure, speed, etc. The data might then be analyzed on either a real-time or historical basis to track system performance or capacity. Industrial processes, such as manufacturing, oil drilling, and chemical processing, often use such measuring systems. Other common uses are diagnostic systems for equipment, facilities, or even people.

Data are typically meaningless unless you know *when* the measurement took place. Problems arise at the year 2000 turnover because the time stream breaks off when the year reverts to 1980 or 1984. Many sophisticated systems will shut down, believing the system has malfunctioned.

4) Maintenance tracking: Many computerized safety- and health-related systems include built-in maintenance tracking and will shut down if maintenance is late. Such schedule-related software is, obviously, date-sensitive. Examples are elevators, medical devices, precision test equipment, and emergency equipment and vehicles. This maintenance-tracking function could easily be unknown to the user.

Consider a heart defibrillator requiring maintenance every four months for safety and medical-liability reasons. If the device exceeds the specified period, it shuts down. At the century date rollover, it might shut down when the chip reverts back to an incorrect year, believing many years had elapsed without maintenance.

5) Satellites: The precise position of a satellite relative to the earth must be constantly monitored and controlled for its solar panels to always be oriented toward the sun to recharge its batteries and for it to be oriented to its ground stations as it reports the data it collects and the status of onboard systems (telemetry) back to earth. This precise positioning is done with computers and is dependent on time, date, and position. Each piece of data is, of course, date/time tagged.

6) Single-purpose systems: Many systems, such as parking, electronic toll-collection, access control, and facility security systems, use personal computers with specialized, date-dependent software. They can also fail because of the year-reversion problem or because they process dates internally. Parking systems, for example, use dates and times to calculate fees.

7) High-level management systems: Many large applications tie smaller systems together for high-level management purposes. It's programmed to know when it's a weekend or after 5 PM. A high-rise office building might coordinate the management of parking, access control, security alarms, environmental controls, elevators, fire alarms, and sprinkler control with a single management computer. This would allow it to disable elevators when a fire is detected, or adjust heating and cooling on weekends when the building is empty. The individual components may not be date-sensitive, but the larger system could be.

Factories, refineries, power and water plants, residential neighborhoods, and transportation systems are other possible examples.

8) Date-programmable devices: The user can actually program the date in many devices, such as VCRs, video cameras, fax machines, and copiers. Some less obvious and possibly more important gadgets, such as thermostats, security systems, bank vaults, and traffic lights, use date-tracking to alter system-behavior on weekends.

These are some of the more common embedded processor uses and potential failures. There are as many more as there are creative programmers in the world. As the results of testing come in, it is becoming clear that the embedded system component of Y2k is by far the most unpredictable because of the sheer number of chips needing inspection and replacement. Widespread infrastructure failures and extensive environmental damage are just two of the more ominous possibilities.

The July 1998 issue of *Byte* magazine, one of the most widely read and respected computer publications, summed up the embedded-chip problem:

The problem is larger than most people think.... Hardware also suffers from Y2k consequences; after all, a chip is just solidified software. One commonly cited problem is associated with gadgets that monitor periodic maintenance. When the clock strikes twelve on New Year's Eve, 2000, these devices might think it has been 99 years since their last maintenance, realize that's too long for safe operation, and shut down. Not good, especially if it's the device that monitors your IV.

Why Can't We Fix It?

Ironically, we know exactly how to fix the mainframe programs. It's not so much a technical problem as it is a management and personnel nightmare that requires the one thing we don't have—time. On July 20, 1998, the *Los Angeles Times* reported:

> Simple as the date problem may sound, the fix is anything but. In mainframe-computer programs, for example, it requires technicians to comb through millions of lines of code written in COBOL and other antique programming languages to identify and rewrite the sections where the two-digit field appears.

Although this task is straightforward, it is monumentally difficult because of the sheer magnitude of the task. It is generally a three-year project from start to finish, we are precariously close to the deadline, and there is a critical shortage of qualified programmers and systems engineers to do the job. More than 750,000 programmers and systems engineers are needed worldwide, but only 250,000 of them are qualified and available.

This shortage has already spawned a feeding frenzy as institutions have belatedly woken up to the problem and started competing for the available talent. Qualified people have gotten signing bonuses of up to $150,000 to change jobs, and government has been the biggest loser. The person in charge of the Y2k program at the Internal Revenue Service (IRS) took early retirement, lured away from the government by a big signing bonus. The IRS has lost almost 10 percent of its people to more lucrative corporate jobs, as it falls further and further behind.

Perhaps the most crucial factor is the inflexible time schedule; you can't negotiate with the calendar. Even a presidential executive order won't influence the calendar and the clock. Because of the magnitude of the repair task and the shortage of programmers, any medium-to-large company or agency that isn't far enough into the repair stage to start testing by January 1999 will not be ready in time, since the testing phase takes about a year. Many of these institutions have thousands of programs to fix. They have to perform a kind of "triage" by identifying their "mission-critical" systems, fix as many of them as time, money, and personnel will permit, then pray that they have done enough to survive until the rest of the systems are fixed.

Y2k could hit you and me where it hurts—in our wallets—because our financial systems are especially susceptible to the Millennium Bug.

The sad truth, according to *Byte* magazine, is that about 30 percent of America's corporations don't even have a Y2k *plan* in place and will not have fixed their mission-critical systems in time. For most of them, that is a death sentence.

What's more, nearly every government agency is hopelessly behind schedule.

Don't Bank on It

Y2k could hit you and me where it hurts—in our wallets—because our financial systems are especially susceptible to the Millennium Bug.

Banks have special problems. Not only do they have thousands of date-sensitive programs, but they also have to interface with other banks' computers, as well as with credit-reporting agencies, government agencies, business clients, and companies and institutions that create the instruments (stocks, bonds, etc.) in which they invest their money.

When you deposit a check to your account, it is cleared at the issuing bank by computer. What if the issuing bank is not Y2k compliant? Importing data from a non–Y2k-compliant computer can contaminate a compliant computer. All computer transactions become suspect.

What if your bank is not Y2k compliant and you have a CD that matures in 2001? Will the computer think it is 1901 and conclude that you can't get your money for a hundred years? Your bank's computers may not be able to verify your balance or clear the checks you write.

And the least discussed but most dangerous threat to the banks is the Y2k status of their customers. What if the bank is Y2k compliant but many of its biggest loan customers are not? Given that the Y2k-repair progress of up to 30 percent of all American corporations is hopeless and that 10 percent to 30 percent of the rest are behind schedule, banks could face the failure of many of their best customers, and a lot of loans may go sour. Many banks are now requiring Y2k-status reports from loan customers. How many bank customers will fail and/or default on their bank loans because of Y2k?

Many of the nation's banks—especially the medium-sized and regional ones—will not be completely ready in time, and although we do know that some of the biggest ones are in pretty good shape, in most cases we don't know which ones will be ready, or which of their many programs will not work as they should.

Broken Brokers

And what about your broker? Will his computers be able to keep track of your account and your trades? In testimony before a Senate subcommittee on technology, Alfred R. Berkeley III, president of the National Association of Securities Dealers (NASD), said:

> In the best-case scenario, systems will fail, causing lost processing time as software is corrected. In the more likely scenario, applications will continue to process, producing inaccurate data and information.
>
> For example, erroneous calculations may impact billing invoices, loan interest payments, or depreciation schedules. Applications dependent on age calculations, such as benefit payments, may be severely impacted.
>
> The systems that the NASD, NASDAQ, and NASDR operate are large and the changes that will be required

will be extensive…. [T]ogether they are responsible for 134 application systems that comprise 18,500 programs made up of 16,600,000 lines of computer code. These systems run on six major platforms and are written in eight major languages. Only about 1/3 of our applications systems are already Year 2000 compliant.

In fact, one of America's biggest brokers, Smith Barney, has already experienced a serious Y2k problem. The company attempted to bring online one program it thought had been repaired. The program had tested out just fine offline, but as soon as it was online it promptly dumped $19 million into 525,000 accounts—to the tune of $10 trillion! Smith Barney was lucky this bug in its repair created such an obvious error that programmers could easily catch and repair the problem. But what if it had been a smaller error, repeated over and over? It could have thrown Smith Barney's whole system into chaos; it could have just as easily been a bug that *deducted* money from your account and really messed up your life.

On the positive side, the financial-services industry is well ahead of most other industries and is making a good-faith effort to fix its computers. In 1998 it performed a public "scripted" test that was widely reported in the media and that seems to have gone well. The bad news is that it was a very limited test, involving only ten major firms and seventeen minor firms, and was programmed not to fail, as a PR gesture. There will be a much more comprehensive and valid "industry-wide" test (covering members of the New York Stock Exchange) on the last three Saturdays in March 1999, and on the second Saturday in April 1999, which will tell us a lot more. There is some hope.

The Lawyers

Already, many companies are refusing to comment on their Y2k readiness "on advice of counsel." They know that the tort lawyers have been sharpening their knives—holding seminars to plan the biggest litigation explosion the world has ever seen or will ever see again. These suits will turn even manageable problems into unmanageable messes, with companies tying up desperately needed resources while fighting for their legal lives, and concealing the problems from the public to lower their profiles as litigation targets.

On June 29, 1998, the *Wall Street Journal* reported that many big accounting firms that have consulting divisions that could help their clients repair their Y2k problems are refusing to do so out of fear of being sued. They don't want to take on projects they know they can't possibly finish on time. The list of accounting firms either refusing to do Y2k work at all or limiting their work to a few selected clients reads like a Who's Who in accounting—Coopers and Lybrand, Deloitte and Touche, Price Waterhouse, Ernst and Young, and Arthur Andersen.

Seeing an opportunity to cash in on Y2k litigation, many lawyers are already tooling up. Salvatore J. Graziano, an associate at the New York law firm of Milberg, Weiss, Bershad, Hynes, and Lerach, forthrightly told the *Journal*, "We have been discussing suits against consultants with potential clients." In plain English, the firms are using the prospect of Y2k litigation as bait on their client-recruiting hook.

The Electric Power Grid*

Our power plants and the grid that connects them are another trouble spot because they are run mostly by noncompliant mainframe programs and embedded chips. The Nuclear Regulatory Agency has warned all the nuclear plants (which produce about 20 percent of America's electricity—40 percent on the East Coast) that if all their systems are not Y2k compliant by June 1999 they will have to start the shutdown process, which takes several months, and many,

---

*I am indebted to Don McAlvany, a tireless researcher and the editor of the *McAlvany Advisor* (P.O. Box 84904, Phoenix, AZ 85071), for many of the quotes on the power-grid problem.

if not most, are years behind schedule. Their management and safety systems are seriously at risk.

But that's far from all.

On June 11, 1998, Senator Christopher Dodd, vice chairman of the Senate Special Committee on the Y2k Technology Problem, said, "We're no longer at the point of asking whether or not there will be any power disruptions, but we are now forced to ask how severe the disruptions are going to be."

U.S. News and World Report reported on June 8, 1998, that a midwestern utility company ran a Y2k-compliance test, and the power generator shut down completely. After three days of programming fixes, the test was run a second time; the system failed again. The problem remains unsolved.

Moreover, according to the March 2, 1998, issue of *Business Week*:

> ...electric utilities are only now becoming aware that the programmable controllers—which have replaced mechanical relays in virtually all the electricity-generating plants and control rooms—may behave badly or even freeze up when 2000 arrives. The utilities are just now getting a handle on the problem.

Because of the domino-like, interconnected nature of the nation's power grid, you could live in Panguitch, Utah, and suffer from power failures, power rationing, brownouts, and unpredictable power surges due to the failure of a computer in Canada or Washington. In testimony before the Senate Special Committee on the Y2k Technology Problem, Michael Gent, president of the North American Electric Reliability Council (NERC), admitted, "Year 2000 poses the threat that common-mode failures... or the coincident loss of multiple facilities could result in stressing the electric system to the point of a cascading outage over a large area."

The *McAlvany Advisor* reported that there are 7,800 U.S. power-generating and distribution organizations in America. In late 1997 two surveys of utilities found that between 32 and 45 percent of them had not yet begun a Y2k analysis, and of those that had started, 37 percent were behind schedule.

Rick Cowles, a computer expert with seventeen years' experience in the electric-power industry and a point man on reporting Y2k conditions in the industry, wrote the following shocking report on February 27, 1998:

> Most electric utilities are still in the awareness stage of Y2k. Some are actually fighting about how to conduct inventory. There is very little upper-management appreciation of the depth of the Y2k issue. That lack of appreciation translates into a significant deficit of executive-level support (resources and funding) for any Y2k projects. Y2k program managers are frustrated at their inability to convince their local or executive management that Y2k is, indeed, an enterprise-threatening problem. There is a sense of urgency at the Y2k-program management level that is approaching panic, but the support is still not materializing.
>
> Not one electric company has started a serious remediation effort on its embedded controls. Not one....
>
> Almost all electric-utility projects are severely understaffed.... This company still doesn't have a single full-time person dedicated to Y2k, and this includes the project manager....
>
> Oh, one other thing. Contingency plan? The industry hasn't started thinking about it yet.
>
> Here's my main message—the electric industry doesn't have the time left to lick this thing.

On June 9, 1998, Senator Robert Bennett, chairman of the Senate Special Committee on the Y2k Technology Problem, said, "If Y2k hit tomorrow, there is a 100 percent chance that the [power] grid would fail. With eighteen months to go, we may be able to get this down to 40 percent."

Three days later, Bennett summed up just how catastrophic this problem could be:

> If the power grid goes down because of connections in the computers or because of embedded chips in certain power plants that shut those power plants down because of bad software, then it is all over. It doesn't matter if every computer in the country is compliant if you can't plug it into something.

Railroads

Our railroads are completely computerized. Railroad companies no longer have the ability to manually run the systems or do the switching. The cars are all owned by corporate or individual investors, and their whereabouts is tracked by vulnerable computers, most of which are time- and date-sensitive and are not Y2k compliant—and repairs are way behind schedule.

Consider just how vulnerable the railroads are: When Union Pacific bought Southern Pacific, the problem of integrating their computer systems created a monumental mess that is still being straightened out. Shipments have been delayed as long as three months, and Union Pacific has had to hire a fleet of more than one hundred trucks to deliver goods.

Now, on top of that, these railroads have to deal with the Y2k problem, and they are woefully behind schedule. If our railroads cannot run, there will be dramatic repercussions on our infrastructure. Our railroads also carry the coal to electric power plants; even if plants were to be compliant, they couldn't operate without coal.

The Government

Almost every government agency is a hopeless mess. The government is required by law to report to Congress every quarter on its Y2k repair progress, and the most recent reports on its "mission-critical" systems are pathetic, to put it kindly. It is impossible to exaggerate how terribly the government has mismanaged its Y2k problem, and how far behind it is.

The bad news is that government benefits and services will be curtailed or even disappear. The good news is that government will be less able to mess up our lives. It may be liberating. We may learn firsthand the wisdom of Will Rogers's sage observation, "Be grateful you aren't getting all the government you're paying for."

The Year 2000 computer problem pervades all aspects of our lives; don't be complacent because you don't think it will affect you.

Realistically, however, we are far more addicted to government services and money than we think we are. The withdrawal symptoms will be far more painful than you can imagine.

Ed Yourdon, a giant in the software field who is the coauthor of *Time Bomb 2000: What the Year 2000 Computer Crisis Means to You!*, bluntly states:

> Nobody seems willing or able to say it in simple language, so let me be the one: *the federal government is not going to finish the Y2000 project*. No maybes, no ifs, ands, or buts. No qualifiers, no wishy-washy statements like "unless more money is spent" or "unless things improve." We're not going to avert the problem by appointing a Y-2000 Czar or creating a national Y-2000 Commission.

Capers Jones is another software legend whose work is noted for its rigor and academic integrity. He literally invented the field of software metrics and has written many books on this arcane subject. His new book, *The Year 2000 Software Problem: Quantifying the Costs and Assessing the Consequences*, is based on data collected from six hundred large organizations working on Y2k. According to Jones:

- 58 percent of federal Y2k projects are behind schedule.

- 14,250 military applications will not be fixed in time.

- The total Y2k cost for the federal government will be $143 billion. (The government's estimate is a paltry $3.9 billion.)

But what does the government say?

Sally Katzen, the Y2k spokesperson for the Office of Management and Budget (OMB) and a lawyer pal of Hillary Clinton, once declared Y2k to be "a nonevent," although she has since changed her tune.

Representative Steve Horn (R-CA), chairman of the House subcommittee on Y2k, recently issued a shocking report card on the federal government's Y2k status. Based on current progress, the Departments of Justice and Health and Human Services won't be ready until 2001 (no FBI, Medicare, or Medicaid). Treasury won't finish until 2004 (no IRS or T-bills for four years), Agriculture until 2005 (goodbye, food stamps), Transportation until 2010 (no air-traffic control), Defense until 2012 (Saddam grins), Energy and Labor until 2019 (yawn).

Even the Congressional Research Service, a branch of the Library of Congress, has concluded, "...due to the lack of time and resources, the majority of... government agencies will not likely fix all of their computer systems before the start of the new Millennium."

History is not encouraging. Only 14 percent of all large government software projects are ever finished on schedule, and Y2k is the largest software project in history. The government is desperately short of time and personnel, the leadership is incompetent or nonexistent, and it will cost many tens or hundreds of billions more dollars than the government has admitted. And, as stated, programmers are leaving the government in droves for lucrative jobs in private industry.

Bill Clinton and Al Gore will be remembered as leaders who talked a great fight on technology but ignored the greatest technological crisis in history for almost six years.

Don't be complacent just because you feel you are not directly dependent on a government check. If you add up all the people who get a check from some level of government (including Social Security and Medicare recipients, veterans, government and military retirees), or work for a company that has government contracts or is a supplier for a government contractor, or live in an economic area that depends on the military or other government agencies for its local prosperity—plus all the dependents of those on the above list—about three-quarters of all living Americans are vulnerable to cutbacks in or the failure of government services. Then, of course, everyone is affected by the impact on the general economy.

Because Health and Human Services and Treasury will not be ready in time, the food-stamp and welfare programs will not be delivered as promised. Cities with large government-dependent populations will be potential tinderboxes.

The IRS computers are basket cases. After eleven years and $4 billion, the IRS admitted defeat in 1997 on its program to modernize its computers—and that project did not even begin to take Y2k into account. Based on its present rate of progress, its Y2k repair will be ready—*four years late!* IRS Commissioner Charles Rossotti has conceded that the IRS has no contingency plan, saying "We have a very thin margin of tolerance to make this whole thing work. There is no plan B." And, as Rossotti has admitted, if the IRS isn't Y2k compliant, the repercussions could be devastating: "If we don't fix [our computers]... the whole financial system of the United States will come to a halt.... It not only could happen, it will happen if we don't fix it right."

Millions of Americans could figure out that if they don't file their returns on April 15, 1999, or if they file fraudulent returns, the IRS cannot catch them. This would give Uncle Sam a cash-flow problem of epic proportions. (I am *not* advocating not filing; I'm merely predicting this could easily happen.)

The Social Security Administration has bragged that the Old Age and Survivors' Benefits program will be Y2k compliant in time. But then it discovered that not all of the systems with which it interacts are on schedule. For example, every government check and automatic electronic deposit, including Social Security and Medicare, is processed by the Treasury Department's Financial Management Services—fifty million checks a month—and its computers are in lousy shape. As of March 1998 it hadn't even finished assessing which of its systems needed to be repaired.

This is a serious bottleneck—a choke point. Since it takes three years from start to finish to complete the typical Y2k project, and government computer projects usually run fifteen months behind schedule, your Social Security check will be in serious doubt, barring a miracle.

The States

The only states I am reasonably sure will be mostly ready are Washington and Pennsylvania, because they took the problem seriously when they still had time to fix it. Many states are following the examples of Nevada and Georgia and are introducing or planning to introduce laws exempting the state from liability or lawsuits relating to Y2k-caused computer failures in state programs.

What makes this even more critical is that most federal benefit programs are administered by the states, and their computers have to interface with each other.

The Airlines

The Federal Aviation Administration (FAA), with its heavily computerized air-traffic control system, is way behind schedule. The global-positioning satellites used for navigation, and their downlinks, especially on international and transoceanic flights, are also heavily computerized. In addition, each plane has about two thousand embedded chips that must be examined. Those that are date-sensitive must be replaced or reprogrammed, and many of them aren't even being manufactured anymore.

Therefore, the airlines will probably ground flights on December 31, 1999. As noted, KLM, Lufthansa, Delta, and American Airlines have already announced that they probably will not fly that night. High-level sources have even conceded that the airlines are planning to suspend flights for at least two weeks because insurance companies plan to withhold coverage from any plane in the air at midnight on December 31, 1999.

Water Systems

Our water systems are totally controlled by computers, and are programmed with dates and times to dump purifying chemicals into the water.

The *Salt Lake City Deseret News* reported on June 16, 1998, that officials in a Utah town were recently testing the computers that run its water system for Year 2000 problems. As they turned an internal clock past 1999, a valve opened and purification chemicals were dumped into the water. David Fletcher, Utah's Year 2000 program manager, said that, if it had continued for another hour, "I could have killed the entire town!"

This is not just a freak, isolated instance. A recent newspaper article in Australia commented on a similar scary incident in Coff's Harbour, Australia, when the town did a Y2k test on the water system:

> Enough toxic chemicals would have been released into Coff's Harbour's water supply to kill its entire population, under a test on the likely impact of the Millennium Bug....
>
> When microprocessors at Coff's Harbour's water-storage facility were turned over to 2000 dates in a simulation, the entire chemical holdings—normally used in carefully regulated amounts to purify water—were

dumped into the water in one hit. Experts say this would have the potential to kill the town's entire population.

The Timetable and the 99 Problem

The millennium rollover is not the only computer problem. On many of these mainframe programs, "99" or "00" means "end of file" or "delete file," which is just one of the reasons we will have problems *before* the drop-dead date of January 1, 2000. September 9, 1999 (09/09/99) could be a big one that confuses a lot of computers. In fact, some programs that deal with expiration or maturity dates in the year 2000 or later are starting to have problems now. Whenever you read about a serious computer glitch somewhere, Y2k should be the first suspect.

The fiscal years on which corporations and governments work may also cause complications. New York State's fiscal year 2000 (FY2000) begins April 1, 1999, as do Canada's and Japan's. The United Kingdom begins its fiscal year on April 6, while forty-six U.S. states begin FY2000 on July 1. Texas begins September 1; Alabama, Michigan, and the U.S. federal government start on October 1. Any of these dates could cause system malfunctions that will trigger unpredictable mass behavior—hoarding, bank runs, a gold stampede, and strange consumer behavior, ranging from crowded churches to "eat, drink, and be merry (and spend it all) for tomorrow we die."

In other words, Y2k will not all happen at once like a bolt out of the blue. The cumulative effect of these creeping deadlines will be front-page headlines long before New Year's Day 2000.

For some, it will not be too bad—especially if they are physically, emotionally, intellectually, and spiritually prepared. But for many Americans, it will be far worse than they thought as the consequences of their lack of preparation sink in.

America Leading the Pack?

As far behind schedule as we are, the United States is ahead of the rest of the world in repair and readiness. Western Europe is way behind, with Y2k on the back burner because programmers have focused on preparing systems to convert to the new European currency, the Euro. Most of Europe's major corporations, government agencies, banks, and stock and bond exchanges have no chance to be ready.

Britain, however, is taking the problem more seriously. Prime Minister Tony Blair said, "The Millennium Bug is one of the most serious problems facing not only British business but the global economy today. Its impact must not be underestimated."

Asia is in worse shape than Europe, with few banks and corporations, even in Japan, even close to being on track. Latin America and Africa are hopeless, with most institutions barely getting started, and, according to President Clinton, many governments not even aware of the problem.

But remember just how interconnected our global, computerized economy is. This raises another Y2k complication. These megacomputers talk to each other and exchange data and money freely. Billions of dollars move around the world at a keystroke in a nanosecond. Take the world's stock and bond markets, for example. If you are John Smith and Company, Stock and Bond Brokers, your computers must interface with the computers that run the Hong Kong and Frankfurt markets—that is, if you want your clients to be able to buy or sell those stocks. But if the Hong Kong computers have malfunctioned due to an unrepaired Y2k glitch and put out inaccurate data that have been accepted by your Y2k-compliant computer, your database is contaminated.

Banks, we know, have similar interface problems. The only rational course of action for a bank that *is* Y2k compliant will be not to interface with any other computers until they can be certified as Y2k compliant. This will have a devastating effect on commerce. Because most foreign institutions will not be ready, I expect the international stock and bond markets and the international system of payments to fall apart, or, at the very least, to curtail computerized interaction.

Y2k and Your Life

I hope I have raised some serious question for your consideration, such as "How will this affect me and my family? What should I do about it, and when? How can I invest in it?"

Will someone invent a magic bullet to fix the problem? No one who has any credibility in this area is suggesting that will happen, because this is not one big problem, but many thousands of smaller problems, each with its own unique technical problems, management culture, funding problems, personnel needs, and schedules.

Will someone invent techniques to at least speed up the repair-and-testing process so more can get done in time? Probably, and that will help, but it is likely to be too little, too late to solve the overall problem, and it probably won't cure the sick embedded chips.

There is no way to know with a high degree of accuracy just which programs will be repaired or when and which chips are compliant or will have been replaced in time. Because of this uncertainty over how the Year 2000 computer crisis will play out, I have outlined three different scenarios: worst case, intermediate case, and best case. But there is no uncertainty over how you can and should act in the face of this crisis, so I have offered a list of steps you can take to protect yourself and your family.

The Worst Case

In our worst-case scenario, your life will be most affected. There will be a worldwide depression, and trillions of dollars in wealth denominated in paper assets or cybermoney will fade like the morning mist on a summer day. Bankruptcies will soar, and millions of businesses will close forever.

The computerized national government will be crippled if not paralyzed, perhaps permanently. That's good news if you are paying more in taxes than you are getting in benefits. If you are one of those whose freedom has been most abridged by a growing, intrusive government, a shrunken government is not a complete curse. But if you depend on a check or other benefits from Uncle Sam, you are in trouble because the government probably won't be able to deliver.

The IRS is almost certain to be unable to calculate or issue refunds for a long time. The government's huge cash-flow crunch that results when millions of Americans discover they can get away

Fortunately, there are a number of steps you can take to protect yourself and your family from the oncoming crisis.

with not filing tax returns will cause Uncle Sam to cast aside all pretense of fiscal responsibility and run the printing presses around the clock.

You will see the surprising spectacle of the IRS and big-government advocates pushing for a national sales tax or a flat tax to try to rescue the government's finances, because the IRS will no longer have the capacity to administer or enforce the present monstrosity of a tax code.

The airlines will not fly, or will fly only on a sharply restricted schedule, and only when there is good weather on both ends of the flight. Dial tones will disappear, or be sporadic, as will TV transmission.

There will be soaring crime and civil disorders, especially in big cities with large government-dependent populations. In such places, benefits will be delivered sporadically at best, if at all, and the jilted beneficiaries will be frightened and angry. Foreign stock and bond markets will shut down for days, weeks, or months—possibly even years. Electricity will become undependable, for the computerized power grid will give us blackouts and brownouts—perhaps over several months. Safe drinking water may not be taken for granted.

Your local supermarket may reopen after the panic hoarding dies down, but there will be only a fraction of the familiar infinite variety of goods on the shelves.

There will be bank failures—not all banks, and not everywhere, but, as we saw in Chapter 2, the real danger to the banks is the *perception* of insolvency. It could start with a small bank a thousand miles from you, but the TV cameras will be there, with breathless reporters interviewing frightened depositors (or "withdrawers"). The contagion will spread, exhausting the resources of the Federal Deposit Insurance Corporation (FDIC), and a bank holiday will be inevitable while the Federal Reserve flies 747s full of cash to meet the demand. Uncle Sam will eventually provide the cash necessary to meet withdrawals, but the printing press will have to run around the clock—assuming the computerized printing operations are functioning—and printing-press money brings big-time inflation!

At home, your heating and air-conditioning may be sporadic or nonexistent, depending on whether it is controlled by a noncompliant chip and whether you have power. In fact, to reduce the demand for electric power it might become illegal to run your air conditioner at all.

In this scenario, it is inevitable that gold will rocket up to $2,000 per ounce; similarly, silver will hit $100 (see Chapter 9). There will be times and places when they will be the only acceptable means of exchange as printing-press inflation undermines public trust in the currency.

In a worst case, the president will invoke several executive orders that are already authorized by Congress, which empower him to rule like a dictator "for the duration" (see Chapter 4).

Even in the worst case, however, I do not expect the end of the world, of western civilization, of America as a dream—but the dream could be a nightmare for several years. I wouldn't know how to prepare for the end of the world, except to repent—something I have a lot of practice doing.

I also have great faith in the strength and resilience of America. Whatever happens, I want to believe we will get through it somehow, even if we have to rebuild on some literal and figurative rubble. That Pollyanna attitude does not, however, persuade me that we will not have a terrible mess—only that there will be light at the end of what may be a long, dark tunnel. I just hope it isn't a gorilla with a flashlight.

The Intermediate Case

In the intermediate case, a lot of the Y2k bombs will be duds. Power brownouts will be infrequent enough to be only an inconvenience. The international stock and bond markets will plummet, and Y2k will exacerbate and prolong the bear market already in progress due to non-Y2k factors (maybe before you read this). But the American financial markets will still function, albeit with delays and computer errors, such as inaccurate trade confirmations or messed-up account balances. But the system will hang together.

There will be runs on some banks, but a bank holiday will give the feds time to shovel cash into the banks to meet withdrawals. The Federal Reserve will throw open the lending window to bail out the banks, and the panic will subside before the banking system collapses. Inflation will peak at around 15 percent.

Protests over stopped government benefits will die out before the cities are in ruins (some cities will be worse than others), and order will be restored just in time.

All-out mobilization of all the programming talent in the United States, rationed and allocated by the Federal Emergency Management Agency, will gradually bring essential services back online, and after a month or so of confusion and danger, we will start pulling out of the mess. In a year or two, things will be back to "normal," but there will be an antitechnology backlash—millions of Americans will decide that a simpler, low-tech lifestyle is not only a lot safer but also more satisfying.

Developing countries in Latin America, Africa, Eastern Europe, and Asia will be in ruins, figuratively and sometimes literally, as international commerce will go back to the old manual-transactions mode, which will devastate the volume of commerce. America will come through in the best shape of all, but a new generation will look upon January 1, 2000 as a watershed, and forever refer to "before Y2k" and "after Y2k," just as those who lived through the 1930s consider that the defining era of their lives.

The one blessing in this mess will be that government will have shrunk, and the income tax will be toast. There will be a political backlash against the politicians who have promised all things from government and can no longer deliver. You will see a national sales tax or a flat tax, simply because it will be impossible to administer and enforce the current bloated income-tax code.

The Best Case

This scenario is the hardest to predict in detail, but here's the best case.

In the best case, technical fixes will be developed that will dramatically accelerate the repair process, and the theoretical consequences of faulty programming will turn out to be just that—theoretical.

Gross Domestic Product will fall as much as 1 percent, the stock bear market will run its course, and there will be intermittent brownouts, some bank failures, and a jump in corporate and personal bankruptcies. For most people, life will go on but will be more scary than before.

Which scenario am I hoping for? The best case. Which do I think is most likely? The intermediate case. Which should you prepare for? The worst case.

Action Steps

1) Move to a smaller city or town at least fifty miles from a large, volatile, government-dependent population, even if it means a longer commute. When the checks and the food stamps are interrupted, even for a few weeks, those who depend directly on the government will be upset. The bigger the city, the more people are dependent on federal, state, and municipal benefits. I feel good about living in a small Utah town fifty miles from Salt Lake City, with a mostly Mormon population, steeped in their pioneer self-sufficiency culture and with a deep respect for law and order.

If you insist on living in a big city, at least spend New Year's Eve 1999 at Grandma's house in the country. If the Y2k bomb is a dud, breathe a sigh of relief and go home!

2) Ensure you can eat. Buy *at least* a six-month supply of nonperishable food—canned, dehydrated, freeze-dried. A year's supply would be better. Chapter 8 explains the what, where, why, and how of food storage. Merchants who sell packaged storable food are listed in the Appendix. Distribution of food and other vital consumables depends on computerized distribution systems and electricity-dependent freezers and refrigerators, which brings me to my next recommendation.

3) Buy a generator and wire it into your home electrical system. Install an underground fuel tank. When the brownouts and power outages happen, you can run your furnace and air-conditioners and your lights.

4) Loan this book to all your family and neighbors, and get organized. Don't try to face this crisis alone as the only one in your neighborhood who is prepared to live well.

5) Prepare for the greatest stock-market crash in history, triggered by social unrest, a rash of bankruptcies, Y2k-caused corporate losses, and market system and bank malfunctions and closures. The way things look as this is written, you should liquidate all your paper investments (stocks, bonds, Treasury bills, CDs, etc.)—except for the stocks of the Y2k-compliant and Y2k-repair companies listed in Chapter 10—no later than August 1999. June would be even better.

6) Buy bullion-type gold and silver coins, using the money you have after liquidating your paper investments. Chapter 9 explains which ones to buy and how to buy them. Hide these coins somewhere safe. When we get to the other side of this mess, I expect everything else to be on the bargain counter; it always is in a deep recession or a depression. Cash and gold will be king.

7) Have a supply of batteries, including rechargeable ones, and other items without which your life would be dangerous, difficult, or merely uncomfortable.

8) Secure the safety of your home. Be sure your windows and doors are all burglar-proof. Buy some guns, and learn how to use and store them safely. Take a gun-safety course.

9) Test your home computer and all of your applications software for Y2k compliance, and upgrade and replace as necessary. Fortunately, this is the easiest Y2k-preparation task. Even a computer klutz like me can do it. Macintosh computers and Microsoft's Windows 95 and 98 are compliant (we think), but your BIOS chip (found in every PC) may need to be replaced. Most computers shipped in the last year are Y2k compliant, but some, amazingly, still are not. PCs more than two years old will probably need to be replaced. Upgrade your applications software with the latest versions.

You can go on the Internet to <http://www.rightime.com> and download a copy of TEST2000.ZIP. It will determine if your machine is Y2k compliant and if it can be made compliant. If you have Windows 95 or 98, don't advance the clock on your computer to January 1, 2000, just to see what happens, without first backing up your critical files.

Check your other electronic systems. I just checked out my new combination fax, printer, and scanner, and found it accepts only two-digit dates.

Before you buy any new electronic equipment or applications software, require a statement in writing from the manufacturer that it is Y2k compliant.

10) Buy James Talmage Stevens's book, Making the Best of Basics. It is by far the best and most comprehensive book on how to prepare your life for a major calamity that endangers our support systems. It's been around for more than twenty years, but it reads almost as if it had been written for Y2k. It also has a comprehensive list of dependable merchants to do business with as you prepare for Y2k. It's available in your local bookstore.

11) Make hard copies of all important documents, such as Social Security and pension deposits, bank balances, insurance policies, investments, birth and marriage certificates, tax payments (state and federal income taxes, property taxes, etc.), mortgage payments and other loan payments, and anything you'd need to prove your age, assets, and credit. Get a fire-proof safe and lock them away.

12) Pray that the worst case doesn't materialize!

The Final Word

Y2k is an extraordinary story, and it's a very difficult one to evaluate. As the months roll on, it will be a shifting story as new challenges and new solutions materialize, and as we have more data to work with.

That's why I urge you not to follow any of the specific investment recommendations in this book until you have been updated by the *Ruff Times*, which, among other things, is the ongoing journal of the Y2k odyssey. The investments are recommended based on their prices when I turned this book over to the publisher, and prices will change, as will valuations, as the story unfolds. The market is a passing parade, not a statue carved in stone—or even in gold. You can get one free update (prepared monthly) by sending in the postage-paid card enclosed in this book, or by writing to me at P.O. Box 887, Springville, Utah 84663.

A word about panic: Some panic is likely—unpredictable and sporadic—as the crisis unfolds. I do not want to add to it, so I urge you to get ready well ahead of time. There are things you should do now, before the rest of the world has decided to do it, such as getting your food-storage program. The commercial packagers of dehydrated and freeze-dried foods were back-ordered as much as seven months in September 1998.

I believe you should liquidate most of your stocks now for non-Y2k reasons, except for those that will benefit from Y2k as described in Chapter 10. Too early is better than too late.

Start buying gold now. It is near historic lows as I write, and there is little downside risk. The guidelines are in Chapter 9.

Get your stock certificates from your broker now and put them away in a safe place. They are your only proof of ownership.

I don't know exactly when you should take your money out of the bank, but it seems to me to be prudent to do it sooner rather than later, when everyone else has the same idea.

This is a time to draw close to your extended family (see Chapter 11); in an intermediate or worst case, family ties will be more important than the government or even your employment.

After you have completed your preparations, keep your eyes fixed on the long-term, and don't lose faith in the future. America has faced and come through huge challenges in the past—a civil war, two world wars, a depression, the Nixon constitutional crisis, 18 percent inflation and 21 percent interest rates in the early 1980s—and emerged safely.

God bless America! She will need it. I hope she deserves it.

Chapter Four

Power to the President

I f Y2k causes a serious economic and social crisis, what will Uncle Sam do, and what *should* he do? Certainly the government would not stand by and watch the infrastructure come unglued without at least *trying* to do something.

In the last few months of 1999, a monstrous, better-late-than-never crash effort will get under way to head off this once-in-a-millennium train wreck. The government will try to rally all of its resources as it becomes apparent that the crisis is a genuine national emergency.

I recently asked a congressman who is a good personal friend and sits on the House Y2k subcommittee, "Is your committee taking Y2k seriously?"

His answer in a nutshell was, "No."

"Is anybody in the House taking this seriously?"

"Only Steve Horn." Horn, chairman of the Y2k subcommittee, has been issuing quarterly report cards on the progress of the government agencies.

As this is written, the only senators expressing any deep concern are Robert Bennett (R-UT) and Christopher Dodd (D-CT)—a couple of unlikely allies.

As we approach the deadline, and a rising tide of Y2k concerns begins to flood the media, scary events will occur and penetrate the public consciousness, especially as the state and federal governments roll over to fiscal year 2000 and the number of computer glitches starts to rise. There will be increasing demands for the president to do something—*anything!* And, in fact, he has some potent tools at his disposal.

There are some things the government *should* do. The president has the power to invoke and implement emergency executive orders that are already the law of the land, but, as we will see, they carry inherent dangers to constitutional government.

The Anatomy of a Crisis

Many not-unlikely events will be beyond the ability of normal governmental processes to cope with:

1) There is a high risk of a banking crisis and a desperate need for a bank holiday.

2) There will be problems with the electric power grid, possibly requiring rationing of electric power in some areas—perhaps even a ban on such "nonessentials" as air conditioning (if you are a retired eighty-year-old living in Sun City, Arizona, you may doubt that air conditioning is "nonessential").

3) The government may need to mobilize all shipping to make sure food and other essentials flow to markets all over America.

4) We will literally have to draft programmers and systems engineers away from other pursuits to save or restore a crippled or failing infrastructure.

5) We may have to have martial law if benefits and checks to large government-dependent populations, especially in the inner cities, are cut off, triggering riots.

Presidential Power

To cope with such an emergency, the president has some dormant but extraordinary powers. President Ronald Reagan issued Executive Order 12656, which replaced EO11490 issued by Jimmy Carter. Among other things, it authorized the president to seize dictatorial powers "*in any national emergency situation.*" It's still in force.

Is there a legal basis for this?

Executive orders have been determined by the courts to be the law of the land when published in the *Federal Register*, and they can be implemented at any time by order of the president. Once one is implemented, it is then in full force for at least six months because during that time the Congress is prohibited from doing anything about it, including repealing it.

To cope with a Y2k emergency, the president has some extraordinary powers that unfortunately carry inherent dangers to constitutional government.

If Y2k approaches even the intermediate case described in Chapter 3, it is genuinely arguable that the president would be irresponsible if he failed to invoke extraordinary executive powers, such as declaring a bank holiday and imposing a new monetary system to replace a shattered one. In fact, this would probably enjoy broad public support.

However, once seized, power is rarely relinquished, which raises extraordinary concerns.

Let's examine the emergency mechanisms.

On July 3, 1995, John Contrubis, a legislative attorney in the American Law Division of the Congressional Research Service, submitted to Congress at its request a report on executive orders and the rationale for them, explaining what executive orders are and how the president derives the authority to issue them.

Article II of the Constitution is generally quoted as the rationale for executive orders when it states: "The executive power shall be vested in a president of the United States of America…. The president shall be commander in chief of the army and navy of the United States… [and] he shall take care that the laws be faithfully executed."

Contrubis points out that executive orders, "if issued under a valid claim of authority and published" in the *Federal Register*, are "in force and effective, and courts are required to take judicial notice of their existence."

President Franklin Roosevelt issued more than 3,500 executive orders, based on his "stewardship theory" that the president is vested with *residual powers* that are neither expressly stated in the Constitution nor assigned broadly to a specific branch of government. To him, they resided in concepts like "national security" or the "public good." Based on this theory, Roosevelt confiscated all the gold in the early 1930s by way of executive order.

FDR said, "My belief was that this was not only his [the president's] right, but his duty to do anything that the needs of the nation demanded, unless such action was forbidden by the Constitution or by laws."

Contrubis states, "...[T]he president has and may exercise a reservoir of *implied powers* created by the accumulation of the total 'expressed powers' vested in him by the Constitution and the statutes [emphasis added]."

The bottom line is that, if the president issues an executive order, we are either in an area the courts have placed within the president's "circumference of powers" or in the nebulous region of "implied powers." But if an emergency is sufficiently dangerous, no Congress will resist an executive order aimed at curing the problem.

State of Emergency

President George Bush declared a state of emergency on August 2, 1990, by Executive Order 12722, to deal with the "...unusual and extraordinary threat to the national security and foreign policy of the United States constituted by the actions and policies of the government of Iraq."

On July 29, 1998, President Clinton extended this state of national emergency. Since it has never been challenged or revoked by Congress, we are still operating under a state of national emergency.

There are also dozens of interlocking executive orders, each order assuming powers from previous orders and broadening the president's authority to cover situations way beyond that which triggered the initial executive or emergency order.

Executive Orders and Y2k

Ronald Reagan's Executive Order 12656 applies to "*any national emergency situation that might confront the nation.*" Y2k certainly qualifies. Reagan's order outlines the responsibilities of all the agencies under what the president, in his sole discretion, defines as a "national emergency."

How could EO12656 be invoked in a Y2k crisis? The language is specifically applicable to Y2k:

> A national security emergency is *any occurrence*, including a natural disaster, a military attack, *technological emergency*, or other emergency that seriously degrades or threatens the national security of the United States [emphasis added].

EO12656 seems to protect due process in Section 102(b):

> This order does *not* constitute authority to *implement* the plans prepared pursuant to this order. Plans so developed may be executed *only in the event that authority for such execution is authorized by law* [emphasis added].

However, the executive orders and acts we have cited have already been authorized by Congress, either by prior legislation or by default—that is, by being published in the *Federal Register*, whereby they become the law of the land. Stating that it needs authorization by law is just a fig leaf. This is very much like a bikini—what it reveals is interesting, but what it conceals is vital.

Under this order, the Department of Defense is given power to implement a military police state under martial law, specifically to coordinate with the attorney general "the specific procedures by which *military assistance to civilian law enforcement authorities* may be requested, considered and provided [emphasis added]." In other words, we could have troops in the streets.

The government could even requisition your personal automobile, as the Department of Transportation shall be prepared to:

> ...allocate transportation resource capacity and emergency control and management of civil transportation resources and systems, including *privately owned automobiles*, urban mass transit, railroads and St. Lawrence Seaway [emphasis added].

Part 15, Section 1501(a), gives the Department of Treasury the power to freeze your bank account, since it must develop plans for:

> ...the continued or resumed operation and liquidity of *banks, savings and loans, credit union, farm-credit institutions*, measures for the *re-establishment of evidence of assets or liabilities*, and provisions for *currency withdrawals* and deposit insurance... [emphasis added].

Treasury is also to develop plans for "discouraging the flight of capital from the United States," so don't plan to send your money to Switzerland *after* the Y2k crisis begins.

If you think you can wait to see if there is a Y2k crisis, and then run off to Tahiti or New Zealand, Section 1502 instructs the secretary of the treasury to cooperate with the attorney general in the "control of people entering and leaving the United States." So don't plan to send *yourself* to Switzerland to be reunited with your money.

Great powers are given to the Federal Emergency Management Agency, a shadowy government organization that already seems to operate in the twilight with extraconstitutional powers. Those guys will really be running things in the name of the president.

The Bottom Line

It could be argued that many of these powers would be necessary in a worst-case Y2k crisis, but there is great potential for mischief here. Whether these are temporary measures or become a permanent part of the American governmental landscape depends entirely on the character of the president and his respect for the constitutional system he has sworn to uphold—and his willingness to later relinquish powers. History tells us that power, once obtained, is rarely relinquished voluntarily.

Troubled times cry out for a Man on a White Horse, and the people, when they are scared enough, will look for a strong father image to protect them. Remember that Hitler got his first good press during the peak of the German inflation crisis in 1923, when the country was flat on its back after losing World War I and devastated by the worst inflation of modern times, when the proverbial wheelbarrow full of money bought the proverbial loaf of bread. Although Hitler illegally seized power from an ailing chancellor in 1930, he was legitimately elected by an overwhelming majority in the next election.

Either Bill Clinton or Al Gore will be president when Y2k starts to hit, depending on the outcome of the presidential scandals. If Clinton is still in the White House, he will have some unusual motivations. Y2k would be a great way for him to change the subject. If he is allowed to limp to the end of his term, he may be so crippled that a Y2k crisis could seem like a Heaven-sent opportunity to show that he is a "strong president" acting at the demand of "the American people."

Although this may seem to be a stretch, a Y2k crisis would also have other benefits for Clinton. Despite the temporary reprieve of the November 1998 elections, Clinton is still under a black cloud and could even face indictment once he is out of office. Outside the White House, Clinton is naked (pun intended), which is why he might have to be dragged from office kicking and screaming. Once his term is over, he will be defenseless. But as long as he is still in the White House, he can still influence public opinion, reward people who might squeal on him, or punish potential enemies by using the full resources and influence of his powerful office, as he has so abundantly demonstrated he is willing to do and capable of doing.

This would give Clinton the incentive to suspend (or cancel) the election in November 2000. Although none of the executive orders explicitly authorizes the president to suspend an election, a really bad Y2k crisis would make the 2000 election hard to pull off. Our elections are highly computerized, electronic affairs, so the president could "suspend" the election "until the computer crisis is over," on the grounds that it is not possible. He could also press for revoking the limitation of a president to only two terms, arguing that it is dangerous to change horses in the middle of a technological crisis.

I asked a congressman friend of mine how most congressmen would feel if the president were to "postpone" the 2000 election. He said that as long as there is a crisis big enough to serve as a fig leaf, lots of them would probably like it, especially members of the House, who have to run every two years, whether they like it or not.

If Al Gore is president when Y2k heats up, he is a lot less dangerous. He has identified himself with the high-tech revolution and bringing the "information superhighway" into every classroom (I imagine when the Starr report was released on the Internet, the Clintons weren't too thrilled about that). But he stood silent about Y2k for six years while this crisis has been creeping up on us, and is at least partly to blame for our lack of preparation.

For Gore to declare a national emergency by executive order— for good and defendable reasons—has undeniable political benefits, because it positions him as America's defender against a national cybernetic nervous breakdown.

Y2k Abuse of Power

What would limit possible abuse of the extraordinary powers given to the president in these executive orders?

First, the president can impose by order only that which he can *enforce*. Our army is derived generally from the lower economic and educational classes, whose families will be most devastated by the failure of government to deliver its promised services, benefits, and checks. They might be undependable.

Moreover, due to the popularity of hunting as a sport, we are fortunate to have a semi-armed population, the best efforts of the anti-gun crowd notwithstanding. A healthy fear of government often motivates pro-gun activists, and that fear of government may not seem so paranoid when the crisis hits.

I repeat: If Y2k comes, the president can, will, and probably should invoke at least some of these executive orders. We will hope the president will do only that which is necessary to get us through the Y2k crisis and will have enough respect for the Constitution and American free institutions that he will not impose a permanent dictatorship.

But two big questions remain: What should we do to get ready for these executive orders; and, after Y2k, where do we go from there?

Action Steps

To decide what to do if the president imposes any of the executive orders, you have to first decide what the likely impact will be on you and your family. Then you have to preempt the problem by acting in advance. The most likely event is a bank holiday.

1) Avoid tying up your money long-term—no long-term CDs, for example. To beat the crowd, by about June 1999 start withdrawing enough money to meet all your cash needs for at least ninety days. That way you will not get caught in a possible panic at the bank doors. Cash will be king because no one will accept a check during a bank holiday. And just in case cash becomes useless, buy the gold and silver coins described in Chapter 9.

If you have a food-storage program as described in Chapter 8, at least you won't have to worry about buying food. You will be panic-proof.

2) If you decide to move to some low-tech country, do it before the crisis reaches the executive order stage. Be sure you have a current passport, and send your money well ahead of you, because currency controls won't let you take it with you.

3) Keep your cars' gas tanks full.

4) Secure, well ahead of time, documentary proof of all investments, mortgage payments, other loan payments, insurance policies and premium payments, securities, tax payments, birth certificates, medical records, car titles, business records, and so on.

5) Buy a six-month supply of necessary prescription drugs and glasses.

6) June 1999 is the time to consider converting all stocks and bonds to cash, if you haven't already done so. If you decide to wait longer than that, at least keep your eye on the news, looking for signs of a deteriorating public mood, and be ready to be quick on the trigger.

Chapter Five

When You Have a Hammer in Your Hand, Everything Looks Like a Nail

E arly in his career, Ray Bradbury, the late and lamented science-fiction writer, wrote a marvelous short story in which man has finally eliminated all violence. He has invented the Watchbird—a network of intelligent flying robots that blankets the Earth, programmed to detect violence before it occurs and strike down the perpetrator before he can do harm. But the people have made one fatal error; they have enabled the robots to transmit their experiences to each other, to learn, and to make increasingly sophisticated judgments.

The Watchbird's first action prevents a New York mugging. Its second prevents the first shot of an African border war, to the cheers of a grateful world. But the third strikes down a hangman to prevent the execution of a rapist. Then the Watchbird network decides animals should not be killed, and destroys a slaughterhouse worker to save a hog. Soon the victims include a surgeon about to make an incision, a child pulling the wings off a fly, a nine-year-old school-yard bully, a mother spanking a two year old, a lion killing an antelope, and a farmer reaping his wheat (since plants are living things).

Within weeks, every predatory animal—every lion, ferret, shark, snake, and spider—is dead, as the ever-industrious Watchbird expands its definition of violence, broadens its mandate, and performs its new self-appointed tasks.

When the people realize what a dangerous thing they have made, they try to deactivate their creation. But the Watchbird concludes that it, too, is a living thing, and to protect itself, strikes down its creators, and soon the Watchbird presides over a perfectly orderly but perfectly silent world.

America's Watchbird Network: The Controllocrats

Government is populated with Watchbirds who distort the decisions of businessmen who are often forced to relinquish a perfectly intelligent, well-conceived business plan because it runs afoul of some mindless government regulation. The costs of those regulations are in the hundreds of billions of dollars a year and passed on in the cost of everything you buy.

The creeping loss of freedom to government regulatory agencies is a real threat to your future that you may not even be aware of.

Government has been chipping away at your freedom for decades. As a businessman, I can tell you out of painful and ugly personal experience that can be like being nibbled to death by ducks. In fact, the creeping loss of freedom to government regulatory agencies is a real threat to your future that you may not even be aware of.

We have been seduced into surrendering our freedom to the government piece by piece because we believed the promises that benefits would follow, and we thought the exchange would be worth it. But when the Millennium Bug strikes, the government may no longer be able to deliver the promised benefits, and we could be left only with regulations. Government will no longer even be able to pretend that it serves the people.

Paradoxically, the coercive structure may fail also. The big question is whether we will be like a circus lion raised in a cage who discovers the door inadvertently left open and is either afraid to leave his safe home or, if he does venture out, is bewildered and totally unequipped for freedom. Government may have left us ill-equipped to survive without the help of Uncle Nanny.

Alexis de Tocqueville, the great French observer of American life who traveled and wrote in America in the 1800s, had prophetic insights into the character, personality, and future of America. He could have written today rather than in the nineteenth century. None of his prognostications about the future of America is more pertinent than his vision of our omnipresent, overregulating government, which, he wrote,

> ...everyday renders the exercise of the free-agency of man less useful and less frequent; it circumscribes the will within a narrower range and gradually robs a man of all the uses of himself. The principle of equality has prepared man for these things; it has predisposed men to endure them and often to look on them as benefits.
>
> After having thus successfully taken each member of the community in its powerful grasp and fashioned him at will, the supreme power then extends its arm over the whole community. It covers the surface of society with a network of small complicated rules, minute and uniform, through which the most original mind and the most energetic characters cannot penetrate to rise above the crowd. The will of man is not shattered, but softened, bent, and guided; men are seldom forced by it to act, but they are constantly *restrained from acting*. Such a power does not destroy, but it prevents existence; it does not tyrannize, but it compresses, enervates, extinguishes, and stupefies a people, until each nation is reduced to nothing better than a flock of timid and industrious animals of which the government is the shepherd [emphasis added].

Freedom and Alphabet Soup

If the American free-enterprise system and the unprecedented climate of freedom, which were the foundation on which our extraordinary wealth and opportunity were built, are compromised by unconstitutional regulatory chains, my financial advice won't do you any good. And your profits—if any—will bring you no pleasure.

Unfortunately, as any businessman can tell you, we have already lost much of our freedom, to say nothing of our privacy, and it's eroding at an accelerating rate. The enemy? The alphabet soup of regulatory agencies run by Washington controllocrats—FDA, OSHA, EPA, SEC, FTC, *ad infinitum, ad nauseam.* More often than not, they are classic, mindless Watchbirds. It isn't just their bad behavior that threatens us; it's their very existence.

They are "independent," which means they are out of the reach of Congress, although the president can influence them because he appoints their top bureaucrats, and, technically, they report to the executive branch (the White House). Once, when a friend from Canada who lived in our home ran into a tortured interpretation of one of the mindless regulations of the Immigration and Naturalization Service (INS), I called a senator who was a good friend and asked if he could intercede. He responded, "INS? No way! They won't even return my calls. We have no influence on them whatsoever."

These agencies are all an end-run around the Constitution in dangerous ways.

No small part of the genius of the Constitution is the "separation of powers." The Founders understandably feared government tyranny—Jefferson called government "a singularly dangerous beast that must be chained"—and so to chain government down they envisioned and designed three separate but coequal branches: the legislative (Congress), to make the law; the executive (the president), to administer the law; and the judicial (the courts), to judge whether the law has been violated. But the regulatory agencies have arrogantly assumed all three functions.

So, how did this sad state of affairs come to be?

When Congress or the president perceives an evil that needs to be corrected or regulated by government, legislation is passed creating an agency with a very broad mandate and sweeping powers. The detailed regulations are left to be written by the agency—a legislative function. The agency hires a swarm of agents and inspectors to go about the country checking on compliance with the regulations—an executive function. Finally, if the agency decides you are not obeying its rules, it can haul you before its own hearing examiners, who judge whether you have sinned—a judicial function. The hearing

Paradoxically, we may find that, when Y2k strikes, the failure of coercive government may be a blessing in disguise.

examiners report to the same agency head as those who bring the charges. This structure was, in essence, the tyranny of King George, against whom we rebelled.

Regulators are accountable only to their own agencies, unlike the president and Congress, who must answer to the voters at regular intervals. In fact, under the civil service laws, a bad apple working for the government is next to impossible to fire. It takes at least two years and a few million dollars in legal costs to get rid of a federal "civil servant," too often a living oxymoron.

The following points may blow your mind:

- For every law passed by elected bodies in the United States, there are now eleven regulations passed by unelected bureaucrats, which are binding upon you and have the force of law, often with criminal penalties, including jail and fines.

- If a regulatory agency brings a legal action against you which is appealed to the courts and it loses, it can repeat the process in another jurisdiction until you are bankrupt. Most defendants knuckle under to avoid the persecution or sidestep bankruptcy. It is easier to knuckle under to the IRS if the money involved is less than the legal fees it would take to fight it.

• Government often wins by default, simply because it can throw its battalions of attorneys—for whom you pay—at you without monetary constraints. A whole industry has grown up in Washington: law firms staffed by former regulators who try to get you or your company through the regulatory maze with minimal damage. The Watchbirds use "consent decrees" to get that which they could not get by statute or even explicit regulations. A consent decree is a document that you sign that in essence says, "I didn't do anything wrong, and I promise never to do it again." This, of course, will be published in a press release, listing all the alleged sins you promised never to commit again.

There is great incentive to cave in because constitutional guarantees don't apply. The Supreme Court has ruled 8-0 that you are not entitled to jury trials in "administrative proceedings."

Let's examine a classic but by no means rare or unusual specimen of the Gestapo-like behavior that is increasingly common with the controllocrats. It involves the Food and Drug Administration (FDA), an agency that is supposed to protect the nation's health and well-being.

Through its internally generated regulations, the FDA claims the power to decree that your health-food store is in violation of labeling laws, because on one shelf you sell a book advocating vitamin C for the common cold, while there are vitamins for sale on the other side of the store. This constitutes "misbranding" of the product by "claiming a cure," which, under the FDA's regulations, makes it a drug. Even though no such law has been passed by any legislature, the FDA has arrested a health-food store owner and clerk, confiscated the vitamins, and burned the books.

You may, moreover, be bankrupted by the cost of the legal battle even if you should win, because you can't sue for damages. Most mom-and-pop health-food store owners don't have the resources to fight, so freedom of speech and freedom of the press are trampled on by bureaucratic whim.

I have had several encounters with arrogant Watchbirds. These true personal horror stories are typical of the government's bureaucratic mentality that threatens our future.

Ruff's Watchbird Encounter Number One

One day I received a call informing me that my checks were bouncing. I immediately called my bank to find out what had happened, since I knew there was more than enough money to cover my checks. I was informed that the IRS had levied funds from my account to pay for an alleged tax deficiency. When I called the IRS, the agent told me that he had levied $12,000 from my account. When I asked him why, he said, "You owe us taxes for two years ago."

"How much?"

"We don't know exactly how much. We're still determining that."

"Then how did you know how much to levy from my account?"

"We just made sure we took enough."

"Why didn't you just call me? This could have been settled without taking money out of my account. I have checks bouncing all over America."

"If we had called you, you might have taken your money out of the bank and hidden it, and we could not have secured our interest."

It was finally determined that, due to a miscalculation in my return, I owed all of $35. It took two weeks to get the lien lifted from my account so I could have access to my funds. In the meantime, my credit was in tatters.

Ruff's Watchbird Encounter Number Two

Shortly after I started the *Ruff Times*, I got a call from the Securities and Exchange Commission (SEC) demanding that I register my newsletter under the Investment Advisor's Act of 1948, a law that was originally intended to regulate money managers but that had been expanded by arbitrary creeping regulation to cover all those the SEC deemed "investment advisors," including newsletter publishers who don't manage anyone's money.

My attorneys had concluded that I could avoid registering if I simply did not recommend specific stocks. At that time in my career I was primarily recommending gold and silver, and I had no intention of personally managing anyone's funds, so we restructured the *Ruff Times* to keep us outside the SEC's regulations.

The SEC finally admitted that I was in a "gray area" and that it "preferred" that I make some changes. We left with an uneasy truce.

The Constitution guarantees freedom of the press and of speech, right? Apparently not. Let me tell you what I could *not* do if I had registered.

1) I could not spend my money as I saw fit. I would be required to escrow 100 percent of the subscription funds I received, and only release them to myself proportionately with each issue of the newsletter—in my case, one–twenty-fourth of the money with each issue. But I spend as much money in marketing and direct-mail costs obtaining a new subscriber as he pays me in the first year, all before I even get the subscriber, betting on renewals. This would have cost many millions of dollars I didn't have. The regulation was impossible for me to comply with. Most old-timer newsletters were exempt from this requirement under "grandfather clauses."

2) I could not make personal investments without first notifying my subscribers. This would have totally inhibited my personal ability to act quickly for my own personal portfolio in fast-moving markets, since the *Ruff Times* was published only twice a month.

3) I would have to disclose the most minute details of my personal financial affairs and those of members of my family and executives of my company, including even our warehouse supervisor.

4) I would not be allowed to use testimonials from George Bush, William Simon, Howard Jarvis, Senator Orrin Hatch, among others, in my marketing.

5) I would have to pass certain examinations and register as an investment advisor (easy enough for me), and so would all my employees (not so easy for them). Then we would all have to pass similar tests in all twenty-nine states that require such registration.

I had two choices: (1) knuckle-down and register, accept the restrictions and raise the capital, and be free to write about individual securities, or (2) refuse to register and never recommend specific securities—a restriction of my freedom of speech. The chilling effect on what I could or could not write was a flagrant violation of the First Amendment.

The net effect? In order to stay outside the SEC's regulatory grasp, I avoided registering by not recommending securities, that being the lesser of the evils. I chose to live another day, and I hated myself for it.

But there is a rare happy ending to this story.

A year or two later, a financial advisor by the name of Lowe decided to start a financial newsletter—from jail. He was incarcerated because as a broker he had added a zero to a client's check and cashed it. In this case, a zero was not "nothing." When he applied to register with the SEC, the commission refused him on the difficult-to-refute grounds that he was a crook.

He took them to court and won. The SEC appealed, and it won—the decision was reversed. He appealed to the Supreme Court, and wrote to me and other newsletter publishers, asking for money to pay the lawyers. Although Lowe was truly sleazy, I decided that the whole issue of registration would probably never come before the Supreme Court again, so I ponied up some money. I prepared an argument and took it to a prestigious Washington law firm, which prepared a brief. I persuaded the ACLU and Ralph Nader, of all people, to submit their own briefs, and the court agreed to hear the case.

We won, 8-0, and I can now recommend stocks. But it's a travesty of justice to have to fight so hard for such a basic right.

Ruff's Watchbird Encounter Number Three

I once received a fascinating letter from Mr. Robert H. Hartline, supervisory agent of the Eleventh District of the Federal Home Loan Bank Board:

> Dear Mr. Ruff:
>
> We understand that during a December 24, 1978, telecast of the program, *Ruff Hou$e*, you made a statement to the effect that people should not put their savings into Savings and Loan Associations.
>
> We request that you provide us with a copy of the text of that statement and any explanation of the reason for such a statement, so that we may determine the *propriety of the statement* and whether it complies with applicable laws. Your early response will be appreciated [emphasis added].
>
> Sincerely,
> Robert H. Hartline

I found it frightening that a Watchbird would believe he had the right to "determine the propriety" of something I said on TV.

In the show under question, I read a letter from a viewer wanting to know whether he should put his money in a federally insured bank or savings and loan. My answer in part was:

No. I wouldn't put it in a bank or savings and loan right now. Your rate of return on those investments will be less than the rate of inflation. That, plus the fact that the "profit" is taxed, makes you a loser.

Second, we're moving into a recession, and possibly into a depression, and our banking system and our savings and loan system are moving into this in considerably weaker condition than when we went into the recession in 1974–1975. I happen to believe that we will see headlines in the not too distant future telling us that there are some very serious things wrong with our banking system, as we did in 1975. If you want to sleep well, no, I would not put money there.

A little research told us that Mr. Hartline's objection was based on a 1938 law that states:

Whoever willfully and knowingly makes, circulates, or transmits to another or others any statement or rumor, written, printed or by word of mouth, which is untrue in fact or is directly, *or by inference*, derogatory to the financial condition, or affects the solvency or financial standing of the Federal Savings and Loan Insurance Corporation, shall be fined not more than $1,000, or imprisoned not more than one year, or both [emphasis added].

This allows an official policy of concealment of the true condition of a bank or the banking system, and allows people to blindly make commercial deposits and buy bank stocks and CDs in troubled or even insolvent banks, while the government works secretly behind the scenes to bail them out.

On my next *Ruff Hou$e* show, I read Mr. Hartline's letter. I then looked sincerely into the camera and said, "Mr. Hartline, I'm not going to send you a transcript of that show. If you want it you'll have to subpoena it. However [dramatic pause], if anyone else would like a transcript of that show, simply write to me...."

I never heard from Mr. Hartline again, and we got several thousand transcript requests.

Some months later one of my associates attended a Washington party at which Mr. Hartline was present. When asked, "Have you ever heard of Howard Ruff?" Hartline answered, "I don't want to ever hear that name again." It seems Mr. Hartline had been bombarded with letters, and virtue triumphed. But most people who are challenged by a government agency aren't so lucky as to be able to rally public opinion and embarrass someone on the tube. I still find the incident chilling.

> If we can no longer control the government that is supposed to be serving us, we have lost something far more precious than money—our freedom.

Free speech might prove embarrassing in the short run, but in the long haul freedom of speech and the press is indispensable to our system. Without it, the system is vulnerable to bureaucratic tyranny. And that's precisely what I walked into.

Trust Your Government?

The above incidents have led me to ask this question of most audiences I address: "How many of you love your country, but fear and distrust your government?" Almost every hand goes up. The people I speak to are middle-class America—the backbone of this country. These are the people who marched off to war in Europe, Okinawa, Korea, Vietnam, and Desert Storm. These are the people who pay the taxes, support candidates, save their money, love their families, give to all the diseases, and personify all the values that have built this country.

And yet they fear and distrust their government. That is an amazing change from my childhood, when we saluted the flag before the first class of the day, said a brief prayer, and venerated our president as our leader. The disintegration of the attitude of

Americans toward their government parallels the growth of regulatory government. The Clinton scandals have accelerated the downhill slide.

Thomas Jefferson said, "I have sworn eternal hostility towards any form of tyranny over the minds of men." If that tyranny comes from our own government, we owe it to the Republic to expose it. As long as government remains our servant, it is a tolerable and necessary evil. When it tries to become our master, we must fight back.

Regulatory government is the arch-enemy of the free-enterprise goose that has been laying golden eggs. When you abuse that goose, she stops laying. If you kill her to have a goose dinner, you can feast on goose only for a little while. Then you have neither eggs nor goose. Not only is free enterprise at stake, free *anything* is at stake.

The usual argument for regulatory government is that it is protecting us for our own good. But as a philosopher once said, "If I knew that a man was coming to my house with the express purpose of doing me good, I would lock all my doors and arm myself against him."

Pioneers Saved!

North Platte, Nebraska (UPI), July 26, 1858—The Federal Trade Commission and Department of Transportation, together with the Department of Commerce, have just recalled all stage coaches of the Wells Fargo Company and the Bison model of the soft-top vehicles manufactured by the Conestoga Wagon Company of Independence, Missouri.

The noted consumer advocate Jim Bridger pointed out that motion pictures taken of an Oregon-bound wagon train being chased by Indians showed that, at high speeds, the wheels tend to turn backwards, creating a safety hazard.

It is anticipated that some families will have to camp along the Oregon Trail.

> Washington has assured the grateful travelers that food-relief shipments, food stamps, and federal troops will be provided. They were also assured that the help would be on its way within two years.

Imaginary? Yes. Funny? Perhaps. But more important, it illustrates a point about bureaucratic silliness and illogic and is not much of a stretch from reality.

Here are the twentieth century's three greatest lies in ascending order of immensity: (1) "My wife doesn't understand me," (2) "My check is in the mail," and (3) "I'm from the government and I'm here to help you."

Why have we allowed government to gain such power over us? We are seeing the fulfillment of the prophecy of Professor Alexander Fraser Tytler, a Scottish economist who studied the great democratic republics and pointed out that the later stages of the decline of a democracy are apathy and dependence.

The public is one corner of a three-cornered unholy alliance, as millions of people demand protection from the vicissitudes of life.

On another corner are our congressmen and senators who want to have their names on a piece of important legislation—and the real plum is to sponsor a new agency. That is their bid for immortality, because their creation will never die.

On the third corner are the Watchbird controllocrats whose very existence, livelihood, and future hopes depend on the creation, extension, and perpetuation of more regulatory programs.

Each year Congress introduces about 25,000 pieces of proposed legislation. Out of these, perhaps 400 will eventually be enacted into law. In short, with 535 legislators on Capitol Hill working full-time, less than one bill per congressional office gets signed into law. (Thank goodness it wasn't *two* bills per office!) Approximately 200 pages of the *Congressional Record* are published daily. But very little of the voluminous *Congressional Record* involves laws that affect your life.

However, every day a book as big as the *Congressional Record* arrives at each congressman and senator's office—the *Federal Regis-*

ter. Unlike the *Congressional Record*, the *Register* means business. It includes regulations proposed by government agencies as well as a few presidential executive orders. Nearly all of these regulations become law, complete with civil and/or criminal penalties. The *Register* is published every workday, fifty-two weeks a year—about sixty thousand pages a year. So we now have a body of law and regulation of such proportion that it often cannot be understood or obeyed. It is too huge and complex. If you are a small businessman or a professional, you could violate the law twenty times a day and never know it. But you could be held liable for fines or imprisonment, or be required to publish "corrective advertising," confessing your alleged "sins" before the world, or suffer any number of other penalties for laws you innocently violated.

We found out during Prohibition that when laws are not respected, law and order breaks down. America is built on a voluntary respect for its institutions and for reasonable laws, based on our conviction that these laws have been enacted by elected representatives who are responsible to us. But today the balance of law-making power has shifted from Congress to the Watchbirds.

Why has the growth of government power defied the best efforts of our last eight presidents to limit it? It's the good old American profit incentive. A government employee's pay and GS rating (the official status that dictates the pay-scale) are based, to some extent, on the number of employees and the size of the budget being supervised by that individual. Consequently, there is a built-in financial incentive to create a multiplicity of regulations that need to be supervised and that require more enforcement, legal, and clerical staff.

Here is how this idiotic system hurts us:

- It increases the costs of government so that the tax burden confiscates the money that might have been spent productively in the free economy to create real jobs.

- It adds to the budget deficit.

- We lose our freedom an inch at a time.

"A Giant Mechanism Operated by Pygmies"

In Jonathan Swift's savage satire, *Gulliver's Travels*, Gulliver was shipwrecked and washed ashore unconscious. When he woke up he was tied down, not by a thick rope or chain, but by thousands of threads, no one of which was strong enough to immobilize him, but which collectively put him in bondage to a race of pygmies.

Today we are experiencing something akin to Gulliver's plight, this time at the hands of government bureaucracy, which, as the French writer Honore de Balzac rightly pointed out, is "a giant mechanism operated by pygmies." We are rapidly drawing close to the point at which our bondage to the pygmies who run our bureaucracy will be total. If we can no longer control those who are supposed to be serving us, then we have lost something far more precious than money—our freedom. And we will find ourselves increasingly beset with the same kind of troubles that eventually destroyed the Soviet world empire.

Regulations never atrophy. They only evolve and proliferate.

Ruff's Laws of Government

I have five principles of government:

Ruff's First Law: Government is not compassionate or wise. Government is impersonal and stupid.

Ruff's Second Law: When government solves a problem, it invariably creates two problems of equal or greater dimensions.

Ruff's Third Law: The true function of government is to make small problems bigger.

Ruff's Fourth Law: It is the tendency of all governments to increase their power at the expense of the freedom of their citizens.

Ruff's Fifth Law: True patriotism requires resistance to the expansion of governmental power, within the spirit and letter of the Constitution.

Let's dig a little deeper into the worst of the Watchbirds.

The FDA Watchbird

The FDA kills people. Many drug discoveries that might have saved the lives of those who suffer from rare diseases quietly fade away because the cost of nursing a new-drug application through the FDA—even for a life-saving drug that might have only five thousand or ten thousand customers—is as much as $500 million, the same as the cost for a blockbuster drug like Prozac that might be used by tens of millions. That makes it uneconomical even to begin to develop, test, patent, license, and market such a drug. Many of these drugs are in common usage in other civilized countries, saving lives every day.

Because of the FDA, you probably pay at least 100 percent more for your drugs, and you are denied the use of effective remedies. If you buy unapproved drugs in countries where they are legal and cheap, and bring them home, you can be jailed for smuggling.

One of the most dangerous aspects of FDA regulation is that many of the regulations prematurely freeze into law areas that are essentially scientific issues still under dispute. For example, the whole vitamin controversy is based on the opinion of mainstream nutritionists who say supplements are useless. But a very talented and respected scientific minority—including Nobel Prize–winner Dr. Roger Williams and Dr. Linus Pauling—have vigorously disagreed, claiming that they are essential to the health of the population.

The FDA holds hearings with compliant "experts" who agree with the mainstream, and it sets up regulations governing potencies,

Recommended Daily Allowances, and legal dosages. The current majority opinion is now frozen into law, and it has become "consumer fraud" to advocate the minority position. It is illegal to compete in the free market with ideas that do not adhere to a government-approved conclusion.

As a result, scientific progress lurches to a halt. Look at the long list of medical and scientific advancements that required great pioneers to go against the establishment: the electrocardiograph, the electroencephalograph, Dr. Lister's germ theory of disease, not to mention Galileo's work.

Today, Lister would have to fight not only the AMA but also the regulatory power of government, which would harass and fine him for his "quackery." New mothers would still be dying of childbed fever because of doctors who go directly from the autopsy room to deliver babies without washing their hands.

Alexander Fleming, the discoverer of penicillin, would never even have reached the human experimentation stage under present FDA rules, since penicillin causes severe side effects in rats and dogs. Dr. Michael De Bakey, the heart-transplant pioneer, has said that under current regulations his pioneering surgery would have been impossible.

Applying my second law, "When the government solves a problem it creates two or more problems of equal or greater dimensions," I am convinced that FDA policies can be lethal because of their chilling effect on the advancement of the frontiers of knowledge.

The EPA Watchbird

When two agencies attack the same perceived problem, the results have, on at least one occasion, been lethal. The Environmental Protection Agency (EPA) and the Department of Agriculture gave us a perfect example of mindless government at work when there was a series of grain elevator explosions. These chain explosions completely destroyed four huge grain-elevator storage complexes, killing more than fifty people. Grain dust is up to fifteen times more explosive than coal dust, and an explosion is easily set off when the humidity drops below 35 percent or 40 percent. The obvious answer is to vent the accumulated dust out of the silos. EPA rules, however, prevent this, since it would "pollute the atmosphere."

Well, okay, let's use humidifiers to raise the humidity level above the flash point. Oops! This is forbidden by the Department of Agriculture, which says that the increased moisture would adulterate the grain. So the dust accumulates, and, as a result, more than fifty families are bereaved, and millions of bushels of grain are gone.

The FTC Watchbird

Sometimes the creeping loss of freedom due to regulatory agencies is so egregious that we can only laugh at it.

> Washington, D.C. (UPI), February 1, 1998—You may have noticed a different pattern in Santa Claus's visits to your children last Christmas. During August and September last year, the Federal Trade Commission (FTC) entered into private negotiations with a Mr. S. Claus of Nome, Alaska. Santa has agreed to a consent decree. Without admitting any wrongdoing, he agreed that beginning on Christmas 1998 he would no longer discriminate between "naughty and nice."

Perversely, the regulatory mess might be at least partially solved by a hearty Y2k crisis. One of its benefits may be a much smaller government. If the government's computers crash and burn, so might the Watchbirds. But if most of those computers survive with the government's systems largely intact and functioning, regulatory government may actually be strengthened by the emergency controls described in Chapter 4, "Power to the President." That would be a tragedy, indeed.

Action Steps

So, what do we do about it?

The broad outlines of a program to reform government and renew America are offered in Chapter 12. As long as these Watchbirds survive and have the power to continue to do their mischief, we have no practical alternative but to try to adjust to their bureaucratic stupidity. But we cannot sit idly by; we must be active in supporting and electing politicians who aggressively move government back toward the vision of the Founders (if you can find any). The trouble in the coming months and years may create a strong, dedicated antigovernment movement that might have the political clout to make the Watchbirds an endangered species.

In the meantime, we should hold to the fire the feet of any legislator who proposes any law or regulation that does not include a "Freedom Impact Statement."

If the Y2k crisis ends the ability of agencies to deliver their promised benefits, we must be ready to exploit the resulting antigovernment sentiment to restore constitutional principles to American life.

Chapter Six

Social Security: The Ponzi Chain Letter

Before we discuss the Y2k vulnerability of the Social Security system, there are some hard truths you need to understand and accept.

If you ask your financial planner to set up a retirement plan, he will include your Social Security benefits in your future income projection. After all, you gave that money to the government through payroll deductions to hold in trust for you, and it will give the money back to you. Right? Wrong.

Social Security is the most dishonest, unsound scheme ever foisted by government on a trusting public—a fraud so huge that it is nearly impossible to imagine.

Try this short True/False quiz:

T   F   Payroll deductions for Social Security go directly into the Social Security trust fund.

T   F   The money deducted from your paycheck will be saved for you and used to pay your retirement benefits.

If you marked both of these "false" you score 100 percent. But most people do not, simply because the Social Security system goes against people's basic assumptions.

Bear in mind that the national economy depends on the Social Security system. It disburses far more funds than any other governmental subdivision. FICA (the Social Security tax) is our biggest single tax. The impact of changes in Social Security payroll taxes or benefits is immense, and if we alter either one, the effects on the economy are complex and painful.

Social Security is a critical area of national vulnerability. Its soft underbelly will be attacked by Y2k.

Pensioners have been trapped into dependency on the system, and they will suffer if payments are not increased to compensate for cost-of-living increases or if they fail to be delivered because of Y2k problems.

The Shell Game: Now You See It, Now You Don't

Here is the fundamental, shocking truth about Social Security.

When the government forces your employer to deduct Social Security taxes from your paycheck, all of this money, along with your employer's "contribution," *goes directly into the general fund.* It is not held separately from other funds for your future pension. It is all used for current federal general expenditures in the year in which it is collected!

In lieu of the money it misappropriated, Treasury issues to the Social Security trust fund a special class of nonnegotiable IOUs, and these constitute the whole fund—approximately $757 billion in nonnegotiable paper as of July 1998. The trust fund has never seen any of that money—only these pieces of paper, which represent the money the government has ripped off and spent. When the government has a cash-flow deficit—which it has, as we will see, despite Clinton's boasting about a balanced budget—that IOU is just a promise to print money.

The trust fund is much less a future source of money than a ticking inflationary time bomb.

These securities, in other words, are a liability of the United States Treasury, secured by "the full faith and credit of the United

States government"—translation: "the printing press." When the fund disburses its monthly benefits, it calls on the Financial Management Services Division of the Treasury Department to issue checks and electronic transfers, and money is created to cover it. *All* the money being paid out has to be newly created at the time of payment.

The government would do this even if there were *no* government IOUs in the fund, and the inflationary cost to Americans would be the same. Everyone feels safer if there are pieces of paper saying the government promises to pay some money in the future, but the so-called Social Security trust fund is nothing more than a glorified set of bookkeeping entries. Just for form's sake, if it has to issue more money than was collected for FICA, the Treasury will merely retire some of those IOUs, and the "trust fund" shrinks.

Social Security is a critical area of national vulnerability. Its soft underbelly will be attacked by Y2k.

How valuable is a Treasury security held by the Social Security system? If you were to write yourself an IOU for $1 million, add it to your financial statement and take it to the bank to borrow against it, you would be laughed out of the bank. We cannot create real wealth by giving ourselves our own IOUs. The Social Security Administration is a division of the United States government holding IOUs of another division of the United States government—with no collateral. This paper represents no value at all. It is not a real asset.

As a result, any debate over whether Social Security checks should be paid from the general fund or from payroll taxes is simply a discussion of cosmetics.

The supposed depletion of the so-called trust fund is not the real threat to the system. The real threat is the rising tide of pension payments, supported by a shrinking pool of workers paying their FICA taxes.

The good news is that Social Security is not currently in deficit. In 1997 it brought in about $100 billion more than was paid out.

The bad news is that Bill Clinton is the political beneficiary of that fortuitous circumstance.

Early in 1998 Clinton began crowing about how his administration had "balanced the budget," and in September he announced that we were now in the black. Even the Republicans took up the cause; as the government began projecting budget surpluses for years to come, House Speaker Newt Gingrich proclaimed a "generation of surpluses." Almost immediately Democrats and Republicans began debating about how to use this alleged extra money, but all the elation overlooked the truth: there wasn't really a surplus.

Because I didn't trust the politicians, I went to the U.S. Treasury's web site on the Internet (<http://www.ustreas.gov>), where you can check out the national debt for any given month in our history. The national debt on January 31, 1997, was $5.313 trillion. Exactly one year later on January 31, 1998, it had risen to $5.492 trillion—a one-year increase of *$179 billion.*

So for calendar year 1997 the true budget deficit—which is how much more was spent than was earned (the same standard any family is held to)—was $179 billion!

So where did our supposed surplus come from? Social Security sleight-of-hand bookkeeping is mostly responsible for it, covering up about $100 billion of the deficit.

Under Lyndon Johnson, we adopted the "unified budget," which incorporates Social Security into the deficit calculation. Johnson did it to make his budget look better. Now FICA taxes are picked up as "revenue," and Social Security payouts are picked up as "expenditures," but the IOUs are not picked up as an offsetting liability. That is like a public corporation reporting pension contributions as revenue, but not recording the future payout obligation as debt—only as an expenditure when it is actually paid out. Any corporate CEO who artificially inflated earnings using the same techniques would go to jail.

And the bottom line is that in 1997 Social Security took in $100 billion more than it paid out, and it was considered to be "income" in the unified budget.

So Social Security is a government slush fund, and that reality stands in the way of honest disclosure and the reform of a monstrous fraud. The government will not permit any reform that would allow you to opt out of Social Security in favor of a private pension plan or allow FICA taxes to be invested in corporate bonds or stocks, as many have proposed. The system would collapse; it desperately needs the money.

The Social Security system depends entirely on your belief that (1) your payroll deductions will directly pay for your retirement, (2) the trust fund consists of real money, and (3) the banking and monetary systems are sound. We have been conned by the government's bookkeeping games. Social Security payroll deductions are simply another method of raising money to fund the government's needs. Your FICA payroll deductions have gone to Defense, Agriculture, FTC, EPA, and the rest of the alphabet soup of federal government, as well as Social Security benefits.

And Now the *Really* Bad News

The system is a gigantic fraudulent chain letter. Chain letters operate under the assumption that when you add your name to the bottom of the list and you send your dollar to the guy at the top, enough other suckers will add their names under yours so that when your name eventually rises to the top you will get money from those at the bottom. It pays off only if others fall for it. Its collapse is mathematically certain, since sooner or later the number of suckers coming into the system shrinks, it sputters to a stop, and the last guys in get ripped off. That's why chain letters are against the law.

Social Security operates under the same principle. The FICA money taken from your check is disbursed to those who are currently receiving benefits, including many who have paid nothing into the system, because the system is now being used to disburse social benefits. Because of that, plus cost-of-living increases in benefits, which have outstripped increases in payroll deductions, the time will come when it can't even pretend to operate on a pay-as-you-go basis. The result? The supposed "depletion of the trust fund."

You hope the system will hang together long enough so that when you reach retirement age, others entering the system will contribute enough to keep your checks coming. You are totally dependent on a continuous flow of new money from new workers entering the Social Security system.

That is an unstable base at best. Decades ago there were ninety workers supporting each person in the Social Security program; early in the twenty-first century, if Y2k hasn't wiped out Social Security, there will be only two. You are making a monstrous bet on your children's willingness to bear that tremendously increased burden, especially since the politicians will buy your vote by increasing your benefits to keep you up with the inflation they will create, thus adding to your kids' burden.

A Social Security Administration press release on April 28, 1998, stated, "The Trustees report that income from payroll taxes will become insufficient to meet all Social Security obligations in 2013." The press release admitted that by 2021 the trust fund will begin to shrink rapidly, and that by 2032 it will be all gone and the income will only be able to pay three-quarters of benefits. In other words, even the fig leaf will dry up and blow away.

It is estimated that, shortly after 2013, keeping Social Security in balance will require FICA taxes of as much as 40 percent. But long before that, we will reach the point at which the government won't dare take any more out of people's paychecks, lest the "pact between the generations" (that's what the government calls it in a candid admission that today's workers are really supporting their parents and grandparents) causes a *war* between the generations. So the government will be forced to pay you by the "inflation tax"— printed money—which will chew up the purchasing power of your money faster than your benefits will increase.

All of these numbers are based on assumptions provided by Rosie Scenario, the nice girl in accounting. She assumes decades of good economic years, a growing workforce, and only minor, transitory recessions—if any. Of course, a deep, multiyear recession or depression caused by Y2k is not factored in. Rosie's scenario is a pie-in-the-sky best case.

Ponzi Revisited

Social Security is the identical twin of a classic fraud case several decades ago when a man by the name of Ponzi raised funds from people by promising huge payoffs from investments in heating oil. He did nothing productive with the money and earned no profits for his suckers, but he paid huge dividends by using the money from new investors to finance the payoffs to old investors, which attracted more investors.

The pyramid eventually collapsed of its own weight, and Ponzi went to jail, but only because he didn't have a printing press and couldn't collect from the taxpayers. It's illegal when private citizens do it, but it's considered compassionate social engineering when the government does it.

As long as enough new suckers provide enough revenue to balance the cash flow, the fraud holds up. But if the number diminishes to the point at which the government cannot or will not balance the cash flow, then the system is inevitably exposed for the fraud it is.

Social Security has gotten away with it for decades because of a large workforce relative to the number of retirees, but the number of retirees is growing and the number of workers supporting each retiree is shrinking, and Social Security will soon become an obvious cause of large government deficits and inflation, and the whole monetary system will be at risk.

Cracks in the Plaster

An old friend of mine, Jesse Cornish, once said, "We always see the cracks in the plaster before the roof comes down."

There are some visible cracks in the Social Security plaster.

To begin with, more people are living longer, so, perversely, every medical advance that prolongs life is an enemy of the Social Security system; a cancer cure would devastate it. With our increasing life span, too few will be paying for too many.

The baby boom of the 1940s and 1950s, which brought a large number of workers into the system in the 1960s and 1970s, is about over. Fewer worker bees will enter the hive while the number of drones will increase enormously, and the birthrate is slowing to well below the replacement rate. If the government continues to increase the payroll to maintain the appearance of solvency, the economy will grind to a halt because of this terrible drag on the spending power of the American worker.

Contrary to the conventional wisdom, our senators and congressmen are really pretty smart. Realizing how unsound the system is, they have their own healthy, fully funded pension program with cost-of-living escalators built into their wages and their retirement. They can afford to vote for inflationary programs and more Social Security taxes and bigger monthly checks because they are insulated from the problems they have caused. Just remember this the next time you vote for a big spender.

I am less worried that the Social Security system will collapse than I am that the Social Security system will cause the nation's bankruptcy-through-inflation because it is the single largest obligation of government. And the debt defies description.

According to the government's most recently available balance sheets, the Social Security system has approximately *$7 trillion* in unfunded obligations (the excess of anticipated lifetime payouts to retirees over expected collections from people paying into the system). That means it will have to pay out $7 trillion more in benefits to those who are presently covered by the system than it will collect in wages. That's roughly equal to 75 percent of everything that everyone in America owns.

Self-Fulfilling Prophecy?

Will I damage the confidence in the system that keeps it alive by telling you all this? It's the old dilemma of whether to tell the terminal patient he's dying. But I trust the truth. In any case, sooner or later the problems will be glaringly obvious, and the dishonest, funny-money Social Security system will collapse of its own weight. Or it may be pushed—by Y2k. You must plan your life on the certain premise that Social Security will be of very little help to you, and it may have done a lot of harm.

For starters, it has discouraged savings, because it takes money away from you that you might have stashed away for your own retirement, and most people feel that Social Security will take care of them. The system has made Social Security junkies out of us because even the most sophisticated financial planners seldom seriously question that Social Security will be there when needed.

> **Sooner or later the dishonest, funny-money Social Security system will collapse of its own weight. Or it may be pushed—by Y2k.**

But there is no question in my mind that eventually Social Security will overwhelm our monetary system through inflation and the loss of confidence in government—if Y2k doesn't get us first. The system is immoral and dishonest, and we have become hooked on it.

What should you do about it? Here are Ruff's Recommendations:

1) Plan your future as though Social Security didn't exist.

2) Realize that if you accept your Social Security check when you don't really need it, you are taking it from some poor guy who had it ripped off from his paycheck last week. You are not getting back what you gave the government—it spent that a long time ago.

Old-Age Welfare

Welfare, by definition, is money given out of tax revenues to those who did not contribute to those revenues. So what's the difference between Social Security and welfare? Nothing!

As a matter of principle, I'm planning not to accept my Social Security check since I can do without it. But there is at least one ethical alternative: accept the money and give it to those who are paying for it—your children. Let them buy the kind of hard assets described in Chapter 9 that will survive the trouble ahead, or contribute it to the political campaigns of those who share this limited-government, free-market philosophy and can help get the Ship of State through the troubled waters without capsizing. Solve the dilemma as you choose, but please recognize that Social Security is welfare, pure and simple. Your FICA taxes paid for your parents' "old-age welfare," and you will collect old-age welfare taken from your kids.

And incidentally, the next time you get all starry-eyed about population control, just remember what it means to Social Security and other pension programs if the birthrate continues to drop and there are fewer suckers for the chain letter.

What Now?

If you are approaching retirement age, cut and scrape and set aside a little each month just in case you should live until the system fails, or the taxpayers revolt, or inflation explodes faster than the benefits increase, or Y2k bashes the system. You could work a few years longer and put something away as a cushion. If you are younger than fifty-five, make your retirement plans as though Social Security didn't exist. For you it doesn't.

If you are still comparatively young, and your parents are approaching retirement age, plan on caring for them if they can't care for themselves.

There must be a special place in hell for the liberal politicians, economists, intellectuals, social dreamers, and others who have made 280 million people totally dependent on an irresponsible, inevitably bankrupt plan, while dissipating the nation's assets. Whatever good has been accomplished by Social Security thus far—and it is considerable—will be offset many times over by the hardship that will come when it is finally revealed that the Social Security emperor has no clothes.

I am by no means the only one, or even the first, to sound the alarm. Way back on November 21, 1977, economics professor Michael Wachter of the University of Pennsylvania's Wharton School said in *The Journal of Commerce*, "Most people under thirty-five have virtually no chance of collecting Social Security and should avoid the system if they can and save for their old age."

Wachter, an economic advisor to Jimmy Carter, said he was scared by the tendency of families covered by Social Security to save less than others: "The government ought to be preparing the younger generation to face the fact that the Social Security won't pay for them, but they can't because then people would not go on paying the higher premiums."

Now, almost two decades further down the same road, I suggest you transform any fear created by reading this chapter into a burning anger for the cynical political opportunists who continue to sell this pig in a poke to the American public. The tragedy that is building will be remembered for generations.

Y2k: The *Big* Crack in the Plaster

The Millennium Bug, of course, could make the preceding moot. Much of what we hear about Social Security's Y2k readiness in the latest quarterly report to Congress from OMB is optimistic, as the Social Security Administration was forced to begin repairing its software way back in 1989 because it ran into problems calculating payouts to recipients expected to live into the twenty-first century.

So far so good, but there are some serious doubts to be resolved. First, the Social Security Administration has not gone very far into its testing, and it has more date-sensitive lines of code than most of the other agencies combined. Also, its computers have to interface with the states' computers, and I am reasonably sure of only two states that will be Y2k compliant—Washington and Pennsylvania.

But the worst problem for the IRS is Financial Management Services, a division of Treasury and a much-ignored component of the Y2k problem. This obscure but pivotal agency writes all the checks for all government agencies, including Social Security. It also handles all the computerized electronic transfers of pension payments to your bank. Its latest quarterly report to Congress on Y2k readiness says that it is way behind schedule and will not be ready by January 1, 2000.

If it is not, Social Security will be forced to develop a system from scratch to prepare more than eleven million checks and thirty-three million electronic transfers every month, probably manually. Mind boggling!

Then, of course, you don't know if your bank's computer will be Y2k compliant and able to receive the electronic transfer and accurately credit your account. We can only hope so.

There is a real chance that the Social Security system will be unable to keep its promises in the year 2000. My advice? If at all possible don't retire when you get to retirement age. Keep up your stream of income as long as possible, and save all you can. The only one you can truly depend on to keep promises to you is yourself.

Chapter Seven

Sin Tax: The Decline and Fall of Western Civilization

A chapter by this same name was in my 1978 book *How to Prosper During the Coming Bad Years.* "Sin Tax" was—and is—a moral and economic argument for traditional morality and traditional family values, and an attack on the sexual revolution. Unfortunately, it was the source of real trouble for me. One incredible incident graphically illustrates the problems I endured, as well as the moral perspective of those who filter the news before it reaches your TV set. It has chilling implications.

In early 1979, when the book was at the top of the best-seller lists, I was scheduled for an appearance on a major network TV talk show. I arrived in New York the evening before and waited in my hotel room for a call from one of the show's producers to go over the questions for the interview. I waited with growing unease as the hours passed—5:00, 6:00, 7:00, 10:00—until the phone finally rang.

It was my publisher's publicist, and she was in tears.

"You're canceled!"

"You mean postponed?"

"No. Canceled. They don't want you."

"Why?"

"Chapter 11."

"Who declared bankruptcy?"

"Nobody. It's Chapter 11 in the book—'Sin Tax.'"

"'Sin Tax'? I thought that would be the most attention-getting chapter in the book and that the media would love it."

"Well, they didn't. It rubbed them real wrong."

It seems that of the twelve producers for the show, ten were among the shock troops in the sexual revolution. If memory serves me right, five were gays or lesbians, five were living with a member of the opposite sex without benefit of marriage, one was an old-fashioned person who was not offended, and I don't remember the status of the other one.

A friend of mine who was present reported that there had been a pitched battle in a production meeting for four hours that evening, with the host, to his credit, wanting me to come on the show, and almost everyone else opposed. Finally, the opposition threatened to resign if I appeared, and the host reluctantly acquiesced.

To compound the sin, the producers called their counterparts at another talk show, and that show also vetoed my appearance.

To put this in perspective, the book was near the top of the best-seller lists for two years and became the best-selling financial book in history. I had multiple appearances on every other show of importance—*Donahue, Dinah Shore, Merv Griffin, Nightline*—all of which welcomed me. And nobody claimed that I was not an interesting interview.

As a postscript, after I reported the incident in the *Ruff Times*, the story was picked up by a major New York newspaper, which asked the powers that be at the network their version of the incident. When they finally responded six months later, they said that the reason for canceling me was my "impractical advice to invest in silver." But the value of silver had more than tripled in the interval.

Being a stubborn cuss when my principles are involved, I decided to update "Sin Tax" and include it in this book. Maybe they will talk to me this time.

John Adams said, "Our Constitution was made only for a moral and religious people. It is wholly inadequate to the government of any other."

Is Adams's statement relevant in an era when most Americans are saying that even though the president admitted his adultery and lied about it to the American people for months—and lied under oath—it is irrelevant to his qualifications for office because "the only thing that matters is the economy"?

The sexual revolution and its corrosive effects on the fundamental building block of American society, the family, will exacerbate the damage to America from Y2k, as millions of Americans will have to face the Y2k assaults on the infrastructure without a stable family environment.

> **The erosion of the family—the building block of American society— will exacerbate the damage to America from Y2k.**

The public's reaction to Clinton's admitted behavior scares the wits out of me. It's more important—and dangerous—than what Clinton actually did, and it has a lot to do with the economy that most Americans say concerns them. Any society's economy and investment environment must be interpreted within the framework of its values and its social environment. John Adams meant that America was built on a broad array of shared values (which are also shared by many who are not "religious"), and the president is expected to represent our most basic values. It is apparent that many of those values are no longer "shared."

The eminent political philosopher Edmund Burke elaborated still further on this principle: "Men of intemperate habits cannot be free. Their passions form their fetters."

The American experiment in self-government has worked for more than two hundred years because there was a general consensus that each of us had a responsibility to the general good, that every man was responsible for his personal welfare, that individuals were to voluntarily be charitable to those who were unable to care for themselves, but not for those who refused to work. We believed that life rewarded those who did honest work. We looked up to those who achieved and did not "fine" financial success by excessive taxation. We were willing to sacrifice security for the opportunities that complete freedom offered us. To be "on the dole" was humiliating, and this attitude spawned great achievements and strengthened society in general. The so-called "Puritan work ethic" was one of our core values, and it had its roots in religion.

We believed in secure, stable money, and several times through hard experience we learned what happens when we violate this principle. Our currency system has collapsed more than once, but the side effects were relatively limited in the past because there was a higher degree of decentralization and independence.

We did not need all-powerful masters and detailed Watchbird regulations to govern us. There was a general consensus as to what was "right" and "wrong" in ethics and morals, especially the rules of sexual behavior that protect the traditional family, which was honored as the basic structural unit of society. The "three-generation" family (children, parents, and grandparents in the same household) was the mainstay of our society, building a bridge across the generation gap. Adultery, unwed parenthood, and sex outside of marriage were universally condemned.

Much of this is no longer generally true. An intangible, "spiritual" consensus determines the strength of the society, and this nation or any nation can become ungovernable if this consensus crumbles. The Founding Fathers who wrote the Constitution took for granted that true freedom required voluntary restraint in private behavior.

Let's zero in on some critical areas where this consensus is unraveling—those that are most likely to give us societal changes beyond our ability to adapt to or cope with... or pay for. They all relate to the crumbling of society's most important unit—the family.

The Evolution of a Revolution

The sexual revolution has been and is an unqualified disaster, a huge threat to the institution of the family, our economy, and our social cohesiveness. We are now feeling its impact, although we usually fail to connect the consequences with the causes. It may be the one factor that undermines all the optimistic assumptions that seek to counter my scenarios.

Every successful society has had basic structural factors that are taken for granted and that must remain stable. In *Fiddler on the Roof*, Tevye understood this when he sang about "Tradition." Everyone in Tevye's village had a role and knew that role and performed it well, so it was a stable and balanced society. And when alien values came into the society at too high a rate, the social structure, first of Tevye's family, then that of their little village, crumbled around their ears.

The sexual revolution is an assault upon the basic nurturing unit of society—the family—and it has social and financial consequences that are awesome to contemplate.

This is not just a recent phenomenon. More than twenty years ago, Professor Urie Bronfenbrenner of the Psychology Department of Cornell University observed the disintegration of the American family:

> Changes of this magnitude have never occurred before except in times of great national upheaval, like wars, depressions and floods.
>
> The family will either become more important again or we will go down the drain like Greece and Rome did. As soon as the family fell apart in Greece and Rome, so did the whole society.

There is an epidemic of violence and vandalism in our schools, divorce and illegitimacy are rampant, and more people are choosing to live alone or cohabit without marriage—often with children—and these disturbing trends must be reversed if we are to survive as a nation. Also, families that have disintegrated due to adulterous behavior—or that never had a man in the house—will suffer the most from Y2k.

When children are born into a traditional family structure in which parents are loyal to each other and devoted to their children, societies remain stable—socially and economically—and are more likely to withstand and recover from economic setbacks. Families stay together, and divorce is infrequent. Reverence for family and ancestors and the associated traditions maintained relative social stability for centuries in the Orient. Khans, emperors, and commissars have come and gone, but the traditional Oriental family structure has survived. Similarly, the nuclear family was the cohesive stabilizing institution in the colonization and development of America. The sexual revolution is an assault upon that institution.

I have long been convinced that religious restrictions against extramarital or premarital sex, which are common to the Christian and Hebrew scriptures, are for the protection of society. They are not there just to please the prudes and killjoys and rob us of our fun. All the rules of sexual behavior, such as those against incest, fornication, and adultery, seem to be designed by a wise and caring Father to prevent the fracturing of our family support structure. The Divine rules against premarital sex are designed to prevent children from being brought into the world without a stable family environment to nurture them to maturity.

These were reasonable, rational attempts to persuade us to restrain our private behavior for the greater good of the society. Whether you believe the rules were man-made or inspired by God is of no consequence to the argument; they were wise rules.

In short, much of what organized religion calls "sin" is a set of essential behavioral standards, the mass violation of which will destabilize any society. This is not a simple matter of opinion or a theological, moralistic position. As we shall see from some of the statistics, violation of these standards leads to fiscal instability, confiscatory taxation, and inflationary ruin. We have no choice but to study human moral and ethical behavior alongside traditional economics if we want to understand the present and forecast the economic future.

Sex, Family, and Taxes

Throughout history, advanced civilizations have had very restrictive, somewhat puritanical sexual codes during their ascendance. At the zenith of these civilizations, as prosperity created leisure time and disposable income, sexual standards began to loosen, and the downhill slide and acceleration of their "sexual revolutions" gained momentum as the societies began their final declines.

In stable societies, codes of sexual behavior were honored by all but a minority. Even when the rules were broken, it was understood that an accepted standard was being violated. But in civilizations in decline, the broken sexual rules became the norm among the upper and middle classes, and the old rules were scorned and ridiculed.

Any society's economy and investment environment must be interpreted within the framework of its values and its social environment.

This is why I was so concerned over the reaction of the public, especially women, who are the traditional defenders of the family institution, to the Clinton sex scandals—particularly after the slimy details slithered out. Even after the sordid truth was revealed, the polls—if you can believe polls—said his sexual behavior didn't matter to more than 60 percent of Americans. Syndicated columnist Mona Charen's analysis is chilling: "If Clinton will just keep us prosperous, we won't hold him to any particular moral or ethical standards."

The issue before us that worries me the most is how we feel about adultery, and the polls give me no joy. What does this tell us about the sexual standards we are imprinting on our children if even the president does it and we don't care. How many fifteen-year-old boys are saying, "Now I *really* want to be president. You get to have sex with foxy interns"?

The Cycle of Democracy

A big part of our exponentially growing public expenditures is the bitter fruit of the collapse of old-fashioned values. Professor

Alexander Fraser Tytler, who wrote about the American experiment shortly after our Revolutionary War, analyzed what he called "The Cycle of Democracy." The core of his studies was the Athenian Republic two thousand years earlier, but his conclusions still apply today:

> A democracy cannot exist as a permanent form of government. It can only exist until the voters discover that they can vote themselves largesse [generous benefits] from the public treasury.
>
> From that moment on, the majority always votes for the candidates promising the most benefits from the public treasury, with the result that a democracy always collapses over loose fiscal policy, always followed by a dictatorship.
>
> The average age of the world's greatest civilizations has been two hundred years. These nations have progressed through this sequence:
>
> From bondage to spiritual faith; from spiritual faith to great courage; from courage to liberty; from liberty to abundance; from abundance to selfishness; from selfishness to complacency; from complacency to apathy; from apathy to dependence; from dependence back again into bondage.

Tytler's quote is not a change of subject. Perhaps the most dangerous economic aspect of the sexual revolution is that it creates an ever-growing, tax-consuming class that is growing faster than the tax-paying class.

Welfare would be a far smaller problem if it were not for the millions of children without fathers, and with poverty-stricken, ill-educated teenage mothers. Yet even as more and more voters are swilling at the public trough, political activists of the Left keep fanning the fires of guilt-driven spending for Aid to Dependent Children, welfare, food stamps, and other poverty programs, with the bills dumped on those who have lived by all the rules and succeeded because of it.

These programs confer legitimacy on sin, while the "advocates for the poor" and their liberal media fellows blame society, racism, sexual discrimination, and so forth for the behavior of the sinners.

Not only are these programs an ever-growing portion of government spending at all levels, we also have built into the IRS code cash payments to those whose income falls below the "poverty level." This means that a rapidly expanding class of voters gets to vote for the big spenders with no responsibility for contributing any of the money it wants the politicians to spend.

This, of course, creates the irresistible temptation to buy votes with money from the public treasury—exactly the problem Tytler exposed. We fought a revolution over the principle of "no taxation without representation." Now we have representation without taxation.

The family is not only the nurturing unit of society, it is also the means by which the values, tradition, and culture of one generation are passed on to the next, and by which the inexperienced young are protected against the consequences of their immature errors. The quality of the family determines whether succeeding generations will be neurotic, criminal, unstable, and a burden to society, or strong, responsible, moral, independent, and emotionally and spiritually stable contributors to society. When we train our children, we are, in effect, training our grandchildren. Adultery brings jealousy and sexual rivalry that can poison or break up the family unit, or, at the very least, make it a loveless environment in which to raise a child, one that severs the lines of transmission of values and traditions.

Adultery is also as much of an integrity problem as it is a sexual "sin," because the adulterer has to lie, sneak around, and violate his most sacred promises. I don't believe anyone can lead a deceitful double life without spiritual and emotional damage. Based on the studies that confirm the epidemic of extramarital sex, we may be becoming a nation of liars and sneaks.

Adulterers are liars, and serial adulterers are brilliant liars. Bill Clinton is a glaring example. It was not as shocking that he lied to cover up an affair as it is that he did it so brilliantly and persuasively. He duped those closest to him—his family, his aides, and his cabinet—even in the face of the mounting pile of evidence. Habitual lying has poisoned the deepest wells of his character.

Teddy Roosevelt said it well:

> We can afford to differ on the currency, the tariff, and foreign policy; but we cannot afford to differ on the question of honesty if we expect our Republic permanently to endure. Honesty... is an absolute prerequisite to efficient service to the public. Unless a man is honest, we have no right to keep him in public life, it matters not how brilliant his capacity.
>
> Without honesty, the brave and able man is merely a wild beast who should be hunted down by every lover of righteousness. No man who is corrupt, no man who condones corruption in others, can possibly do his duty by the community.

Bad Numbers

When society relaxes or abandons its restrictive taboos against premarital or extramarital sex, as we have done today, there is an explosion of unmarried family units without long-term legal ties and financial or emotional commitments.

According to the U.S. Bureau of the Census, in 1996 there were 19.7 million children under the age of eighteen living in unmarried family units, mostly with teenage parents. That number is up from 14.7 million in 1986, 11.1 million in 1976, and 5.8 million in 1960. Of those totals, approximately half were children of divorced parents or had been abandoned, and about one-third of the parents had never been married.

Though the climbing divorce rate has flattened out, it seems to be because the most unstable elements of our society, which would be the most likely to divorce, don't marry. They live in those unmarried households, which are the ones that will break up, leaving father-less—sometimes motherless—children, and no statistical divorce trail.

When society condones casual sexual relationships that create children without a father role model—with little girls missing out on safe male affection and little boys not experiencing father-son bonding—the end result is generally promiscuity, illegitimacy, and the accompanying burden on society. The most stable and productive members of society end up paying the bill.

Loosening sexual morality has hit Americans right in their pocketbooks.

I know what it is like to grow up without a father. My dad killed himself when I was six months old. When I became a husband and father, I had no role model in my past. I had to learn how to do it all by myself, and the result was a lot of mistakes. If I became an okay father, it was against tough odds and because of Kay's tough tutoring.

Loosening sexual morality has hit Americans right in their pocketbooks. The exponential growth of welfare costs and property taxes can be directly traced to the sexual revolution, and it is the major contributing factor to juvenile crime, gangs, alcoholism, abortions, drug addiction, and disruptive schools riddled with violence. It has turned the hearts of our great cities into social, financial, and moral wastelands—bottomless sinkholes for your tax dollars.

This is anything but a new problem. More than twenty years ago, Peter Schuck, at that time deputy assistant secretary of Health, Education, and Welfare, said, "There is definitely a high correlation between out-of-wedlock births, welfare costs and many of our most pressing social problems."

The intervening years have not only confirmed that he was right, but have also seen matters get much worse. In late 1998 the Family Research Council published some horribly depressing statistics:

- Women who bear children out of wedlock are far more likely to be on welfare and to spend more years there, as will their children.

- The illegitimacy rate among black Americans rose from 26 percent in 1965 to 68 percent in 1997—and it's still climbing. Among white Americans, the illegitimacy rate rose from 2.29 percent in 1965 to 22 percent in 1997.

- Nine out of ten unwed mothers land on the public assistance rolls, which is many times the rate for married mothers. Too often the children run wild for lack of supervision, and mothers become mired in a life of poverty, alcoholism, drug addiction, and child abuse, which they pass on to their own children. Fatherless children are the biggest cause of juvenile crime and teenage pregnancy.

One study at the Utah State Prison showed that nearly 80 percent of the inmates grew up in a home without a father. More than 70 percent of all juveniles in state reform institutions come from fatherless homes, and the likelihood that a young male will engage in criminal activities doubles if he is raised in a home without a father.

An Equal-Opportunity Employer

We often hear that the unemployment rate in our inner cities is horrendous—as much as 70 percent. But I submit that it may be much lower than that, because many are gainfully employed in activities—sometimes very lucrative ones—that don't show up in the official business and income statistics. They are criminals.

No one knows how many people in the big city ghettos are numbers runners, low-level drug dealers, prostitutes, muggers, gangbangers, or burglars, but it is not unreasonable to speculate that if we ever stamped out all crime in the inner cities, many of their legitimate businesses—where the criminals spend their money— would suffer from falling sales.

Crime has several advantages:

- It's an equal-opportunity employer; there is no discrimination on the basis of race, gender, or social status. The profession confers its own social status.

- Its proceeds are tax-free.

- It rewards hard-working, risk-taking entrepreneurs.

- It escapes the oppressive burden of government regulation; no OSHA, no handicap parking, no environmental-impact studies, no tax lawyers or accountants to keep track of the business and file mountains of reports to satisfy government snoops.

But as Dr. Bronfenbrenner has pointed out, "These people are going to put a growing burden on our society, not only to sustain them, but to repair the social and economic damage they do." The total cost to society is impossible to calculate exactly. You would have to add up the cost of food stamps, Aid to Dependent Children, local and state law enforcement for juvenile crime, the cost of trying and incarcerating the youthful debris of single-parent homes, various and sundry welfare programs, and so on. It's many billions of dollars every year.

Our old-fashioned value systems have survived for thousands of years because they are good for societies. Strictly from the perspective of a social observer, I don't know whether relaxation of these values is a consequence or a cause of a declining civilization. It may be both, but it is, at the least, an accompanying factor to the rate of decline.

Be Good, or Else

This raises an interesting question. Does society have a right to enforce its traditional morality by laws as a protective measure to save itself, if that enforcement interferes with the human right to "sin"? The answer is that if the majority of the people in a society has chosen to violate these stabilizing standards, passing laws will only drive these people underground, making the forbidden fruit that much more attractive. Prohibition proved that. Again, we get back to John Adams's apt analysis: There was an invisible consensus that made it unnecessary to depend on laws to regulate the details of our lives. The people themselves responsibly regulated their own lives.

The Constitution was thus not an experiment in government but an experiment in freedom. It was not designed to regulate our lives, but to protect us from an oppressive government so we could freely choose how to conduct our own lives.

To attempt to control morals by law raises grave questions of freedom. But at the same time, permitting the mass flaunting of aberrant behavior gives social respectability to social disintegration and raises equally grave questions. I feel threatened in either case.

That is why the crusade to force or shame us into accepting homosexuals' "alternative lifestyle" as equal in legitimacy to heterosexual marriage is profoundly disturbing. Homosexual sex is by its very nature profoundly antifamily, and society's approval lends legitimacy to the whole idea of sex outside of marriage. Nevertheless, laws attacking homosexuals are an assault on freedom, and I feel in jeopardy when society is forced to choose between these two alternatives. And of course, hate or violence against anyone is an affront to God. Jesus said, "Inasmuch as ye have done it unto the least of these, my brethren, ye have done it unto me."

But remember, it is always the nature of government to expand its mandates in all directions—when you give it a hammer, everything looks like a nail.

Any society that does not have a general consensus that sex is reserved for heterosexual marriage will reap a harvest of unstable relationships that shift like the sands, leaving children the bewildered, crippled victims. But if the invisible consensus to which John Adams alluded breaks down totally, a free, democratic society cannot enforce laws regarding sexual behavior without becoming a police state.

The Role of the Model

The lack of effective male role models in the home doesn't just affect the children in that home. It leads to unstable second and third generations. Marriage is a tough enough learning ground for amateurs, even if they grew up *with* role models.

All we can really do to insulate ourselves from the general moral collapse is to create oases of sexual stability and fidelity in our homes and churches. If we don't, the next unstable generation will bleed us even drier in welfare costs, crime, drug addiction, alcoholism, violence, police costs, fire costs, legal fees, and gigantic government efforts to deal with these problems. If we sow the wind, we will reap the whirlwind.

A society that collectively makes dysfunctional decisions in the area of sexual morality is on a collision course with financial and social disaster, to say nothing of the moral and religious implications. No moral authority can be exercised over America by its elected leaders that has not voluntarily granted them by virtue of their exemplary lives.

Based on the above principles, and on economic grounds, I am terribly concerned about pornography, sexually explicit films and TV, and bringing children into the world without the emotional, financial, moral, and legal commitments of marriage. I am especially concerned about publications advocating the "new morality," such as *Playboy*, *Penthouse*, etc., which have gained such respectability that you can buy them in almost any drug store or convenience store in America. They have greater potential for evil than hard-core pornography, which everyone knows is dirty, without question.

Playboy pays premium prices to respectable authors to write articles on serious subjects to provide the rationale that many people need in order to justify buying sexually explicit soft-core material. The resulting tolerance by much of the American mainstream tells us more about Americans than it does about the publications. The universal acceptability of such trash, which enables people to buy it without having to go through a door marked "XXX," has corrosive power to influence sick attitudes and rot society at its core.

I am concerned about the consequences of a middle-aged man comparing his loyal wife, as she loses the battle with gravity and adds wrinkles and pounds, with the forever-young, physically perfect, immune-to-the-effects-of-gravity-and-aging centerfold, and finds that his faithful spouse does not measure up to this fantasy-land ideal. No woman can compete with that, and this fantasy may be the reason for so much male sexual dissatisfaction and infidelity, and for so much unhappiness in the home.

Fortunately, the pendulum can swing both ways. The 1920s were a period of great sexual license and moral disintegration. Isadora Duncan, with her free-love philosophy, was a much-admired heroine of her times. The movies were really quite explicit for their times, and there was a growing underground market for hard-core pornography. But when we were hit by the Great Depression in the 1930s, the nation swung back into a puritanical backlash, and illicit sex had to retreat and go underground where it belonged. This puritanical period lasted almost forty years.

We can only hope that our age is just another swing of the pendulum, albeit considerably worse than during the 1920s. We can only hope that the pendulum will swing back during the hard times ahead because most people will simply not have the time, leisure, wealth, or emotional energy for the hedonism that now surrounds us.

I hope I have conveyed the fundamental concept of the social, economic, and freedom-constricting consequences of moral disintegration. It was brought home to me when it cost me thousands of dollars every year for several years to care for three children of a woman friend of our family who had joined the sexual revolution. These children, who were conceived by two different fathers, without benefit of matrimony, ended up in my lap. When she could not keep her crippled family together for a variety of reasons and came to my wife Kay and me for help, we couldn't say no, for the sake of the children. Moreover, of the eighteen foster children we have had and the four teenagers we adopted, several experienced sexual problems in the home. We have seen the sexual revolution's devastating consequences firsthand.

Not only will the direct and indirect costs of the sexual revolution have to be numbered in the hundreds of billions of dollars and some day in the trillions, but it is an unimaginable waste of precious human potential.

When Y2k hits, someone will have to help the fractured families that will be hurt the most. And if that isn't an economic issue, I don't know what is.

Part Two

Prescription

Chapter Eight

Panic Proof

If you are at least partly persuaded that Y2k is really serious stuff, you have some very important decisions to make, especially if you believe the intermediate- or worst-case scenario in Chapter 3 is possible. But if you honestly believe that there will be no bank closures or holidays, that our computerized banking system will remain stable and liquid, that there will be no electrical failures and/or brownouts or disruption of the railroads, that you will be able to drive to your supermarket, make a selection from an almost infinite variety of goods on the shelf, pay them with your personal check, drive home, and store them in your dependable, electric-powered refrigerator, then you can ignore the rest of this chapter.

If, however, you think our systems are vulnerable to the Millennium Bug, this chapter contains the most important advice in the whole book.

In truth, I hesitated before including this chapter because it may be perceived as "doom and gloom." Many in the media will be saying, "There he goes again."

I've been recommending emergency food storage for twenty-five years, but not for apocalyptic, end-of-the-world reasons. It arises out of my Mormon, nineteenth-century, pioneer, self-sufficiency heritage. In the coming months a lot of people who have an emergency food-storage program may well find out why it was a good idea.

Unfortunately, for years the storage of food has also been advocated by the real end-of-the-world apocalyptic believers, and I will probably be tarred with their brush. But, despite my fellow travelers, it is still a sound principle. Buying food for storage is much like paying for an insurance policy. You spend hundreds of dollars every year to insure your cars against the accident you fully expect not to happen, and you can't eat the canceled checks. You pay life insurance premiums, betting that you will die prematurely, and hoping you will lose your bet and the insurance money will be wasted. Food storage is the insurance you can eat. It will never have to be wasted. And to give you one more perspective, if the Y2k problem causes a bank holiday and disrupts the system, won't you want your neighbors to have a food-storage program?

> **In the coming months a lot of people who have an emergency food-storage program may well find out why it was a good idea.**

I don't know which or how many cybernetic systems will fail on or before January 1, 2000, or which ones will be repaired in time, because we are still too far away from that fateful date, and as the deadline draws near, there will be a huge "crash-prevention" effort. We know some systems will be repaired and tested; some will be repaired but not tested and subject to the inevitable bugs and programming errors that crept in during the repair process; and many (number unknown) critical systems won't be ready at all. Nor do we know which parts of the country will be affected by power shortages, if any. We don't know which banks will be closed due to technical failures or just because of panicky bank runs, or even whether someone will invent a magic bullet that makes Y2k look like silly, end-of-the-world fantasizing.

"Uncertainty" is the operative word here. Unfortunately, the marketplace and the economy hate and fear uncertainty even more than confirmed bad news and can react badly and unpredictably. But even if only some of what we've discussed here ever happens, there is a very good chance that the market system that has brought to your local supermarket the incredible variety of goods that you take for granted will have glitches with consequences that may last hours, days, weeks, or even months.

I cannot for the life of me understand how people can believe my diagnosis has a real chance of being accurate and still be willing to literally bet their wealth and well-being that the marketplace will still function efficiently by not having an emergency supply of food on hand.

The marketplace is like a hardy, tough-to-kill weed; it will always be there. But because of Y2k, we can't be positive that it will always function dependably, and it is highly likely there will be at least some partial and periodic disruptions. Most of the time, food will be available, but perhaps not what you would prefer to eat. You might have to stand in line for scarce goods. Computer problems could upset the complex and delicate chain of transportation, distribution, credit, and payments that restocks your supermarket shelves every night.

Back in 1962 I was driving across the eastern Colorado prairies on a business trip when I turned on my radio and heard President Kennedy announcing the Cuban Missile Crisis. When he told us the Soviets had missiles in Cuba and had put the Strategic Air Command on alert, my stomach turned over, and I was hit with a cold chill, since we lived only fifty miles from Strategic Air Command headquarters in Colorado Springs, an obvious target.

I stopped at the first gas station, called Kay, and asked her if we had any food in the house. That's a rather embarrassing question for a Mormon to ask because we are counseled to have a year's supply of food, just in case, but back in those days we didn't feel we had enough money to do it. When she said we didn't have very much, I told her to go down to the supermarket and buy everything she could with whatever money she had.

When I got back to Denver, the markets were jammed with people buying everything in sight. Even the anchovies, pickles, caviar, and paté were gone by the time I got there. Newspapers reported fights and minor rioting because securing a food supply was the first instinctive response.

I also got caught up in a panic when we had a brief meat shortage in California in the early 1970s. One day I stopped at the supermarket to pick up some groceries for Kay. As I walked by the meat tray, which was an empty, glistening chrome wasteland, suddenly one of the clerks came up with a cart full of plastic-wrapped packages of hamburger and dumped them in the tray in front of me. There must have been an announcement over the store PA system that I didn't hear, because as I was deciding if I wanted any, I was literally swarmed over by a fierce crowd of pushing, gouging, elbowing women, all grabbing for hamburger. Entering into the spirit of the occasion, I began grabbing for all I could, while doing my share of pushing and shoving, and charged off to the check-out counter with my arms full. After I paid for the ten packages of hamburger I had managed to corner, I suddenly realized I didn't even like that store's hamburger. I had been caught up in a small panic, and I didn't like what it had done to me.

Perception can be as bad as reality in its effect on the marketplace. An old stock-market adage says, "Buy on rumor, sell on news." Johnny Carson once created a month-long toilet-paper shortage with a joke about such a shortage on the *Tonight Show*. The American people tend to swing between total apathy on the one hand, often accompanied by a near-total refusal to acknowledge real problems, and overreaction on the other hand.

This chapter is designed to panic-proof your life, to keep you calmly above the fray when everyone else is losing his head. We should start with our most basic and critical need—the production and distribution of food. You are vulnerable simply because going without food for a few weeks is not an option. Food is perishable, and the distribution system is sensitive to delays and disruption.

To prevent misunderstanding and overreaction, let's put to rest some irrational fears. America won't ever have an African-type famine, with people dropping dead in the streets. We will always produce enough food in the vast agricultural areas of California and the Midwest to feed our people. We could have a 60 percent failure of our wheat and corn crops and still have enough to feed ourselves, since we export that much. But all this abundance is of no use if it is not efficiently distributed. Distribution is the weak link in the food chain, and if that were crippled, prices would go sky-high, and you might be intermittently reduced to a rather strange, unbalanced diet because of spot shortages and scarcity..

Most food shortages or even famines are caused by politics and economics. Consider the horrible famines in places like Somalia, where there have been tiny tots with matchstick arms and legs and distended bellies. In this world of incredible abundances and surpluses, people are still starving. Hundreds of thousands of people have died in Eastern Africa, and the physical and mental growth of children has been permanently stunted by lack of protein and calories. The reasons are instructive.

The world is producing much more food than it can consume and could produce several times more, and America and other prosperous nations have been willing to send more than enough food to Somalia. But even after nations sent food and it arrived safely in the port cities, the people still starved. African politics and distribution systems were either unprepared or unwilling to deal with the problem. In some cases, food supplies were hijacked by the warring parties to feed their armies during fratricidal civil wars, making pawns of dying people.

This is an extreme but classic example of how famines are usually caused by political, social, and economic forces, rather than natural disasters. In fact, in October 1998 the Nobel Prize for Economics was given to an expert on famines who came to this same conclusion—that famines' roots are economic and political.

In America computers have blessed our lives and given us thousands of minor miracles that we take for granted and hardly notice, but the computerized world is like a duck, floating serenely on top while paddling like crazy underneath.

In 1964 I bought a plane and learned to fly. Later someone convinced me I would be a lot safer if I had two engines instead of one, so we bought a twin-engine Beechcraft Baron, under the assumption that if one engine quit, the good engine could get me to an airport in one piece. Great idea, but I soon made an interesting discovery; going from one to two engines more than doubled the complexity of the plane. Complexity increases vulnerability exponentially, so you have several times the chance of something going wrong. For that reason, the rate of fatal accidents is higher in twin-engine aircraft than in single-engine planes. A twin with an engine out can fly, but a split-second mistake can ruin your whole day.

Our food-distribution system suffers from this same problem: The risk of malfunction has soared as complexities have multiplied. Food in the supermarkets now depends on an increasingly complex, computer-dependent distribution and marketing system that functions beautifully as long as all the engines are working and there is no severe high-tech turbulence.

Imagine what would happen to that system if the banks were in trouble, or even were only *perceived* to be in trouble, and payment and credit were in doubt. The possible repercussions are staggering to consider.

Would food be delivered to the grocery stores? Every day shoppers spend hundreds of millions of dollars in all the supermarkets of America, and the next day, as if by magic, those shelves are full again and ready for more hordes of shoppers. The complex system that brings food to the supermarkets of America—and into your home—depends on normal credit and a sound banking system. This allows the farmer to deliver his wheat on credit to the elevator operator, who delivers it on credit to the barge operator, who takes it down the Mississippi, and so on up the chain of processing, credit, and transportation to the supermarket, which trusts you and the banking system enough to accept your check for a loaf of bread.

And even if your supermarket could get food, would it routinely accept your check at the check-out counter? Would credit be routinely extended at every point in that complex chain?

What if the truckers believed they couldn't depend on their paychecks because of uncertainties about the banks, and went on strike and set up a gauntlet of picket lines at any of the critical and sensitive distribution points?

What if the banking and credit system became unworkable, even for a short time? We would have to totally reorganize the system by which people are paid for their products or services, and the changes would be monumentally disruptive and would take time.

If you panic-proof your life, you can stay calmly above the fray when everyone else is losing his head.

What if Y2k bugs in the government's computers crippled its ability to deliver welfare checks, food stamps, Social Security, Aid to Dependent Children, etc., even for just a little while?

For example, what if a small bug in the Social Security system's Y2k repairs (or those of Financial Management Services, the agency that actually writes the checks and makes the electronic transfers) resulted in 10 percent of the checks not being delivered, or being for the wrong amount? How would the Social Security system handle five million phone calls, especially if our telecommunications system was impaired or suffering from glitches and bugs and chronic busy signals?

Do you believe that large government-dependent populations will take this sitting down? Some people might, but a lot won't. There will be angry people—especially in the big cities.

Would food move safely into your local supermarket every day, and could you safely walk in with your money and walk out with your food?

What if there are brownouts or blackouts, even for a couple of days? Are you sure you will be able to buy fresh meat or milk? Every day? Any time you want?

How do you buy food if there is a bank holiday? Or if your supermarket won't accept your check? And what if your supermarket's computers, which tie into the register at the check-out counter, are unable to function and track the inventory as they ring up the purchases?

And what about American farmers? If they can't get their food to market, there will be a rash of bankruptcies in the farm belt. What if the government's computers can't calculate and pay the subsidies on which American farmers now depend?

The American food-growing industry has become almost entirely dependent on massive applications of hydrocarbon-based fertilizers, pesticides, herbicides, etc. made from petroleum and natural gas, most of which is transported by train.

It can truly be said that the food chain begins in the sands of Saudi Arabia or in the bowels of the earth below the Gulf Coast of Louisiana. We import more than half of our oil from the OPEC nations, about two-thirds of that from the Persian Gulf, and that percentage has been rising steadily.

What if farmers can't get those hydrocarbon-based fertilizers pesticides and fungicides that are so essential to the American food-growing industry? Modern oil wells and supertankers are computer-controlled and infested with embedded chips—and we don't know how many or which ones are not Y2k compliant. Remember that some of those oil-rig chips are next-to-impossible to inspect, reprogram, or replace because they are in drill heads thousands of feet underground or deep in the earth's crust under three thousand feet of ocean.

Pesticides and fungicides to protect plants that were bred for yield, not resistance to insect infestation and disease, are hydrocarbon-based. What if farmers cannot run the pumps that pump the water that irrigates the crops that were bred for yield and not for hardiness and drought-resistance? If we cannot in effect pour back into the soil eleven calories of hydrocarbons for every calorie of food we take out of it, the nation's food production will be crippled.

Stored Foods

Over the twenty years I've been publishing, hundreds of my subscribers have said, "I agree with your philosophy and would like to ask you a question." Then they ask my advice about money. When I suggest an emergency food-storage program as a backup position, they say, "I haven't gone that far, but I have some silver coins. I will always be able to buy food with silver coins, even if the currency collapses."

But you can't buy it if it isn't being transported. You can't buy it if there is panic at the supermarket with a crowd standing around waiting to storm the delivery trucks. You can't buy it if there is a banking panic or a bank holiday. You can't buy it if it isn't there. I know that sounds unthinkable, but Y2k raises at least the possibility. Panic buying can occur even if there is no real problem and people only anticipate one. There are all kinds of less-than-apocalyptic reasons for having an emergency supply of food on hand. For instance, in 1968 my speed-reading business went down the tubes when my franchise was abruptly canceled, and I was forced into bankruptcy. I went to work rich and came home broke, which ruined my whole day. Fortunately my wife had squirreled away some food-budget money and accumulated a supply of food that helped sustain us during the next several months until I could establish a new income and get on my feet. If we had not had that food, we could not have used what little money I was able to earn or borrow to continue to make mortgage payments and maintain some stability for our family during that difficult period.

If we have a Y2k-driven recession or depression, some unknown number of you will lose your jobs or your businesses, or your employers may go out of business. The peace of mind that comes with an emergency food supply in a period of vulnerability makes it worthwhile, even if you never have to eat it. Just being able to stay home for a few days during a big-city civil disorder can be important to your personal safety and peace of mind.

Moreover, a food-storage program bought now will give you an outstanding tax-free return on your investment; your profit consists of the money you don't have to spend later to buy expensive food if prices explode due to shortages and uncertainties about the currency. They can't raise prices next year on the food you bought this year.

Odds

As we have seen, there are fragile links in the food-distribution chain—oil and gas production, the railroads, and the transportation from the farmer through that whole complex chain of food distribution to the supermarket, where it will have to be paid for with a check drawn on your possibly non–Y2k-compliant bank.

One or more of these problems could likely materialize; the odds favor it. We just don't know which ones, or how many. In addition, we don't know how many repaired computers will be corrupted by bad data imported from unrepaired computers. But we are certain that thousands of corporate and government computers will crash or regurgitate bad data.

If you put a gun to my head and made me bet which are weakest links in the food chain, it would be transportation and the banks.

You should start right away to exchange some of your money, not just for food, but for all those things without which your life would be difficult or uncomfortable.

But start with food.

Hoarding versus Prudent Preparation

Prudent and timely food storage is not hoarding. Of course, that's what the media will call it. But it's hoarding only if you wait and try to buy food later when it is scarce and everyone else wants it. If you buy it now during a time of abundance, you are not hoarding.

I would bet that most of my newsletter subscribers who have at least in part accepted my assessment of Y2k have not taken the logical leap of storing food, and that is sad because it is the only riskless piece of advice in this book. It is an essential part of your financial planning, and if you are not willing to do that, you probably don't *really* believe the rest of this book.

If I'm wrong, the worst thing that could ever happen to you is that you would eat your food and save some money. But if I'm right, you will eat it and save your health.

Modern storage foods are a far cry from old K-rations. Dehydrated and freeze-dried foods are almost indistinguishable from the fresh product. They are also economical because there is no waste; everything in the can is 100 percent edible.

Implicit in the concept of storing food are many moral and technical questions:

Q: Isn't it likely that if I store food and Y2k disrupts food distribution, hungry people will try to take it away from me and I will have to defend my food with guns?

A: I often hear that rather dumb question, usually coming from a TV-show host. It's almost hard to take it seriously. It assumes a worse-than-worst case, which is far from a done deal. It assumes that I think hordes of people will cast aside all civilized restraint. It assumes you can defend yourself against a mob. And it lumps me in with right-wing militia types and apocalyptic cults whose beliefs I do not share. I take at least partial exception to each of these assumptions, though it does make for more interesting TV.

Although I believe one of the consequences of a Y2k worst case will be a soaring crime rate, including burglary and house break-ins, I'm not worried about hungry mobs scouring the countryside. I would, however, be concerned about temporary disorders in big cities with large government-dependent populations.

My worst case tells me that *if* we see such civil disorders, they will mostly be limited to the core of the big cities. The odds are that you won't be in great personal danger if you stay home during the worst of it, especially if you live in a small town. There may be brief periods of panic if the food-distribution chain is disrupted, and a lengthy period when food prices will be terribly high, and/or choices severely limited, and/or many commodities in short supply.

Small towns and cities—with populations of fifty thousand or less—are more likely to have smaller government-dependent populations. They are perhaps too small to make up the critical mass of angry people necessary to sustain civil disorders; they are more likely to have a tradition of law and order, making such mass lawlessness less likely. Such towns also tend to be more self-sufficient, especially ones with diversified, agriculturally based economies.

I expect to use my food-storage program to tide me over during brief periods of shortages and possibly a lengthy period when the variety and quality of food I need to maintain optimum health may not be consistently available. I can supplement available supplies by intermittently dipping into my food storage when necessary over a period of months or even years.

This is not preparation for the end of the world; that's impossible. It is preparation for a period of personal hardship, possible loss of job or failure of business, temporary disruptions of food distribution, and an indeterminate period of national convalescence in which you may not be able to buy what you want when you want it, in the quantity and quality you want.

I would also like my neighbors to have a food-storage plan, and I have stored some extra food to help members of my extended family, although they are mostly in good shape. The best way I know to help prepare them is for you to loan them or buy them a copy of this book. It could be a better persuader than you.

Q: Is it moral to store food when other people don't have any? If everyone took your advice wouldn't it create shortages?

A: There is enough surplus grain now to provide between 100 to 150 pounds for every man, woman, and child in America. Whole wheat is one of the basics of my food-storage program.

Storing food in times of surplus is, of course, merely prudent preparation. It is hoarding only when supplies are limited, and besides, the government may even make that illegal by rationing. Moreover, when people store food in times of plenty, they will not be competing for food in times of scarcity. There will be more for everyone else, including the poor and the profligate. I'm sure the people in my town will be glad not to have me and my big family standing in a food line ahead of them. Food storage is good for you and good for America.

Q: Where do you store your food, and how much space does it take?

A: Concentrated dehydrated or freeze-dried foods need only one-seventh to one-quarter of the space of an equivalent amount of fresh foods. If you use a proper mix of grains, beans, supplements, and dehydrated and freeze-dried foods for a balanced and interesting diet, a year's supply of food for one person could be put under two card tables. It can easily be stored in the bottom three feet of your closet. Properly prepared, it requires no specialized storage facility, and doesn't take up a lot of room.

The peace of mind that comes with an emergency food supply in a period of vulnerability makes it worthwhile, even if you never have to eat it.

Q: How long will this food last?

A: Nitrogen-packed dehydrated food has a nutritional shelf life from four to seven years, which means it will not start losing nutritional value for at least four years, depending on the temperature at which it is stored. Wheat, if kept dry and protected from the weather and insects, will last for two- or three-thousand years. Some that was found in King Tut's tomb was still edible, and it even germinated. I have been told by farmer friends that it is one of the modern ancestors of the ubiquitous hybrid grains.

Q: How much does a good food-storage program cost?

A: If you prepare a complete do-it-yourself program, you can set aside a year's supply of food for one person for as little as $200 to $500. If you want an interesting and varied diet which falls somewhat short of gourmet fare but is reasonably appealing, using some dehydrated and freeze-dried food, a year's supply for one person would cost about $1,500. That is very close to the cost of feeding your children for a year while shopping at your local supermarket.

If you want a really luxurious freeze-dried food-storage program, complete with beef stroganoff, shrimp creole, and sirloin steak, you can pay as much as $5,000 per person. It all depends on your pocketbook and your inclinations. But it still isn't a heck of a lot compared to what you are now spending on food. And you can buy your program a bit at a time.

Q: When should I buy this food?

A: You already know the answer—buy it *now*! I'd rather be a year too early than a few days too late. It wasn't raining when Noah started building the ark. Do it before you follow any of my other advice. As this is written, due to the Y2k fears of a small number of families, commercial food-storage programs are back-ordered for as much as seven months. As awareness grows, it will get worse. If your money is limited, just do the best you can. It's your surest investment from a strictly dollars-and-sense point of view, and it's the one indispensable piece of advice that applies to everyone. Disruptions in the marketplace due to computer failures can come with stunning swiftness and could create problems overnight. Of course, you might not need it for a year, or two, or three. Or perhaps never. But then again, you might need it next week.

You can't get insurance when the roof's on fire, and the best insurance is to become food self-sufficient.

There are three basic ways to do it:

1) Nineteenth-century style: If you live on a farm or have an acre or two, you can become self-sufficient by using intensive methods of organic gardening and raising chickens and rabbits. You will then have less need for a food-storage plan, although you might want some commercially prepared foods set aside for winter and spring when supplies may run low, or as a protection against crop failure. If there is hunting or fishing close by, so much the better. If you have the land, skills, and inclination, that's a great way to go.

2) The do-it-yourself food-storage plan: Most of you can't be self-sufficient in food production, although almost everyone can grow something, even if it's only in a window box or a sprouter. You buy bulk basics such as wheat, powdered milk, honey, salt, and beans, and you purchase containers and prepare them for long-term storage. This approach to storage is a lot of work, and not exactly gourmet fare, but it can be a real money-saver.

The most outstanding book on the subject is *Making the Best of Basics* by James Talmage Stevens, which you can order through any bookstore. It is a classic reference work on self-sufficiency. It belongs in your library.

3) Commercial dehydrated or freeze-dried food-storage plans: These programs are prepared by firms in the business of preparing dehydrated and/or freeze-dried foods. They also have some grain. They range in price from $2,000 to $3,000 or more for a year's supply, and $5,000 or more for a complete program of choice freeze-dried meals, which are indistinguishable from those you would consume in a middle-quality restaurant. You can have fair variety and taste in the $1,500 to $2,000 range. There is a tremendous variety of choices for your pocketbook and palate.

Most commercial packaged units have some nutritional holes to be filled, for some value is lost in processing and over time, as I will discuss in a minute. With some prudent nutritional supplementation with vitamins, minerals, and protein supplements, you can prepare a rather austere year's supply of food for one person that will keep you healthy for several months for a few hundred dollars—$40 to $100 a month—a pretty good bargain.

Dependable food-storage dealers, with contact phone numbers, are listed in the Appendix.

Nutritional Problems

As I said above, most commercial food-storage programs have nutritional holes that need to be filled in by food supplements.

Back in 1973 when I began thinking about the implications to my family of a food shortage, I instinctively turned to commercial food-storage programs, because I'm not a farmer, and I don't have the time or inclination to do a lot of do-it-yourself stuff. But I do have a deep interest in health and nutrition. I was in the food-supplement business in the early 1970s, and for more than a quarter of a century

I have been an obsessive reader of nutritional literature, ranging from the far-out natural-food freaks to the mainstream scientific and professional journals. I felt reasonably able to evaluate and choose a sound program.

I found, however, that commercial plans were at least partly at odds with the healthy nutritional lifestyle I had chosen for myself and my family. There wasn't one I could buy as a "unit"—which is the way it was being sold—and meet my own nutritional standards. I would have to supplement my own unit.

Also, a rising tide of underground concern about Y2k has already strained the resources and production capacity of many of these companies, and you may have to wait a while for a balanced, nutritionally sound program.

Let's look at the dos and don'ts of food storage. First the don'ts.

Thou Shalt Not

1) Don't depend entirely on canned and frozen goods. They both have problems for storage.

The calorie is the measurement of the amount of energy you derive from food. Canned goods are high-cost calories; they usually consist of more water than food. Also, the taste and color are generally inferior to that of dehydrated or frozen food, especially the vegetables.

The nutritional shelf life of canned goods is also somewhat in doubt, despite the claims of the industry. By "nutritional shelf life," I mean the length of time you can count on the food having the same value it had when it was canned. The nutritional value starts degrading long before the food begins to deteriorate enough to become unpalatable or dangerous. And even to begin with, the nutritional value of canned goods is lower than that of dehydrated foods due to the heat used in canning.

It's fine to make canned goods a part of your program, especially sources of high-quality animal protein, such as water-packed (because the shelf life is longer) tuna, as long as you use and rotate them, but you need to compensate for the nutritional losses due to processing and the passage of time with good natural multivitamin supplements and plenty of extra vitamin C, plus a high-quality protein powder.

Frozen food has an even shorter shelf life than canned goods, to say nothing of its obvious vulnerability to Y2k-induced power interruptions. I would not want my food supply to depend on an unbroken flow of electricity to my home.

Canned and frozen foods can be part of a short-term storage program, but for longer-term storage, there are much better alternatives. Because we don't know just how much damage to the infrastructure will be caused by Y2k or how long it will take to repair, you would want to make sure you could safely eat your stored food with good nutritional results several years after its acquisition.

2) Don't buy just any "food unit." Never buy from a food-storage dealer without following the guidelines in this chapter. Many of the units are based on economic consideration rather than sound nutritional principles. Even those companies that have made an effort to be nutritionally sound have generally relied on government nutrition tables, which, unfortunately, have little relation to reality. I haven't seen anything yet the government has not been able to foul up. Also, in my opinion, the FDA is the most biased, industry-influenced regulatory agency of all. It is a captive of the food-processing and sugar industries it is supposed to regulate, and that bias is reflected in the industry-financed studies it publishes. I don't trust its nutritional evaluations.

3) Don't put a neon sign outside your home advertising "FOOD HERE." It would be best to be discreet. You don't have to be paranoid or extreme about it; just don't go shouting to the world that you have an emergency food-storage program.

4) Don't let your food sit there. Rotate it! Use it and replace it regularly as long as replacement foods are still available. There are good reasons for this: (a) it will have higher nutritional value when you use it if you constantly replace it with fresher products, and (b) if the time should ever come that you must rely on it for your family, the transition will go a lot smoother if you are accustomed to it. A sudden change of diet to unfamiliar foods can be stressful. Get used to using whole wheat, beans, and protein powders. They're healthy, and it is a fine way to save money, since foods bought in bulk are a lot cheaper than those bought every week at your supermarket.

Thou Shalt

1) Prepare a seventy-two–hour kit. Pack enough food in a duffel bag to feed your family for seventy-two hours. Keep the bag where you could grab it and run in an emergency. Also include flashlights (with *good* batteries), utensils, plates and cups, a good knife, a non-electric can opener, matches, a sewing kit, toiletries, toothbrushes and toothpaste, medicines, a first-aid kit, and a change of clothes.

2) Set aside a six-month to one-year supply of food. Even in my theoretical worst case, the nation would not be without food for a year, but there is a distinct possibility of intermittent and unpredictable shortages—possibly days or weeks at a time—for several years, or at least until all the computers are up and running again. It doesn't take very long to get hungry. I would be able to draw from my emergency food supplies over a period of several years to replace those foods that may not be available in the quality or variety of choices to which I am accustomed.

I also feel I should have enough to share with those I love who will not believe my message in time—and I want some available for barter.

You will obviously have to work within your own financial limitations, but food is your number-one priority, and it comes ahead of any of my investment recommendations. I wouldn't want to be the richest hungry man on my block.

3) Be sure your program is nutritionally sound. Nutrition may bore some of you, but if you don't want to do your nutritional homework, maybe someone in your family will, so delegate the responsibility.

This may incur the wrath of the vegetarians, but most vegetable protein is incomplete. Sixteen amino acids make up a complete protein, and they have to be in balance with each other or the body can't use the protein for the things that only protein can do—make muscle, connective tissue, enzymes, hormones, antibodies, etc. The body can only inefficiently convert incomplete proteins to sugar and burn it for energy.

Most vegetable proteins are short of one or both of the "limiting amino acids"—lysine and tryptophan—without which you cannot have a complete protein. There are two ways to solve this problem:

- Mix and match them. In the same meal you can combine foods that complement each other. Corn and beans, or corn and rice, or rice and beans, or wheat and rice, taken together in the same meal, make a fairly complete protein.

- Eat or drink a protein supplement in the same meal. These protein powders are usually derived from soy beans and milk sources to make a complete protein. If you dissolve it in reconstituted powdered milk, you have a tasty milkshake.

Powdered milk can be an important part of your program, but there is some evidence that the limiting amino acids are damaged by the heat used in processing, so don't depend on it for all your protein.

I have used the Neo-Life protein supplement for years. It is tasty and of the highest quality. You can buy it from Norvel and Joann Martens (800-824-7861). (Two decades ago I was a distributor for Neo-Life, but I have no further interest in it, except as a user of its products.)

Now, what about vitamins and minerals?

Any time you might be forced to consume your stored food would, by definition, be a time of high stress, and stress increases certain nutritional requirements. You need a good natural antistress multivitamin supplement, and extra vitamin C.

I don't have any one to recommend over all others because there are several good formulas sold through independent distributors. I especially like those sold by the Neo-Life Company (Joann and Norvel Martens, 800-824-7861), Usana (John Carstensen, 800-481-4900), and Meleleuca (Tim Ruff, 888-846-7833). I have no financial interest in your purchases, although my son, Tim, sells Meleleuca. You can usually get a sizable discount by signing up as a distributor, and this does not obligate you to sell anything.

I believe that a good supplement program, when added to your basic storage program, increases the odds that you will stay healthy during a stressful time. Supplementation is a good idea anytime.

Sugar: A Negative Nutrient

A typical food-storage program has too much sugar (sucrose, glucose, corn syrup, dextrose). Many programs rely on gelatin for protein, and most commercial gelatins are half sugar and have very low-quality animal protein.

Sugar is not just a bad nutrient, it's a negative nutrient. You require substantial amounts of the B complex to metabolize it in every cell of your body. Sugar contains no B complex, so your body must rob its tissues. Sugar actually creates an excessive need for these nutrients.

Sugar is also a stress factor. Because sugar is so rapidly absorbed, the body sends out the alarm to produce excessive insulin to reduce the blood-sugar levels, causing stress to the body and resulting in a rapid conversion of sugar to stored fat, rather than energy. I see no merit in adding more stresses if we really have to use our food storage.

Honey

You can store honey in place of sugar. Common table sugar (sucrose) is a compound sugar consisting of approximately 50 percent glucose and 50 percent fructose. Fructose is at least twice as sweet as sucrose, and provides most of the sweetness in your common table sugar.

Honey sugars have a much higher ratio of fructose, so you can do the same sweetening job with less sugar intake. Do not think of honey as food, but as a relatively healthful condiment. Honey also contains trace minerals and B vitamins that are used to metabolize it, eliminating some of the negative-nutrient aspect that plagues sugar.

Once you have used it for a while, you will probably prefer its taste over sugar's. We've used it for years as an all-purpose sweetener.

Honey keeps virtually forever. Bacteria doesn't seem to be able to live in it. It does crystallize and become solid, however, but that is readily corrected by putting the container in a big pot of water and heating it until the honey liquefies. In warm weather you can just put the container in the sun for a couple of days.

Brain Sugar

When you are under stress, the water-soluble vitamins (C and the B complex) are rapidly depleted. These vitamins, particularly the B complex, are involved in the process that fuels and powers your nervous system, including your brain. Brain cells can only use blood sugar for energy, and this requires the B complex for metabolism.

There is much evidence now that shortages of these vitamins can produce states of anxiety, fear, and even schizophrenia. One team of researchers, when visiting the Pellagra wards of African hospitals (Pellagra is the B vitamin–deficiency disease), found that most of the patients were exhibiting mental and emotional disorders that were indistinguishable from paranoid schizophrenia.

Summing Up

To sum up my advice on food storage:

1) Prepare a seventy-two–hour kit.

2) Store a six-month to one-year supply of food.

3) Be sure that it is a nutritionally balanced antistress program, and that vitamins, minerals, and protein supplements are an important part of it.

4) Don't rely totally on canned or frozen foods.

5) Rotate your food supply and replace as needed.

6) Buy it now. The food-distribution chain is vulnerable to computer breakdown, and as the world wakes up to Y2k, the commercial food-storage companies will get even farther behind. Even if you acted today, it would probably be several weeks before your food was delivered.

Buy your food before it is "hoarding," at a time when it is readily available and the marketplace is functioning normally. And if I am wrong about our future, the worst thing that will happen is that you will eat your food-storage program and will be amazed when you find some of it indistinguishable from the food served in some pretty good restaurants.

Miscellaneous Self-Sufficiency

We can't store everything in the world, but we can look about us and determine those miscellaneous items that are crucial to our comfort and well-being and our ability to function in a disrupted society.

If you are going to prepare realistically for a worst-case Y2k crisis, a lot of items you take for granted may not be there to buy, or will be priced out of sight. I have a few fundamental recommendations.

Energy Self-Sufficiency

There are so many ways that our gas, electricity, and heating oil supplies are vulnerable to HAL that I think it is simple prudence in a cold climate to have a modern wood-burning stove and a supply of fire wood. The new millennium begins in the dead of winter.

Modern wood-burning stoves are a far cry from the old Franklin stove. They are air-tight, and the rate of burn is controlled by regulating the amount of air that enters, which is an extremely sophisticated form of draft.

If you live in a moderate climate in the Sun Belt, you could probably get along without one for heating, but at the very least you should have a good charcoal grill for cooking, along with a substantial supply of charcoal. Don't use the grill indoors without adequate ventilation; the carbon monoxide can kill you.

You can install efficient wood-burning heating units in your existing fireplace. You can't heat a house with a typical fireplace, because there is more heat lost up the chimney than is gained through radiation into the room. When the fire is burning, the hot air rises up the chimney, drawing air out of the room, and cold air is drawn into the house through cracks and openings, and the net effect is that the rooms away from the immediate vicinity of the fireplace get colder. But there are fireplace inserts that will recirculate hot air back into the home, allowing you to heat a pretty good-sized home with a fireplace.

You can generally find fireplace-mounted heating units in your Yellow Pages under "Fireplaces."

Water Storage

If you are storing dehydrated or freeze-dried food, it takes a lot of water to reconstitute and prepare it, and our water supplies are vulnerable to Y2k. We will also probably see increasing terrorist activity as those who hate us see our struggles. Terrorists would be utter fools if they didn't target our pumping stations.

During the New York City power failure and blackout in the early 1970s, most buildings were not able to get water from the faucets above the third or fourth floor. If this happens for just a few hours, it's a minor inconvenience, but if it lasts more than a day in the hot summer, it gets serious. Emergency water storage is another of those harmless ideas that cost you nothing but could be lifesaving.

Store at least two weeks of cooking and drinking water, more if possible. Use spare containers to store drinking and cooking water—at least two gallons per day per person. Add a couple of drops of chlorine to each container, and buy some inexpensive portable emergency water filters. The best ones use silver-impregnated activated charcoal.

Odds and Ends

Go through your house, room by room, drawer by drawer, cupboard by cupboard, and list all those items that would make life difficult or uncomfortable if you couldn't buy them on a regular or recurring basis; then stockpile them. Where you would ordinarily buy one, buy three. Buy spare parts for your car, such as fan belts, hoses, plugs, tires.

Hunting and Fishing

I'm often asked if you should store guns. No, I don't think you should store guns; you should *use* guns. Anyone who wants to be truly self-sufficient should be a hunter or fisherman. I'm not a killer, but I fish and will learn to hunt so I can supplement my family's diet in an emergency. It also doesn't hurt to own some guns to have the security of knowing you could protect your family if necessary. And

I doubt if there will be a better barter item in a period of currency breakdown than standard ammunition. It may be the best possible investment you could make, not just for barter purposes, but for price appreciation in a terminally ill monetary system.

Medications

If you have a medical problem, stock plenty of the appropriate medications. Check the *Physician's Desk Reference*—every doctor has one—for the shelf life so you can rotate it at appropriate intervals.

Also, assemble a complete first-aid kit. Be sure you have a broad range of over-the-counter and prescription medications, including painkillers, so you could deal with an emergency.

I am a fan of alternative medicine and believe you should have a homeopath prepare you a good homeopathic first-aid kit. These do work and can be an important adjunct to your health program.

We can always hope for the best, but we should be prepared for the worst.

If you live in a cold climate where an interruption in electric power could create real hardship or danger, buy a dozen extra blankets, warm socks, and caps to help keep your family warm in difficult times.

Paranoia or Prudent Preparation?

Some of these things will sound nutty unless you have bought my premise that we stand on the edge of a precipice whose depth is presently unknowable. But there is nothing I've suggested here that wouldn't be useful to you even if the worst case didn't materialize.

If you live in or within fifty miles of a big urban area with a large government-dependent population, move. If you are not ready to take such a radical step, including a change of job or profession, then at least arrange to visit Grandma over Christmas and New Year's 1999 until you know it is safe to go home.

Life in much of America can go on, at least on the surface, pretty much like it did before 2000, but big-city life is really at risk.

You must choose whether you agree with my best case, my intermediate case, my worst case, or don't believe me at all. Then act accordingly, realizing you may be betting your family's well-being on your decision. I would prepare for a worst case and then be thrilled to death if it didn't materialize. We can always hope for the best, but we should be prepared for the worst.

Chapter Nine

Gold: $2,000 in 2000?

In Chapter 2 I recounted gold's extraordinary monetary history. We traced the evolution of money from a pure barter system, to gold coins, to gold in the warehouse, to receipts representing gold, to receipts representing nothing, to cybermoney in banks.

If the Y2k problem destroys confidence in the banks, we could go back to using gold and silver coins as a means of exchange and a store of value for days, weeks, months, or possibly years. Those who don't own gold and silver may have to resort to barter until the old system is propped up or a new monetary system evolves.

Paper currencies, shells, beads, wampum have come and gone, but gold is always there. Even when it isn't actively being used as money, it is always lurking in the background, and it can perform several important functions:

1) Gold can (and should) be backing for our money.

2) Gold can and will be a means of exchange and a store of value when other monetary systems break down.

3) Gold is a fine investment at certain points in the monetary cycle, especially with a fiat currency.

A Gold Standard?

My main purpose with this book is not to lobby for a gold standard—America is simply not ready to accept a gold standard yet. We abandoned it in the first place when we no longer wanted to be restricted by the discipline gold was supposed to provide. Deficit spending and the subsequent money printing had created so much paper money that there was not enough gold in the central bank to redeem all the dollars that foreigners, worried about the stability of the American dollar, were bringing to the Fed to swap for gold. This run on our gold stores became so serious that President Nixon acted to conserve our gold reserves by "closing the gold window," officially severing the connection between the dollar and gold.

We will have a gold standard only when we collectively surrender to the need for discipline over the money-creation process and are willing to quit spending more money than our real wealth justifies. This discipline will probably materialize only after our present monetary system is in tatters.

I will address this subject briefly in the last chapter. The key question for now is, will gold again be *de facto* money?

If the worst case described in Chapter 3 comes about as a result of Y2k and there is a huge shortage of paper cash, gold probably will serve as real money. The Fed, in order to preempt possible future bank runs, announced in August 1998 that it was printing enough paper money to meet panicky withdrawals from the banks—$200 billion worth. But this could be only a drop in the bucket; the Fed could be forced to print many times more than that. Paper money will shrink in value because of its abundance (inflation), history will repeat itself, and gold and silver will again become real money.

Of course, this is *not* a 100 percent certainty, but it is a distinct possibility—one you must prepare for. You should have a supply of gold and silver coins, just in case. As with food storage, you won't be hurt by preparing for a possible crisis even if it doesn't come. If the current monetary system survives, your gold and silver coins will probably pay off anyway, since, at this writing, they are so cheap they are almost riskless.

I believe Y2k could drive gold to record levels in the year 2000, to the tune of $2,000 per ounce—$2,000 in 2000.

Inelastic Gold

Gold as an investment vehicle is unique. Many "investments" have an elastic supply; as demand increases, production can increase to meet it. Not so with gold, because the supply of gold is severely limited. Remember, all the gold ever mined in the history of the world would fit in a cube less than fifty feet square, and that includes the gold in your teeth, the gold used in industrial processes, and the gold at the bottom of the ocean in sunken Spanish galleons. It takes years to find a new mine, test out its reserves, and put it into production.

Y2k could drive gold to record levels in the year 2000, to the tune of $2,000 per ounce.

From 1932 to 1972, gold was price-controlled, fixed at US$35 per ounce. Starting in 1969, as savvy foreign investors and central banks became nervous about rising inflation, a two-tiered world gold market developed: one tier with an official fixed price of $35— the price at which central banks traded gold—and a worldwide free-market price that applied everywhere but in America, where since 1932 citizens had been denied the right to own gold.

In 1972, however, it became legal for Americans to own gold again, and, as concern grew over the value of paper money due to monetary inflation, more and more investment money began to flow into gold, starting a bull market. Gold went from a low of $35 an ounce in the early 1970s to a high of $850 an ounce in 1980. Fortunes were made by those who bought early and unloaded at the right time, and fortunes were lost by those who bought at the top and held on through thick and thin, eventually selling out under $400 in the 1980s or 1990s.

There is a lesson here: Don't confuse gold as an investment with gold as a crusade for a return to a gold standard. To many gold bugs, gold is always a crusade. They are the ones who gave back all their 1970s profits in the 1980s and 1990s. Investors have to be more pragmatic about gold; sometimes it is a terrific investment, and sometimes it is not. Although my book and the *Ruff Times* helped popularize gold in the 1970s and we made a lot of money, I've been bearish most of the time since 1980, which turned out to be a good idea. Now, because of Y2k, I'm bullish again.

Magical Gold

The gold and silver mystique is expressed in language, legend, fairy tales, clichés, and value judgments. It is natural to speak of silver linings, the golden boy, the Midas touch, the pot of gold at the end of the rainbow. No matter how cleverly governments assure us that paper and ink and a computer-generated bank statement are real money, whenever a small but significant segment of the world's population gets worried, these people want gold and silver. It doesn't take much interest in the metals to bid up the price, since there isn't much around.

Gold and silver tend to be countercyclical to paper investments—they move in the opposite direction from paper. When paper-based economies are booming and everyone is confident that inflation is under control and no one sees any real dark clouds on the horizons, the price of these metals tends to fall, which is precisely what has happened during most of the 1980s and 1990s. But if inflation is accelerating, the dollar is falling, war is imminent, or people are uncertain about the stability of their political institutions or their banks, the price of these metals has traditionally risen.

Nevertheless, some of the old factors that moved gold can no longer be depended on (during Desert Storm, gold hardly blinked), and lots of wealthy, safety-seeking foreigners who used to buy gold when worried about their currencies now buy U.S. Treasury debt. There is no Cold War to scare people into gold.

Gold and silver also have industrial and jewelry uses—silver much more so than gold. But although supply and demand for gold as a commodity are still important, if there is to be a real bull market in gold, demand will have to come from investors and calamity hedgers, not jewelry makers.

Gold still needs a falling dollar and rising worries over the safety and the value of our currency in order to take flight again. I believe Y2k will do just that. When the Y2k crisis hits, if only 1 percent or 2 percent of the money fleeing the stock and bond markets in a market crash goes into gold, you will see that $2,000 gold in 2000.

The old adage "Buy low, sell high" is still true with any investment—stocks, real estate, whatever—but it's even more true of gold because it pays no interest. Real estate will pay you rent, bonds will pay interest, but gold returns nothing but capital gains—and peace of mind.

As this is written, gold has been in a terrible environment, drifting just below $300 for many months. The stock market has boomed, inflation is low, and all the forces that traditionally drive the gold price have been hibernating for years. But because gold has been able to hold its price at these levels without breaking down, there is very little downside risk. The sellers have sold, and gold is in strong hands.

Gold is also a safe investment because it is very cheap right now. Look at the "suit standard." In the 1920s you could buy the best men's suit of clothes in New York for one $20 American gold coin. In 1980 you could still buy the best suit of clothes in New York for one $20 gold coin—gold had kept up with inflation. But since the Great Gold Bear Market during the disinflationary 1980s and 1990s (inflation was still there, but at lower levels), it has taken as many as four gold coins to buy an equivalent suit. If you buy now, you will be buying low.

The silver and gold risk/reward ratio for the patient investor is awesome.

Gold or Silver?

Gold and silver share several economic characteristics that determine their value, but there are also some significant differences that I will address later. In a metals bull market, both gold and silver will go up, but which one will do better?

The gold/silver ratio—the number of ounces of silver an ounce of gold will buy—is one way to determine which is the better buy. Historically, if the ratio is above thirty-to-one, silver is the better buy.

As this is written, the ratio is more than sixty-to-one; silver, therefore, has twice the profit potential of gold.

Silver is also the poor man's gold. It is especially suitable for the small investor.

Your Core Position: Gold and Silver As Insurance

Everyone needs some gold and silver for insurance. This is your "Core Position"; it's your backup in case the banks fail and people lose confidence in paper money or their bank in a Y2k (or other) crisis. It's the ultimate spending money for the worst case. And it doesn't require a worst case for it to be worth owning because it will also be a fine investment in a best or intermediate case. It has everything going for it, but most of all, peace of mind.

I recommend a Core Position of silver coins and gold coins—about $3,000 (at current prices) for each family member, split between gold and silver.

About half should go into "junk silver" coins or silver "rounds." This is your spending money in a currency crisis.

Silver Linings

The United States stopped minting 90 percent silver coins after 1964. These dimes, quarters, and halves have been scrounged out of circulation by now, but are available from coin dealers by the "bag" or "half bag." A bag consists of $1,000 in "face value," weighs about 55 pounds, and contains 714 ounces of silver. The coin industry calls it "junk silver."

But the bags are worth a lot more than their "face value." As of our publication date, one $1,000 bag (face value) sells for around $4,800. You are not paying an inflated price for $1,000 worth of coins; you are merely paying the current market price of that much silver, *plus* a "scarcity premium" (which can rise or fall with demand), plus a 2–3 percent commission to the dealer. Over

The silver and gold risk/reward ratio for the patient investor is awesome.

the past twenty years, bags of coins have disappeared into vaults and safe-deposit boxes or have been melted down for their bullion value.

Because of this scarcity premium, the price of bags could rise, even if the price of silver were to fall. For many years the world has been mining less silver than it is using. Warren Buffett, a legendary billionaire and one of the world's most consistently successful investors, recently bought 150 million ounces of silver because of that.

We have been bridging the silver production shortfall by recovering and recycling silver, coins, jewelry, etc., which has kept the price from going through the ceiling. Also, when economies are booming, especially near the peak of the business cycle, industrial use of silver increases, so it can do fairly well during boom years. There are myriad uses for silver in the electronics industry because it is a fine conductor of electricity, and huge quantities are used for photographic film.

But since silver also does well when people become concerned about the utility of paper money, it has significant price support during hard times. During periods of hyperinflation or a paper-money collapse, silver coins of all nations circulate freely. For instance, in China immediately after World War II, inflationary paper money was rejected almost everywhere, but despite almost nonexistent communications and the raging civil war between Chiang

Kai-shek and Mao Tse-tung, silver coins of all nations were universally accepted by merchants, and an invisible market consensus as to their purchasing power spread over the entire giant country almost overnight, as if by magic. Everybody knew what a dime was worth.

Your silver coins will serve several basic functions:

1) In a worst-case total collapse of the banking system, or merely an epidemic of distrust of the currency due to the mountains of paper the Fed will print to meet the demands for cash, you will be able to purchase goods and services at pretty much the same price (measured in silver coins) as before the collapse. A head of lettuce might cost several paper dollars—or one 90 percent silver dime.

2) For either brief or extended periods in a Y2k worst case, silver coins may be the best universally acceptable means of exchange to buy necessities.

3) Silver will help preserve the purchasing power of your assets until such time as a new universally acceptable (gold-backed) currency is established by the world's governments.

4) Even if we fall short of a worst-case calamity, silver will continue to be an excellent inflation hedge and a profitable investment.

I choose coins in preference to bullion for several reasons: (1) they are more easily divisible into spending units; (2) they weigh no more and take up no more space; (3) they do not require an assay when you sell or spend them, as bullion does. Commonly circulated "junk silver" will be accepted without question. Counterfeiting of these scruffy, worn coins is almost nonexistent.

Other Ways to Buy Silver

In addition to junk silver, you can buy either silver American Eagle coins or silver rounds from any coin dealer. Eagles are pure ".999 fine silver" one-ounce coins made by the U.S. Mint. Eagles have one advantage over rounds: "Hard assets" like gold and silver have not been legal retirement investments, but Eagles are legal investments for IRAs and other retirement plans. The reason is simply that the Treasury decided to make a little money by selling gold and silver coins, so, to help sales, Congress allowed Eagles to be part of IRAs and retirement plans.

The disadvantage is that your trustee will not let you take physical possession of your IRA coins, so you shouldn't buy your core holdings in your retirement plan.

You can also buy Millennial Trade Units. These rounds were created by Liberty Mint (of which I am a minority shareholder) as a different way to buy silver in small denominations. Each one is one troy ounce of .999 fine silver. They are conveniently packaged twenty-five to a tube and five hundred to a box. You pay the spot price of silver on the day you give Liberty the order, plus a premium of $0.47 to $0.75 per coin, the average being $0.55 (about 11 percent) with no commissions, depending on the amount you buy.

This compares very favorably with the silver American Eagle premium, which, as this is written, is around 40 percent, plus commissions, and the junk silver premium is about 33 percent on a $4,800 1,000-ounce bag.

When you sell, the current premium goes with the coin. It is not automatically lost, like a commission.

Call Liberty Mint for a breakdown (800-877-6468).

How Not to Buy Silver

Don't buy coins "on margin" (with a small down payment) and leave them with the coin dealer to store. During the big inflation of the 1970s, a lot of people did this, assuming they could use the leverage to make more money by buying more silver. Those who bought early in the inflation cycle and sold out at the right time did just that. If you could buy a bag of coins for $2,000 and put down only $400, when silver rose to $4,000 a bag, you would have a $2,000 profit on your $400 investment (500 percent profit). On the other hand, those who bought their coins outright for $2,000 and sold them for $4,000 only doubled their money (100 percent profit).

But some of the biggest coin dealers couldn't resist the temptation in this. By selling on margin, and promising to store the coins for you, these firms could sell you four or five times as many bags, and earn four or five times as much commission and profit on each sale. One huge dealer headquartered in Las Vegas got caught when it was discovered that there were no coins in his vault. The company, rather than buying and storing the coins, had lost the customers' money speculating on silver futures. The scandal forced the company out of business. Nearly all the customers lost their money, and the owners went to jail.

I played a big part in exposing one of the biggest of these scams, Bullion Reserve. This company was selling coins on margin and allegedly storing them in a huge vault carved out of a mountain near Salt Lake City. I had an occasion to visit that storage facility and asked to see Bullion Reserve's stored silver. I knew how much silver Bullion Reserve had allegedly sold—it was more than $40 million worth—but there was only a pittance actually in the vault. So I, along with Dan Rosenthal, publisher of the *Gold and Silver Report*, blew the whistle, and Bullion Reserve came crashing down. A lot of people lost a lot of money, and I got anonymous death threats, but far less money was lost than if we had not uncovered the fraud. The president of the company claimed he was doing nothing different from what the banks do with your money—but, of course, the banks tell you they will use your money for other purposes.

The most basic rule is to pay for your coins in full and take delivery at the time you pay for them. Keep them in a safe deposit box (for now, as long as the banks are relatively stable), or in a private vault or safe in your home. Don't speculate on margin with your core holdings. You need one bag of fully owned silver coins for each member of the family.

Buying silver is second in importance only to food storage. It is also a very close second in being low-risk. If the price of silver should drop—which, of course, is possible—you still at least have the face value of the coins. A quarter will never be worth less than a quarter.

Hold your survival coins through thick and thin, through every up-and-down in the silver market until the world stabilizes. This is not so much an investment as it is an insurance policy. If at some future time you realize some losses, look at those losses as the premium you paid for the insurance you never had to use and the peace of mind it gave you.

Survival Gold

If you have enough money, you should have an equivalent dollar amount invested in bullion gold coins. Their price will be the price of gold (the "spot price") plus a small premium (usually around 5 percent), which can fluctuate, depending on demand.

Gold coins also perform several functions in your investment program:

1) *They are "survival money" in the same sense* as silver coins, because they can be spent for big-ticket items. They are the functional equivalent of $100 bills and do not take the place of your small-denomination silver coins.

2) *They are a "chaos hedge."* If bank failure is the chaos we have, gold is a hedge against that. If deflation is the chaos we have, it's a hedge against that. Traditionally, it's the world's scared money. In recent years, U.S. Treasury securities have performed that function, but if Y2k screws up the Treasury's computers, gold coins will again be acceptable in a breakdown of the fiat money system.

3) *Gold is countercyclical:* It does well when other things are doing badly. Even if my worst case doesn't materialize, it is a fine investment when the world *fears* a possible worst case. If Y2k problems overwhelm us, the price of gold will skyrocket. In a real hyperinflation, gold will be worth thousands of dollars an ounce.

4) Gold transports your wealth safely from one side of the Y2k gulf to the other—when things return to normal, which, of course, they will.

5) Gold and silver are the only monetary instruments that are not some government's promise to pay. Their value does not depend on the value of something else; it is intrinsic.

Gold is roughly sixty times as valuable as silver, so you can store more wealth in a smaller space. Coins are an easily measured amount of money that do not have to be assayed when they are sold—unlike gold- or silver-bullion bars.

Everyone needs some gold and silver for insurance. They have everything going for them, but most of all, they offer peace of mind.

Gold is more closely linked to the fear cycle than silver, since it does not have the heavy industrial demand when times are good, so it is a much more direct fear hedge and is more likely to decline when things get better.

Although your survival gold should be bought and held through all circumstances, this is not true of your investment gold, which you buy and sell according to price performance and market conditions.

Gold coins of all nations can be bought through almost any coin dealer, and the price of the coins has no relationship to the fortunes of the country that minted them. The value of a Krugerrand would remain the same even if South Africa ceased to exist. It's just an ounce of gold.

While the monetary system is still hanging together, if you wish to sell some coins, any coin dealer will buy them. If the monetary system has collapsed, your coins can be used to buy whatever is available.

Some people are worried that the government will call in all the gold as it did in the 1930s. Perhaps, but I doubt it. If the government decides to do that so it can establish a new gold-backed money, and if I believe Uncle Sam *really* means it, I will willingly exchange my gold for an honest gold-backed currency. I don't care what you call money as long as everyone is willing to give me something of value in exchange for it.

What Kind of Gold?

The most popular and most liquid of all gold coins is the U.S. Gold Eagle, struck by the U.S. Mint. Next comes the Canadian Maple Leaf, which rapidly grew in popularity when in 1986 South Africa became an international piñata and the Krugerrand was boycotted. Krugerrands are now okay.

Which one do you buy? An ounce of gold is an ounce of gold, so buy the one with the smallest premium over the spot-metal price.

There are other less popular gold coins worth exploring, but only if the premium is less than the Eagle, Maple Leaf, or Krugerrand.

A new bullion coin hit the market in 1989—the Austrian Philharmonic. At this writing, it has a legal-tender value of 2,000 Austrian schillings, or about US$240. This gives the coin a floor value; even if the price of gold were to fall below $240, the coin would still be worth $240. But be wary. Governments can't always be trusted. Canada broke its legal-tender promise when silver fell below the face (legal-tender) value, so take the promise with a grain of salt. It will still pay to shop for the lowest premium.

The Australians are minting the Kangaroo Nugget (I told them to call it the Krugerroo or the Koalarand, but they didn't listen), which is another acceptable choice. It is competitively priced, but not as popular in the United States.

The Austrian and Hungarian 100 Coronas and the Mexican 50 Peso are also marketed in a limited way, but since the Corona is slightly less than an ounce and the Peso is slightly more than an ounce, it is difficult to calculate comparative dollar values, which has limited their popularity.

Avoid the French Rooster, Dutch Guilder, and Swiss (gold) Franc. These are smaller than the standard one-ounce coin and usually have very high mark-ups, even though their real value is limited to the price of gold bullion.

Since the Krugerrand peaked in popularity in the mid-1980s, U.S. investors have preferred U.S. Eagles over the bullion coins of other countries. High premiums have melted into big losses for those succumbing to glitzy promotions of nonnumismatic foreign coins.

I have two recommended dealers for various forms of gold and silver: Investment Rarities (800-328-1860) for junk silver, gold coins, and silver Eagles; and Liberty Mint (800-877-6468) for silver rounds (Millennial Trade Units). They completely understand and agree with the philosophy expressed in this book.

(As is always the case, I disclose any personal interest in my commercial recommendations; I have an interest in Liberty Mint, since it was founded by my son, Larry, and I have a minority position in stock and options.)

Do some price-comparison shopping. They will generally have the lowest prices, but there will be times when you can beat their prices slightly. But if you are dealing with any other firm, observe all the precautions expressed in this chapter. Both these recommended firms tend to resolve legal disputes in favor of my clients, since they value my support.

Scams

When the metals take off over the next few years the con artists will come out of the woodwork. Each new gold bull market brings new scams, but a few time-tested, basic rules will protect you.

When Bullion Reserve went bankrupt, the bankruptcy trustee claimed that recent customer liquidations of stored metals were a "preferential payment to creditors," and customers had to give the money back. So they still lost their money, even if they had liquidated before the scam was exposed.

My hardest lesson was much closer to home.

Several years ago I founded Ruffco, a coin and bullion company, of which I owned a controlling interest. We had metal-storage programs, both "fungible" and "nonfungible." Because I knew we were honest, I figured our clients were safe. But after about three years I sold my interest in Ruffco to a man who checked out as clean. I then announced the sale loudly and repeatedly in the *Ruff Times* so that everyone would know I was no longer managing the company. I let the new owner keep the Ruffco name—big mistake!

Although I remained on the board of directors as an "outside director," I had only the financial information the new owner gave me. Suddenly, four years after I sold out, he bankrupted the company with only twenty-four hours' warning.

Worse, even though all the precious-metals storage was in apple-pie order when I turned the company over to him—the new owner, an accountant, had personally audited it—he had liquidated millions of dollars' worth of customer-stored metals within days of taking over. The new owner was convicted and sentenced to several years in a federal penitentiary. Although the sentence included making restitution, I doubt if any money will ever be recovered.

The lesson in all this is that if you do things that are inherently unsafe you can get hurt, even by well-intentioned people, if they get into financial trouble or if control passes to someone else. It was a hard lesson for me. I will be licking my public-relations wounds for a long time. It hurt to see my friends hurt.

Ruff's Ten Golden Rules

Ruffco is one of the most painful chapters of my life, but you can learn from my experience. If you do all of the following, no crook or incompetent dealer will ever be able to hurt you. These "never violate" rules will leave you exposed only to normal risks in the volatile gold market, which is quite enough.

1) Be wary of coin dealers with glitzy, expensive advertising. Some are perfectly legitimate, but all costs must be factored into mark-ups. Dealers with expensive promotions and higher expenses usually have higher mark-ups.

2) Don't trade bullion coins for numismatic (rare) coins. A complicated grading system, plus supply and demand, determines the value of numismatic coins. Some dealers will pay you the spot price for your bullion coins, then sell you numismatic coins with at least a 20 percent markup—and proportionately high commissions and profit-margins. Then you need a 20 percent move just to break even with where you were with your bullion coins.

Also, never trade numismatics for other numismatics. The buy/sell spread is big enough without doubling it. If you don't want the rare coins you now own, just sell them.

3) Don't buy numismatic coins in a pre-Y2k environment, because if we start having to use them for money, they will be worth only their bullion value. But if you decide to buy them for their collectible or investment value, buy only U.S. coins. Non-U.S. coins have very limited appeal here, and most of them quickly sink to bare-bullion prices.

4) Don't buy "new issue rare coins" from a foreign mint. Chances are, in the anticipated environment, you will lose all of the premium.

5) Never buy gold stocks from telephone solicitors, especially if they are calling from out of state, unless you enjoy making unsecured loans to strangers. They are either outright frauds or grossly overpriced.

6) Avoid "leveraged contracts." These contracts are heavily advertised, especially when gold is rising. They are as risky as futures, probably more so. As much as *70 percent* of your down payment goes to commissions, and you may pay exorbitant finance charges on the balance. The longer you go, the behinder you get. Only if gold were to go straight up from the day you bought it might they be a good deal. But I'm never so lucky.

More often than not, these boiler rooms go out of business (or shut down, only to set up elsewhere with a new name), particularly when the metals go up and customers start taking profits, and they must pay up. Nothing hurts more than calling to liquidate a contract to take profits and hearing that voice on the phone say, "The number you dialed has been disconnected or is no longer in service."

A few banks offer leveraged contracts. The odds are that they are not crooks, and there is a much smaller commission, but even if the bank doesn't go under during a Y2k crisis, carrying costs can still eat you alive.

7) *Don't use "purchase plans,"* making a down payment and letting the dealer hold the metals awaiting final payment. If he goes broke before you take delivery, you will lose everything.

8) *Never fall for an offer of gold "under the spot price."* It's probably a fraud, or at best a loss leader come-on to upsell you to overpriced rare coins.

9) *Most important, avoid storage plans.*

10) *Finally, if the deal sounds too good to be true, it is!* Tell all telephone solicitors you just filed for bankruptcy, and they'll hang up.

More Bang for Your Gold Bucks

The most profitable time to buy gold is when it is still in the ground. That's what you get when you buy the shares of a gold-mining company. Gold stocks are essentially a piece of ownership of gold that has not yet seen the light of day, but that we know (or hope) is there.

I'll cover gold stocks in the next chapter.

Chapter Ten

Opportunity: Investing for the Year 2000

had often heard the cliché that the Japanese symbol for crisis is a composite of two symbols—danger and opportunity—so I checked with my daughter Debbie, who spent eighteen months in Japan, majored in linguistics, and minored in Japanese. She confirmed it.

We have talked about the dangers. Now let's talk about the opportunities. I believe with all my heart that this cosmic Y2k event will provide the greatest opportunities for savvy and gutsy investors and entrepreneurs in my lifetime. Volatility is always the father of opportunity. Even in the Great Depression of the 1930s there were commerce and opportunity, and some smart and gutsy people got rich.

But before we get into specific recommendations, a word of warning is in order. You will probably read this months after it is written, and some pre-Y2k events may be history. Nothing is forever, especially in the volatile environment I expect. No investment is always a good buy at any price, so, with the exception of gold and silver core holdings discussed in Chapter 9, check the *Ruff Times* or the monthly update on this book (one time only) before you buy any of these investments to be sure I still recommend them, or to see if others have become better buys. You can receive the update simply by sending in the postage-paid card enclosed in this book.

The months leading up to the year 2000 may be the most volatile, interesting period in the history of modern markets.

A Sea Change: Stocks and Interest Rates

For years it has been generally accepted that when interest rates fall, the stock market goes up, because businessmen can borrow more cheaply to expand operations or improve productivity and consumers can buy more stuff, which stimulates the economy. If you apply the conventional wisdom of the 1990s to the Great Depression of the 1930s, crashing interest rates should have been good for the stock market back then, but the Dow Jones collapsed 90 percent from a peak of 381.17 in September 1929 to 41.22 in July 1932, and stayed down for years. Almost at the same time, Treasury bond (T-bond) yields were crashing from 9 percent in 1929 to 1/2 percent in 1934, and, when bought on the secondary market, sometimes actually had negative rates of maturity, since they were looked on as capital-preservation havens.

Volatility is always the father of opportunity, and Y2k will provide great opportunities for savvy and gutsy investors.

Unlike in recent years, when falling interest rates have been considered the infallible remedy for a falling stock market and a weakening economy, I believe that the link between interest rates and the stock market is becoming more and more tenuous. What we will see is likely to be much more like the 1930s. Interest rates will crash, and so will the general stock market.

Before the World Wakes Up to Y2k

The following recommendations will only be good *before* the world wakes up to the Y2k crisis. For example, the operations of utility companies are likely to be hit hard by the Y2k bomb as the year 2000 dawns, but before it dawns on investors that Y2k will hurt utility companies, these companies can be relatively safe havens in the general bear market which is likely in the months before Y2k hits. As this is written, the American stock market is teetering on the edge of an abyss, worldwide interest rates have been falling for months, and the world's stock markets and currencies have come unglued. This is an ideal environment for utility stocks. It's also great for T-bonds.

So what do you do in a falling pre-Y2k stock market?

You can do two things: (1) Buy traditional defensive investments, and (2) feast on bear meat. You can shift your money into industry groups that are generally resistant to market declines and benefit from falling interest rates, and/or you can actually profit from falling markets.

Defensive stocks are those in industry groups that savvy investors historically gravitate toward when they believe the stock market is headed downward. They are defensive because these companies almost always produce things we need in any economy, or because they benefit from falling interest rates, which are highly likely in a slowing economy.

I prefer utility stocks and T-bonds as defensive investments, even though, ironically, those will both become very bad investments once the Y2k bug begins to bite hard.

Utility stocks tend to move as a class, and are a good defense because: (1) their earnings are very stable since there is always a demand for electricity, water, telephone service, etc.; (2) they benefit from falling interest rates because they are highly leveraged—these companies are constantly rolling over their debt or replacing matured debt, and falling interest rates mean lower debt-service costs on the newly acquired debt. This improves their profits and can increase their dividend payouts; and (3) utilities are generous dividend payers, making them much easier to evaluate than so-called "growth stocks."

Certain utilities have a superior history of performing well in down markets. The ones I like are:

FPL Group Inc. (NYSE:FPL)
IPALCO Enterprises (NYSE:IPL)

Energy East Corp (NYSE:NEG)
Rochester Gas and Electric (RGS)
United Illumination (NYSE:UIL)

Thirty-year T-bonds are also a great pre-Y2k investment, because when interest rates go down, T-bond prices go up. In a weakening economy, I expect long-term rates to continue to fall, even though as this is written, thirty-year T-bond rates are at all-time lows.

There have been times when these ultraconservative investments, which rich widows buy for safety of capital and for income, have also been excellent capital-gains vehicles, *especially* if they are bought near the peak of an interest-rate cycle.

If you had bought thirty-year T-bonds when I first recommended them in 1981—when the prime rate peaked at 21 percent and T-bonds' market yield to maturity was more than 20 percent— and held them over the next few years, not only would you have had incredible 20 percent per-annum yields on your investment, but also those bonds would have appreciated as much as 100 percent because of the falling rates.

Up until the Y2k crash, long-term T-bonds will be terrific winners. But when the Millennium Bug bites hard, neither bonds nor utilities are likely to be very safe places for your money.

When the Millennium Bug Bites

The U.S. Treasury Department is one of the government agencies that has fallen the farthest behind in Y2k repairs. Bonds are U.S. Treasury instruments, so their long-term future is cloudy at best. When the Treasury's computers begin to do strange things, the bond market will suffer because liquidity will be threatened.

I also plan not to own any T-bills when the Y2k crisis hits because with those you don't even get a certificate—just a computer-generated printout that tells you you bought them. At least with bonds you get paper certificates that you can hold until Treasury patches things back together. T-bills maturing by October 1, 1999, however, will probably be okay.

As you remember from Chapter 3, in the year 2000, electric and water utilities will probably have big technical problems, the whole stock market may be technically challenged, and there is a chance there might not even be quotes or liquid markets for these stocks, depending on how well the financial-services industry handles Y2k. Of course, there is some reason for optimism because, generally speaking, the financial-services industry is in better shape than most other industries. We will know a lot more after the industry-wide Y2k test in March and April 1999. In a best Y2k case, the U.S. stock markets may function fairly well, in which case we might keep our utility stocks.

> **Don't just prepare for danger. Also look for opportunities. There will be plenty of both.**

We will watch events develop, especially the technical Y2k progress of the utilities, the financial-services industry (brokers, banks, money managers, mutual funds, etc.), and the U.S. Treasury Department.

Don't Get Burned in the Y2k Firestorm

Tony Keyes has looked deeper into Y2k-sensitive investments than anyone else. He has a radio talk show on a big Washington, D.C., station and has written a book on Y2k investing called *The Y2k Advisor*. He also publishes a newsletter, *The Y2k Investor*. I asked him to address this issue here:

A tinderbox is smoldering in anticipation of the Y2k change, and the cybernetic Cinderella will turn into a pumpkin at the stroke of midnight on December 31, 1999. There will be many investment losers and winners. It's fairly easy to identify the companies and industries that will prosper, but I'm most concerned about the places where investors will lose their hides.

Actually, most commerce will suffer right after the year 2000 comes, and when investors awaken to this inevitability, they will head for the exit doors, looking for cash. Liquidity will be treasured above everything else. There will be a general market crash, but, as always, some stocks will be immune—assuming that the markets are still functioning and there are good quotes and liquidity.

Investors face two basic threats: "implied impact" and "impact in fact." Markets move in anticipation of *perceived* future events. Most stock prices will move well in advance of any actual Y2k problems, so you have to be alert to threats to investments on both fronts.

I have identified the high-risk industries to avoid, but I also offer some ideas on the phoenixes that will rise from the ashes of the coming digital fire. Some common themes when analyzing Y2k vulnerability are:

1) *Remediation status and pace:* Some industries are later than others in addressing the Year 2000 problem. Further, some of these same industries have no sense of urgency. They are in the "avoid-like-the-plague" category.

2) *Supplier/customer dependencies:* Manufacturers will have big problems with their supply lines. Even companies that have cleaned up their own computers will have trouble finding suppliers and customers with on-time conversions that are compatible with their own.

3) *Liability:* Some industries will be incredibly vulnerable to shareholder liability, product liability, and personal-injury suits.

4) *Sensitivity to an economic downturn:* Some industries will be more sensitive than others to the devastated economic environment that will follow the Y2k digital forest fire, as well as the dawning Y2k awareness that will precede the actual event.

5) International trade: Certain industries rely heavily on raw materials from, or sales to, foreign markets. They are very exposed, as the rest of the world is much farther behind schedule than the United States.

6) Government contractors: Those companies and industries that depend on federal revenues face an enormous threat. State and local governments are also in trouble, with some states better off than others, but most municipalities are way behind the Y2k curve. Contractors and suppliers that look to any level of government for most of their business will be hurt.

The Fire Marshall's List of High-Risk Industries

When investing, avoid certain high-risk industries:

Airlines, shipping, and railroads: Transportation will suffer greatly from the Y2k firestorm.

Airlines in particular are exposed, for reasons discussed in Chapter 3. At this late date, it is impossible to repair the international maritime fleet and all the facilities that support it.

Railroads, still untangling themselves from the merger of Union Pacific and Southern Pacific, face enormous challenges.

Apparel: We import 75 percent of our apparel, much of it from the high-risk region of Asia.

Construction and building materials: In a languishing, perhaps depressed economy, new construction will come to a near standstill.

Others at risk: Auto manufacturers (despite the $500 million General Motors is spending on Y2k. Who will buy its cars?), chemicals, banking, finance and broker-ages, PC and semiconductor manufacturers, general merchandisers, health care, insurance, package and freight delivery, pharmaceuticals, travel and tourism, and utilities.

Perhaps it will be easier to understand why the stock market will crash if you consider the following by James Dale Davidson, editor of *Strategic Investment Newsletter*:

> [T]here is really no alternative to computer pro-cessing as the economy is now structured. Most businesses large enough to require a mainframe to handle their transactions are dependent on transac-tion volumes that could not be managed with old-fashioned nineteenth-century paperwork systems. If such businesses were forced to revert to shuffling paper, they could expect to complete only a fraction of their normal transaction volume. The revenue shock which would result from such a drop-off in business would endanger the survival of all but the most highly capitalized companies.

Y2k Fallout Shelters

But all is not lost. There will be big winners, but the fol-lowing assumes there will be a functioning stock market:

Apparel: We import 75 percent of our apparel, much of it from the high-risk region of Asia.

Advertising: This is for the post-2000 period. This industry recovered quickly from the crash of 1929 and the subsequent depression. Competition was fierce, and companies had to fight vigorously for scarce consumer dollars.

Computer and data services and outsourcing: These companies will continue to flourish through the entire century transition. I also like: publishing and printing, temporary employment services, tobacco, toys, trucking, and truck leasing.

Y2k Repair Companies

My number one Y2k stock pick is Keane, Inc. (KEA-Amex). This company has been around since 1965 with a consistent growth record in revenues and profits. It is in the Y2k repair business.

I have watched the near-perfect execution of the Y2k strategy it outlined for me two years ago. Keane is using its Y2k services as a wedge to enter new markets without letting that dominate its image or business. It has sold $1.75 of non-Y2k business for every $1 of Y2k business in new accounts. Keane will be a solid play into the next century.

CACI International, Inc. (CACI-NASDAQ), provides systems integration, Y2k services, electronic commerce, product-data management, software development, and re-use and market analysis. CACI is very aggressive.

Horizons (CHRZ-NASDAQ) has a strong client base in insurance, telecommunications, and manufacturing. It recently acquired Princeton Softech and its Y2k solutions for the distributed desktop environment. Horizons turned in record revenues and earnings in the first quarter of 1998.

TAVA Technologies (TAVA-NASDAQ) helps factories with the computerized systems that control automatic manufacturing processes and has added Y2k services to its offerings to its client base. TAVA deals with the chemical, oil, aerospace, mining, and other industries. Its major customers include Coca-Cola, Nabisco, Boeing, Nestle, and Hershey. TAVA will be a clear market leader in helping companies sort out the factory-floor Y2k mess.

In addition to Tony's recommendations, I would add my two favorites, ZMAX (ZMAX-Amex) and Wareforce (WFRC:OTC/BB). ZMAX is a pure Y2k play—that's all the company does. It has landed several big contracts with Fortune 500 companies and has plenty of cash and excess capacity for expansion. Wareforce provides total technology solutions, including Y2k, for clients like Hughes, TRW, Disney, NBC, Pacific Bell, and Bank of Japan. With lots of operating cash in the bank and an aggressive growth-by-acquisition strategy, Wareforce is a potential big winner.

There aren't enough of these companies to go around, and when the severity of the Y2k problem starts to sink in, they will be the happy recipients of a feeding frenzy as the bidding begins for their services. Their stocks will soar, even as the rest of the market goes south.

Tony and I both like the Homestate Group Year-2000 Fund (call 800-232-0224 for a prospectus). This is the only Y2k mutual fund, so no comparative industry analysis is possible. It's also small. The greatest percentage of the portfolio consists of Y2k service providers. Homestate also likes the staffing and testing sectors of the industry. Even if you love some of the individual companies named here, you should still have some of your money in Homestate for diversification in a volatile industry.

The way things look as this is written, I plan to consider liquidating any paper- or computer-denominated investments by August 1999, although there will probably be exceptions that have not yet come up on my radar. Some of the hitherto safest and most conservative investments will have become as dangerous as coiled rattlesnakes.

Deploying money in the years before, during, and after New Year's Day 2000 requires a good defense and a good offense. Don't just prepare for danger. Also look for opportunities. There will be plenty of both.

Stop-Loss Orders

The one inviolable principle of investing is to protect yourself against big losses, because "he who fails to take small losses will take big losses." The best way to protect yourself is through "stop-loss orders."

A stop-loss order puts a floor under the potential loss on a stock purchase, so that if you have made a mistake in stock-picking or simply a mistake in timing, you can automatically cut your losses.

A stop-loss is simply a "limit sell order." For example, you buy XYZ stock at $50 a share, decide how much you are willing to lose if you're wrong, then place a sell order at that point. For example, if XYZ is at $50 when you buy it and you have predetermined that you don't want to lose more than 20 percent, you place a stop-loss order with your broker to sell if the stock hits $40.

Sometimes, of course, the stock will barely touch $40, trigger the sell order, then turn around and head higher. That can be frustrating, but most of the time when the stock hits the stop order, it heads even lower, and you're glad you got out.

The one inviolable principle of investing is to protect yourself against big losses; the best way to do this is through "stop-loss orders."

Stop orders will be automatically executed on exchange-listed stocks, but it doesn't work with NASDAQ and Bulletin Board stocks. With them, you must place a stop-loss order in your head, watch the stock closely, and sell without second-guessing yourself if the stop level is violated.

How far below your sell price should you place your stop? This is the toughest question of all.

One simple way to decide is to get a chart of that stock over the previous year or two and draw a straight line connecting last year's lows. Place your stop at the trend line. That gives it enough room to breathe within a normal volatility range.

The more volatile the stock, the more room you need to give it to breathe so you don't get whipsawed out on a short-term move.

The *Ruff Times* places and constantly revises stops on all of our Back Page portfolio recommendations, except for my speculative category called "Potential Home Runs"—young, emerging companies that I believe have great futures unrelated to the stock market as a whole. So, with that exception only, stop losses are critical.

I saw the value of stop-loss orders in August and September 1987—the two months preceding the huge, one-day 508-point market crash on October 19, 1987. The Dow fell 500 points in those preceding two months, so, including "Black Monday," the market dropped more than 1,000 points, from around 2,700 to around 1,700.

My *Ruff Times* subscribers and I had made a lot of money in the preceding months, and I had moved our stops up behind the stocks (trailing stops) to preserve profits in case the market took a downturn. Sure enough, after the market peaked in August and started down, we began to be stopped out of our positions. At first I was upset, because at the time I did not believe we were headed for a big bear market, but I soon learned that a stop-loss system had protected me and my subscribers from my own errors in judgment. We were stopped out of stock after stock, nailing down some pretty big profits long before that fateful day in October, when the market dropped 500 points so fast that it was impossible to execute our remaining stops at the stop price. Our three remaining stocks hadn't been stopped out yet, so they "ran the stops," and we took some bigger losses than we had planned. But fortunately, most of our profits were already safely in the bank, and our portfolio losses were more than offset by the money we had already made. Because of stop-loss orders, we had averted financial disaster, even on the worst day in Wall Street history.

Think of a stop-loss order as a protection against your bad judgment—or mine—and as a way to preserve your profits.

Gold Stocks

Gold stocks will be among the biggest winners in the months leading up to the year 2000, and perhaps after that—*if* the stock markets remain viable. Investing in mines can be immensely profitable
if you know how to pick them because you will make many times
more money on mining stocks than you will on bullion in a gold
bull market.

There are several varieties of mining companies, ranging from
Producers (those that are actually mining gold) big and small, to
Exploration companies (companies that are looking for gold). The
best of the Exploration companies have found gold and have done
or are doing the necessary drilling to verify the size of the reserves.
Eventually they will either turn into producing mining companies,
or more likely be bought by the big producers, which can be a huge
windfall for shareholders.

Then there are the Holes in the Ground Surrounded by Liars,
most of whom are domiciled in Vancouver, Canada. The Vancouver
Exchange is the hotbed of gold-mining stocks; that's where the
money is raised for legitimate exploration companies, but it's also
where the charlatans go to fleece unsuspecting gold investors.

I'll give you a list of legitimate mining and exploration companies that have real prospects of finding gold. That's where the big
money will be made when gold rouses from its years' long slumber.

Why is investing in mining stocks more profitable than buying
bullion?

If you paid $300 an ounce for bullion and it went to $600, you
would double your money. If, however, you bought stock in a gold
mine with a $275-an-ounce cost of production, with $300 gold the
mine would be making $25 on every ounce produced. But if gold
doubled and went to $600 an ounce, the mine would now make
$325 on every ounce of gold produced, a twelvefold increase in
profitability. The stock could multiply twelve times while gold had
merely doubled.

Two good gold-mining stockbrokers have stood the test of time for me and other gold-oriented investors: Global Resource Investments (800-477-7853), a brokerage firm specializing in natural resource stocks, and National Securities (800-532-7574).

Here is a list of the most promising gold-mining stocks. For advice in selecting the potential winners, I have relied upon three men who know how to separate the real deals from the dead ends: Rick Rule, the president of Global Resource Investments; Bob Bishop, the former managing editor of the *Ruff Times* who graduated from us to become one of the most respected mining-stock experts and editor of his own mining-stock newsletter, the *Gold Mining Stock Report* (510-283-4849); and Mr. X, the sophisticated and successful mining stock investor who writes a regular column for the *Ruff Times* but who wishes to remain anonymous.

The following list is a composite of their recommendations. Each company on the list has been recommended by at least two experts:

Seniors (big, established mining companies with track records as producers): Newmont Mining and Newmont Gold (about to merge); Barrick Gold (ABX/NYSE); Euro-Nevada (EN.T); and Goldfields of South Africa (GDFDY), Rick's favorite.

Junior production companies (smaller, well-managed producers): Viceroy Resources (VOY/TSE), Manhattan Mining (MAN/TSE), Western Copper (WTC/TSE), and Aurizon Mines (ARZ/TSE).

Exploration companies (companies with very promising properties, in various stages of finding gold): my favorite, Madison Resources (MNP.V); Manhattan (MAN/TSE); Rio Narcea (RNG.T); Miramar (MAE.T).

Also mentioned (by at least one of our experts): Golden Star Resources; Battle Mountain; Nevsun; Solomon; Kinross; Iamgold; Ariel; International Northair; High River; Mansfield Minerals; Golconda Resources; Romarco; Farrallon; Altoro Gold; General

Minerals; Golden Queen Mining; Fairfield Minerals; Rayrock Yellowknife; and Franc-or.

Build your portfolio on a base made up of one or two seniors and one or two junior producers.

Next select two or three recommended exploration companies.

Then, make up a complete list of the "Also Mentioned," stick three or four pins in the list with your eyes closed, and invest in the holes, because nobody knows which ones will be the big winners. The odds are that in a gold bull market you will make more money with the also-rans that make it big. You now have created your own little personal mutual fund to diversify your risk.

In a gold bull market the big producers will rise first, followed by the junior producers, and then the exploration companies will have their day. As the winners emerge, we will prune out the losers and double our bets on the winners, and if this gold bull market runs true to form, we will make a ton of money.

Check with the *Ruff Times* for the current portfolio recommendations, because this book will have been written a few months before you read it, and things can (and probably will) change.

Gold Mutual Funds

If all this is too overwhelming, consider buying gold-stock mutual funds. You get professional management, a diversified portfolio, and generally low fees. Gold funds do not, however, try to "time the market"; they are generally 100 percent invested in mining stocks in bull or bear markets, so you must decide when to buy or sell.

Because of the volatility of the metals and the leverage in the mining stocks, gold funds can soar like eagles one year and then anchor the bottom the next year. Don't give back profits by holding on too long. You must watch mutual funds as closely as individual stocks or bullion.

One caveat: Whether you stay with mutual funds when the Millennium Bug begins to bite hard depends on whether the Vancouver and Toronto Exchanges are Y2k compliant, because they will be the only places to get real prices and liquidity.

Most of the larger mutual-fund families have a gold fund, and all gold funds generally go the same way at the same time. However, depending on the quality of the market and the particular focus of the fund, overall performance can vary significantly. Some gold funds hold South African shares exclusively. Some hold everything *but* South African shares, and some hold a combination of shares from around the world. A very few funds, like the Lexington Gold fund, hold gold bullion along with stocks.

Choose only no-load funds, because your holding period for a gold mutual fund may be short, and a load or commission can really eat away your total return. Check the back performance of several gold funds over several years before making your final move. Call for a prospectus, an application, and a quarterly report that will list the fund's current portfolio.

There is one closed-end fund that Rick Rule especially likes— BGR Precious Metals (BPTA.T), because it is a great performer and, as this is written, is selling at a big discount to the value of its portfolio (Net Asset Value, or NAV).

Mining-stock mutual funds are the easiest way for most investors to participate in a rising metals market. Some of my favorites are: Benham Gold Equity Index fund, specializing in North American Shares (800-472-3389); U.S. Gold Shares, which consists exclusively of South African shares (800-873-8637); and Invesco Gold, which combines all regions (800-525-8085).

Feasting on Bear Meat: Short Selling

There are several ways to make money in a bear market. Some of them are complex and require detailed explanations and are for only the most serious investors and speculators, so I have limited this discussion to some relatively simple strategies.

Few people even try to make money in falling markets using "short positions." They just fail to sell out soon enough and end up giving back their profits. Let's take a close look at short selling and how it works.

The Concept

The only way to make money investing is to *buy low and sell high*, but when you short a stock, you do it backwards—*first* you sell high, *then* you buy low.

The principle is simple: When you think a stock will go down, you sell it, even if you don't own it. "Shorting," or selling what you do not own, has been done for hundreds of years. To short a stock, a short seller borrows shares from his broker (who borrows stock left with him in "street name" by his clients) and sells them in the market. He must return the borrowed stock to the lender some day, but he hopes to buy it back at a lower price, return it, and profit from the difference.

Fortunes will be made by short sellers in the Y2k bear market.

For example, if you think the market or the economy is headed for trouble, General Motors (GM) probably will not sell a lot of cars, and its stock should fall. Therefore, selling GM short at $55 should be profitable. Your broker then lends you one hundred shares of GM stock, which you sell for $55 a share, or $5,500. You must return the stock some day in the future.

Let's say you're right, and GM falls on tough times, dropping to $35. You then buy one hundred shares, "covering" your short, and your broker returns the stock to the lender. The purchase cost $3,500, so your net gain is $2,000, less commissions. You *sold high* and *bought low*.

If you're wrong, however, and GM rises to $65, you could cut your losses by buying stock to return to the lender. One hundred shares at $65 costs $6,500, giving you a net loss of $1,000, plus commissions. You *sold low* and *bought high*.

A short seller's liability is technically unlimited. Theoretically, the stock can rise forever, and he can lose a lot more than his initial outlay, although in the real world you can limit those losses with stop-loss orders. More on that in a minute.

Shorting on Margin

On short sales, brokers require an initial cash deposit, or "margin," equal to at least half the current value of the stock you sell short. Your margin deposit is due no later than the settlement date—usually five business days after the sale. In lieu of cash, some securities firms will accept T-bills or marginable stock to meet this requirement, so check with your broker.

If the stock rises, your initial margin deposit may not be enough to protect the broker with a cushion against losses, and each broker has a minimum, or "maintenance" level, for margin accounts. If the stock rises sharply, you'll get the only unqualified piece of advice a broker ever gives—a margin call. This is a sure sign that you're on the wrong side of the market, so you should cut your losses, cover your shorts, and never meet a margin call.

In fact, you should set a stop-loss order close enough to get you out *before* you get a margin call.

Your broker can open a short-selling account just as easily as a regular cash or margin account. Actually, it's really a margin account. You just need good credit.

Borrowing Stock

Selling something you don't own seems vaguely wrong, but it's an honorable, legal, institutionalized procedure, and is the key to making big money in a falling market.

When the market starts to nosedive, most investors either take their lumps and hope it's just a temporary decline, or make a mass exodus for the sidelines. But this is the point at which sophisticated short sellers move into the market—borrowing and dumping those stocks they think are heading south.

Hectic trading activity creates back-office paperwork problems for brokers, especially if a seller fails to deliver his stock by settlement date. To avoid these "fails," your broker must be certain he can borrow enough shares of a stock before he can execute your order to sell it short. It can take anywhere from a few minutes to a few days to determine whether stock can be borrowed, and your broker's approval may be necessary before you can sell short. Brokers' policies vary, so ask your broker about his approval requirements. The bigger the firm, the more likely a short sale will be automatically and quickly approved.

Large capitalization issues like IBM, GM, and most exchange-listed stocks can be easily borrowed, as brokers hold large quantities of customer-owned shares registered in street name. If your broker doesn't have the stock, he'll borrow it from other firms. He may be unable to borrow a stock if it's a smaller company with few shares outstanding and small volume—and, therefore, he won't be able to execute your short sale.

If your broker can't borrow the stock and doesn't hold any in-house for his clients, check with other firms.

The Uptick Rule

Even if you think a stock is headed for a free fall, you may not be able to short it immediately, since exchange-traded stocks can be sold short only on an "uptick" or "zero-plus tick." The uptick rule does not apply to over-the-counter stocks.

An uptick occurs when a stock trades at a price higher than the immediately preceding trade. If the prior trade was an uptick, a trade at the same price is known as a zero-plus tick. "Downticks" and "zero-minus ticks" are just the opposite, as shown in this sequence of trades:

Trade #1	22-1/2
*Trade #2	22-3/4 (uptick)
*Trade #3	22-3/4 (zero-plus tick)
Trade #4	22-5/8 (downtick)
Trade #5	22-5/8 (zero-minus tick)
*Trade #6	22-7/8 (uptick)

*Possible short sales

In the above example, trades #2, #3, and #6 could be short sales. The ticker tape and office quote machines don't separate short sales from other trades. Brokerage firms report them later to the stock exchanges.

Before the uptick rule—such as in the crash of 1929—bears could drive the stock down with relentless selling. At that time, well-heeled traders sold stock until the declining price triggered margin calls (10 percent margin was usually the rule), forcing more selling and even lower prices. Short sellers covered their short positions by buying shares only after the price had plummeted in the panic sell-off, and made fortunes.

These "bear raids" are still possible in the over-the-counter market, but margin requirements higher than in the 1930s (50 percent as opposed to 10 percent), greater trading volume, and the requirements to borrow stock *before* shorting make old-fashioned bear raids a lot harder.

Placing an Order

When you instruct your broker to short a stock, you either use a "market order," telling him to sell immediately at the best price possible, or a "limit order," which must be executed at the price you specify, or higher.

Buying stock using a market order is fast and easy, but short selling is different because of the uptick rule. A market order to sell short may not be executed at all, or it may be executed at a much lower price than you wanted.

Let's say you give your broker a market order to sell short one hundred shares of XYZ, which sells at 50. However, the stock nosedives to 42 before it "upticks." Though one uptick does not even guarantee an order execution—there are probably lots of brokers trying to sell—you could not sell short before XYZ hit 42. You have lost a big chunk of your potential profits right out of the chute.

The safest way to sell short is by using a limit order, which sets the limit one or two points below the current price. Your broker will sell at the best price (even if it's above your limit, which would be terrific), and you won't inadvertently short at too low a price if the stock tumbles before your sell order is executed.

Selling a stock short near its current price should be routine under "normal" trading conditions, but market volatility caused by Y2k could create "abnormal" conditions, and a stock could plummet or soar in a few minutes. Use a limit order to be safe.

Stop Orders on Short Sales

A stop-loss order is important when you own stock, but absolutely essential when you are shorting. This is the only way to limit your theoretically unlimited potential loss.

A short-seller's stop order instructs the broker to buy stock to cover the short if the share price rises to a certain level. If you short one hundred shares of stock at $60, and are willing to risk $10 a share, tell your broker to "buy one hundred shares at $70, stop." Your order then becomes a "market" order, and is executed at the best possible price immediately after the first trade at or above your stop price.

Brokers will accept a "good-until-canceled" (GTC) stop order for stocks traded on organized exchanges, and the order will remain in effect until you cancel it or it's executed. You can change the stop anytime; however, it will automatically be lowered each time a cash dividend is paid, or a stock is split. A $1 dividend lowers your stop price $1.

Stop orders are not accepted for over-the-counter stocks, so you must choose a "mental" stop, and watch closely. Never raise the stop to give the stock "a little more room to breathe." Set your stop and stick with it.

Always lower a stop on a short position to preserve your profits as a stock falls.

In times of unusually heavy trading, a broker may refuse to accept new stop orders on very actively traded stocks, and may even cancel existing stop orders.

Shorting and Dividends

Once you short a stock and it drops, you are winning your bet— unless the price decline is due to dividends or stock splits.

If you sell a stock short, and a dividend is declared, the buyer receives the dividend directly from the corporation, as he is the registered owner of the shares. Since the stockholder whose stock you borrowed usually doesn't know his broker lent his shares to you—and you sold them—he expects to receive his dividend as usual. So you must reimburse him. The broker will do that automatically out of your account with him.

Let's say you decide to short one hundred shares of GM. Your broker lends you one hundred shares that are held in the street name for John Q. Public. You sell the stock to Jane Doe through your broker; she becomes the registered owner.

GM then declares a $1 dividend. Jane owns one hundred shares of GM, has the stock certificate to prove it, and GM will send her the dividend directly. But John, who lent you the shares, still owns one hundred shares of GM. It still appears on his monthly brokerage statement, and he expects to receive the dividend. Since you borrowed his shares, you owe John the dividend.

Stock splits also lower the share price. If a company declares a 2-for-1 stock split, reducing its stock price from $80 to $40, you will be short two hundred shares at $40 instead of one hundred shares at $80—so you won't gain or lose.

Short Strategies

Once you overcome the natural aversion to selling something you don't own, how do you choose which stocks to short? Like porcupines in love—very carefully!

1) The overall market, or at least the industry group, must be in a downtrend. Never buck the primary trend by selling short into a bull market.

2) Once you've established that the market or group is in a downtrend and most stocks are heading south, focus on stocks or industry groups that are breaking down, and don't try to catch the exact top and sell stocks short at their exact highs. And don't "chase weakness" by trying to short stocks that have already fallen out of bed. As my friend Jim Dines says, "Never try to catch a falling safe."

3) After establishing that the market is in a clear downtrend, you still must find the best stock to short. A good short candidate could be devastated in a recession, and the stock could plunge. Most short candidates will be stocks in industries that are hurt by a down-cycle in the economy. The inevitable Y2k recession will wreak havoc on cyclical industries, like autos, housing, durable goods, chemicals, and other basic industries. Interest rate–sensitive groups, like banks and insurance companies, also have pronounced cycles.

There are certain stocks you should *not* short, even when all your other ducks are in a row.

1) Don't short utilities and other high dividend–paying stocks, unless you expect the dividend to be cut. These are usually mature, stable companies that don't fluctuate enough to make them as interesting to short as other companies. Also, they may continue to pay high dividends—even in a recession. Since you must reimburse the lender for all dividends, it's expensive to short these stocks. Dividends will eat up your potential short-sale profits.

2) Avoid possible takeover candidates. A corporate takeover or leveraged buyout can send a stock's price soaring overnight and make life unbearable for a short seller.

3) Steer clear of stocks with a big short interest (your broker can check that out for you), even when the fundamental and technical picture is deteriorating. They're just too volatile.

Shorting Made Simple

Now comes the easiest way to bet against the market.

There is a mutual fund called the Rydex Ursa fund (800-820-0888) that shorts the market. As the market goes down, Rydex Ursa will go up. You simply open an account with the fund and buy its shares. Rydex has a $10,000 minimum. The mutual fund is perhaps the simplest way to do it.

This bull market has seemed immortal, and bearish forecasts have always come up short of expectations, but it will break down sooner or later, and now it looks more like sooner than later—if it hasn't already caved in by the time you read this.

You can be the only kid on your block who goes to the office and brags, "Boy, the market fell 500 points yesterday. Isn't that terrific!" A few smart investors made a fortune in the bear market that began in 1929, but most Americans didn't. They knew nothing about short selling. Fortunes will be made by short sellers in the Y2k bear market. It's just a matter of time.

As I said in Chapter 1, Y2k is a time of great opportunity, perhaps the most potentially profitable period in your lifetime. It requires that you be liquid, preserve your capital, watch for opportunities, and have the guts to pounce when the time comes. I'll be right there with you. It will be exciting.

Part Three

Making a Brave New World

Chapter Eleven

Rebuilding the Shattered American Family

H illary Clinton wrote a book called *It Takes a Village*, based on an African proverb that says the whole village must share the responsibility for each child. In some African cultures, children had no fixed home and could sleep or eat with any family where their fancy took them. Perhaps this works in a simple, even primitive society, but when Mrs. Clinton transferred this wholesome-sounding, one-hundred pound marshmallow of an idea to modern America, "village" became, for all practical purposes, "government."

Politicians and academics of the philosophical Left have always looked to the federal government to solve problems. The government, in turn, has created bureaucratic programs that have steadily preempted the duties and responsibilities of smaller units of society, starting with the states and cities, to private charities, and now even families. The Watchbirds are trying to federalize education, taking the agenda away from the local school boards and preempting the parental duties with day-care centers as they move inexorably toward the Swedish model (to be discussed in a moment).

None of these ideas and programs would have even gained a foothold if churches and families had performed their traditional work. Unfortunately, as too many mainstream churches have evolved from their traditional mission of saving individual souls into social organizations pushing the trendy cause *du jour*, and more and more mothers have left the home to seek careers, these critical institutions too often fail to do their duties. This has left irresistibly tempting vacuums for social busybodies and reformers to fill. These so-called reformers have willingly leaped into the breach, planting their flags on what they claim is the moral high ground.

After having preempted much of the powers of the states and cities with national programs that have been more or less tamely accepted by those smaller institutions, these do-gooders have turned their eyes toward our families.

The American family has big-time problems that seem to be crying out for someone to take charge and "do something." Unfortunately, the government is the least capable institution to tackle the job. It is big, impersonal, inefficient, cold-hearted, power-hungry, and jealous of its prerogatives, and it is far-removed from the problems of those it professes to want to help. Worst of all, the government is philosophically and legally committed to secular solutions to what are essentially spiritual problems.

The family is a crumbling institution that is ill-equipped to stand against the Y2k tide that will assault our government support structures.

Case in point: In 1995 the Department of Health and Human Services decided to launch its own version of the twelve-step programs like Alcoholics Anonymous that have successfully treated various forms of addiction and compulsive behavior, such as alcoholism, drug addiction, gambling, and compulsive sex.

Cooperative efforts between the government and faith-based programs were forbidden, striking at the heart of what made those programs successful—the cornerstone belief that the addict must surrender to "a higher power as we conceive him." By removing this key concept, the government transformed the enormously effective twelve-step programs into futile and ineffectual eleven-step programs. The idea of separation of church and state has been extended to its illogical conclusion, that not just churches, but also

God, must be separated from the state—a dubious constitutional interpretation. Predictably this misbegotten, antireligious bigotry failed, and was scrapped.

Do we really need government to crowd out private solutions that work and replace them with bureaucrat-run, taxpayer-funded programs that rule out the central concept that makes the programs work?

The American family is the nurturing unit of society, and a critical component of the glue that holds it together is the faith-based conviction that we will some day be accountable for our sins, including the sins that tear families apart.

The family, rather than being the rock-solid foundation that holds society together, is now too often a crumbling institution that is ill-equipped to stand against the Y2k tide that will assault the government support structures we have come to rely on. The American family must regroup and recreate the strengths that will allow it to be again the independent bulwark against the secular and statist assaults on traditional roles.

In Chapter 7, "Sin Tax," I discussed the impact of the breakdown of the American family. Study after study has demonstrated that when religion and church attendance are an integral part of a family's life, divorce is far more rare, as are teenage sex and pregnancy, alcoholism and drug use, crime, child abuse, marital infidelity, and other pathologies that assault our families.

Will there be some kind of massive government crash program to reverse the destructive trends that are assaulting the American family? I hope the government doesn't even try; remember Ruff's Second Law of Government, "When government tries to solve a problem, it creates two or more problems of equal or greater dimensions." If a cabinet-level Department of the Family is ever created, I will seriously consider moving to New Zealand or someplace equally remote.

Early on in my publishing career, I learned of a proposal before the Swedish parliament to outlaw spanking and allow children to "divorce their parents." That seemed worthy of attention, so I called an old college buddy, Senator Orrin Hatch of Utah. He arranged with the Swedish government for me to go to Sweden to interview the people who were behind this law, so I set out for Stockholm with one of Orrin's assistants.

It was an amazing look at the future of America.

The Swedish family has disintegrated. The tax laws are deliberately structured to punish families with only one breadwinner and reward them when both parents work outside the home. This has given the government charge of nearly all children of school age in government-operated day-care centers. There the government's secular, antireligious views are pounded into the children's heads. Value-free sex education is taken for granted, and teenagers are actually officially encouraged to experiment sexually.

And yes, it turned out to be true that in the name of ending child abuse, not only was spanking now against the law, but so was "psychological abuse." This, one female member of Sweden's parliament told me, included withholding a kid's allowance as a punishment.

Even though there is a state church (Lutheran), it has little if any influence in the lives of the people and the upbringing of the children. Other Christian churches are valiantly swimming against the tide in this relentlessly secular country but are touching the lives of only a small minority of Swedes.

And what is the result of all this "progressive" conditioning?

For starters, the Swedish suicide rate, especially among the young, is second only to Russia's. Ditto alcoholism. Most children are born out of wedlock, and many of them grow up without fathers in their lives. Teenage pregnancy is barely frowned upon and is only slightly inconvenient because of the day-care centers. Children that have a hassle with their parents can call the authorities with a complaint and can even "divorce" their parents, forcing parents to consider awful legal and social consequences before resorting to traditional disciplines—hitherto considered their duty. Consequently, Sweden has a generation of beautiful, blond, lawless, alcoholic, drug-ridden, promiscuous teenagers and young adults. And the government is nearly bankrupt, with the highest tax rates in the world.

This is the inevitable result of turning the duty of raising our children over to "the village." We are not as far gone in family matters as Sweden, but we are following the Swedes down the same path and seeing the sad early results of the secularization of America.

I believe with all my heart that there are no secular solutions to spiritual problems. The American family crisis is a spiritual crisis that can have only spiritual solutions rooted in the individual family. Attempts to restore the traditional family to supremacy must have their roots in faith-based individual action. Your own home has to become a serene oasis of old-fashioned values in the moral desert that surrounds us. There is no other road to family security.

How can you protect your family from these terrible, secular, immoral trends?

I come from a religious tradition that is rooted in the family. In my church, the smallest official unit is not the congregation, but the family, and the whole program of the church is designed to support the mission and values of the family.

As one who has raised a ton of children, especially teenagers, I can tell you that the level of persistently applied dedication necessary to help a child navigate through the shoals of contemporary society is immense. It cannot be delegated. It takes unconditional love, serial forgiveness, stubborn dedication to principles, consistent reassessment of time and financial priorities, an uncompromising and unhypocritical behavioral example, and a unified team effort between husband and wife—and this is far easier if there is religious training in a church and in the home.

So how does the Ruff family try to do it? Let me count the ways.

Ruff's Rules for Family Success

1) Make a unified, carefully articulated decision that nothing is more important than the family unit and the extended family, and that the measure of its success is the character and spiritual and moral health of its members. Note that I said "articulated." It has to be communicated to the members, and then your actions have to prove it over and over.

2) Make love the central principle of the home. Demonstrate that love by gentle words and demeanor, touching, hugging, and especially showing love and affection to your spouse.

3) Make God a tangible presence in your home, through family prayer and daily scripture reading. We kneel morning and night as a family, and also as a couple, in addition to our personal prayers. Then we try our best to live the principles we espouse in our everyday lives so there is no cognitive dissonance between what we profess and what we practice.

4) With the above as a foundation, erect a specific structure to pass on your values and family identity and traditions to your posterity. It won't happen by accident or by osmosis. It has to be done in a planned and systematic way.

Our structure is the Family Night. We have set aside Monday night for this. About half the time we go out to dinner or a movie or engage in some other activity. The other half of the time we have a lesson, usually derived from the scriptures, to teach an important principle. It might be honesty, chastity, movie and TV standards (R-rated movies are out, as are sexually provocative PG and PG-13 movies), modest dress standards for sixteen-year-old Terri, charity, and more. The important thing is to make it involving and interesting, leading to lively discussions. The consequences can be far-reaching. I know that when I am teaching my children, I am teaching my grandchildren.

The wonderful thing is that as our offspring have become adults, they have all chosen to duplicate our pattern and pass it on to their children.

5) Have regular extended-family activities. We try to get all the family that is within driving distance to come to our house about once a month, usually on a Sunday afternoon after church. This is where our children and their children socialize and bond with each other. This important family tradition is enjoyed by all.

6) Create extended-family structures. Start with a formal family organization, complete with a family newsletter, social director, historian, and correspondence secretary. As the children become financially independent, you could include a family disaster fund to help someone in need of a financial boost, or a college fund for a grandchild.

If the Y2k bug bites hard and other support structures fail, the family can be your prime source of emotional, financial, and spiritual support.

We are all on e-mail, and I try to create a monthly epistle (one of our grandchildren wanted to know if an epistle was the wife of an apostle) from the Patriarch to share with each family member the principles I care about. I recently wrote about Y2k preparation and food storage.

7) Disinherit the IRS. If you are fairly affluent, talk to a financial planner about setting up a family partnership, a family trust, and other estate-planning instruments to help you pass on your assets to your children.

8) Create a family history and a personal life story on paper or audio tape to help bond the generations. Among my most precious possessions is an autobiography my maternal grandfather dictated to my grandmother while bed-ridden and dying of cancer. In her seventies, Grandma went to night school to learn to type so she could prepare that precious history for her posterity. We will be forever grateful to her.

Members of our family have assembled genealogical information and bits and pieces of history and written up some fascinating and valuable histories. Recount your mistakes so your family can learn from them. I am not suggesting that you air all your dirty laundry; some things are too private. But you have learned a lot that can be valuable to those who read it. If all we learn is that which we experience ourselves, we won't learn much. A family that doesn't systematically pass on its values, traditions, and lessons might as well not be a family at all. The family is the God-ordained structure that must do this. No one else will. It's the whole reason for families. If we don't do this as a nation, the next generation will create an alien world unattached to the one you care about.

We have traveled as a family to the funerals of distant relatives so Terri can meet and feel connected to a family even bigger than the one she grew up with, and it has worked. She especially adores her ninety-four-year-old Great-aunt Erva, who still has all her marbles and a great sense of humor.

9) Teach your family about America—its painful birth and its Constitution. A wise man has said, "Those who cannot remember the past are condemned to repeat it." I am appalled at how little American history is taught in public school. If I didn't teach our daughter Terri, she would never know what is precious about America, and she would be a sucker for demagogues, charlatans, social engineers, and despots who could seduce her into voting for them or supporting their programs.

Your family cultural and personal history is a part of that heritage. In our case, we belong to a church that was persecuted, driven from place to place, and sometimes even massacred. I want her to know about that so she will never become bigoted and will respect all of God's children, especially those who look different or believe differently from her.

10) Teach your family about Y2k, and make all family members part of the planning for that most uncertain day. Give or loan them a copy of this book. Twenty years ago, *How to Prosper During the Coming Bad Years* changed a lot of lives, as evidenced by thousands of letters and phone calls I have received. Young people had their eyes opened to sound economic principles and a world view that they didn't get from TV or movies, or, unfortunately, the schools. I hope this book can do the same.

11) Get involved in your children's education. Know what they are taught in school, especially if they go to a public school. Look over their textbooks and their homework assignments, especially their optional reading assignments, so you will be ready to counter some of the soul-destroying garbage they are exposed to. You might consider homeschooling, especially if you have a child who is having social or academic problems or falling in with the wrong crowd.

For further information on homeschooling, contact your local homeschooling organization. To find out how to get in touch with your local organization, you can contact the national office of the Home School Legal Defense Association (P.O. Box 3000, Purcellville, VA 20134; 540-338-5600).

You should also use your home computer as a teaching device. There is a whole world of educational CD-ROMs that are excellent teachers and are engaging and engrossing for the children. CD-ROMs can teach math from first grade to college level, as well as writing, reading, history, and religion. They can be used to supplement a public-school education, or to make homeschooling practically painless, especially when you are trying to teach a subject you got a D on in eighth grade.

A list of particularly valuable educational CD-ROMs is provided in the Appendix.

12) Protect your children from the porn monsters on your PC. Home computers are not without their hazards. Pornography is everywhere on the Internet. The clever perverts who create them have found ways for you to stumble over them by accident. They often set up web sites with addresses that are only slightly different from legitimate web sites and databases. For example, for a while if you wanted to know more about the Mormon church and opened

"Mormon.com," you got a porn site, until a rich member bought it out and gave it to the church.

You can, however, protect all but the most talented and persistent young hackers from these booby traps by installing programs that filter out the hard-core garbage. The ones I like the most are Cyber Patrol and Net Nanny. I use Cyber Patrol. You can buy these programs at any well-stocked computer store. They do use up to sixteen megabytes of RAM, so you may have to add some memory, but it's worth it. They can even tell you how long your child spent on the computer and list by address all the sites he or she has visited.

If you decide to use your computer as an academic teaching device, follow the instructions on page 70 to check your PC for Y2k compliance.

Now, a disclaimer.

I know I talk a better fight than I actually fight. The foregoing list of events and structures is a lot easier to talk about than it is to implement. In an age when family members are going in every direction at once, coordinating all the family schedules is hard. Family prayers and Family Night are especially hard. We have had dry spells in our family life where we were less than regular in doing what we knew we should do. It is usually my fault, since I am often so professionally preoccupied with research, business, and writing.

I too often forget to be affectionate and tender with Kay, but writing this chapter has reminded me of what is most important in my life and renewed my resolve to repent of my neglect. I hope Kay will be happier for it.

Our twelve living children (one drowned as a toddler) have generally done well. Eleven of them are married, and Terri, our late-in-life surprise, is a drop-dead gorgeous high-school sophomore. (That's scary because I will be seventy when she is eighteen). They have all performed church service, most of them have at least some college education, and eight have college degrees. All of our home-made or adopted kids are dedicated parents, and all of them and their little ones are fixtures in church on Sunday. I just want to be a block off the old chip.

Before you conclude we are qualified for family sainthood, I hasten to stipulate that we have not been immune to problems. There have been two divorces, and one successful remarriage. Also, not all of our eighteen foster children have gone on to good lives. Most of them came to us like wounded birds, carrying heavy burdens of neglect, rejection, and abuse, and some of them are still lost souls. We have had our share of tough-minded teenagers who rebelled at what they saw as dull activities and unreasonable restrictions. One of them even makes me wonder sometimes if all good deeds do not go unpunished. But sometimes we succeeded.

Sometimes I've been a less-than-perfect example, and I've too often fallen short of my self-imposed spiritual goals. There have been things in my life I am not proud of. But fortunately, I married better than I deserved. I am the head of my family, but my wife Kay is the heart, the spiritual backbone. She is the only person on earth I fear, lest I fall short of her high expectations.

None of our family successes has been an accident. Each was the result of a premeditated plan. From the beginning Kay and I knew we wanted a big family and covenanted with each other and our Father in Heaven to make molding our children's character our most important mission in life. A lesser commitment would have fallen short.

We had to overcome a less-than-ideal start, as both Kay and I came from less-than-ideal families. Her parents were divorced when we were married (they later remarried—I guess this was one of those divorces that just didn't work out). My father killed himself when I was just six months old; my ten-years-older brother and I were raised in poverty by a single mother. Kay and I were both determined to surmount these handicaps, and have worked hard at it.

I'm sure that millions of families have done a lot better than we and are better qualified than we to teach you, but they don't have this bully pulpit, so I guess I will have to do.

If the Y2k bug bites hard and other support structures fail, the family can be your prime source of emotional, financial, and spiritual support, but it won't happen by accident. You must systematically plan for it, implement your plan, and persist.

There are no luggage racks on hearses, and when we die, the only things we will be able to take with us are the things we have given away, and I don't mean earthly goods. I mean love, service, dedication to principle, fidelity, faith, and other such intangibles. I seriously doubt that anyone will face God regretting that he didn't spend more time at the office or on the golf course.

What would you rather have written on your gravestone: "I TOLD YOU I WAS SICK" or "HE HAD A RIGHTEOUS POSTERITY AND GAVE THEM HIS BEST"?

Chapter Twelve

Renewing America

Assuming that you have secured the home front, have a food-storage program and gold and silver coins, have adjusted your investments for the new millennium, and have organized your family, we can turn our attention to the broader question of America's future.

I have outlined many problems that must be addressed in *any* future scenario, Y2k or not—Social Security, government agencies, our fiat money system, the sexual revolution, the stock-market crash, the public-education crisis, and other disaster areas. Unfortunately, both major political parties are clueless about such things as total freedom in the markets and the dismantling of regulatory government.

Renewing America is a monumental, daunting task, but that is no excuse for not doing what must be done. Though we may feel as if we are helpless in the face of the problems that are assaulting our society—a continually growing government leviathan, politicians whose only concern is their next election, the failure of our educational system, moral decay, and so much else—we must be vigilant about maintaining an America that is true to the vision of its Founders. Only by becoming politically active—and by electing a political party that strikes at the heart of these problems—can we bring about the necessary reforms that will restore America to its true greatness.

Perversely, a real wipeout in a Y2k intermediate- or worst-case scenario may be a huge (but painful) blessing in disguise, a once-in-a-lifetime opportunity to create a better world. Perhaps just a good scare might be sufficient.

Even in a best Y2k case, it is likely that many government systems will fail, the income tax system will be unworkable and unenforceable, the regulators will be unable to regulate, and the public will begin to think unthinkable things.

We face many problems that must be addressed in any future scenario, Y2k or not.

There is a legend, possibly true, about Alexander the Great. He was shown the great Gordian knot, which had defied the efforts of the wisest and most powerful men in the world to untie it for hundreds of years.

Alexander sliced it in two with one stroke of his sword.

Y2k may be the sword that slices through the Gordian knot of the encrusted, malignant, metastatic government superstructure that has defied the best efforts of the best-intentioned presidents, including the sworn foe of big government, Ronald Reagan.

An equally apt analogy may be that of Hercules and the Augean stables. These stables had been so befouled for thousands of years by the horses of the gods that no one could clean them. Hercules knew he couldn't shovel it out faster than the horses could manufacture it, so he simply built a dam and diverted the legendary River Styx through the stables.

Y2k may be our River Styx. The entrenched bureaucracy and regulatory structure, reinforced by an income-tax structure so complex even those who administer it don't understand it, are so huge and entrenched that only something as cosmic as Y2k could wipe it out and give us a fresh start.

Here is Ruff's Program for building a better America.

The Starting Point: The Freedom Party

Y2k or not, we need a new organized political party. The Democrats and the Republicans have both failed miserably to protect our constitutional liberties. The Democrats are tone deaf to the music of the free markets and highly attuned to the siren song of big government. The Republicans differ from them rhetorically, but when it comes to stemming the erosion of freedom from the growth of government, they would take us in the same direction, only a bit slower. The Libertarians have much too narrow an agenda, and too often carry their freedom agenda into the blind alleys of moral relativism. Most (not all) Libertarians I know believe that pornography and prostitution have no moral dimension and should be resolved by the market. Many are indifferent or hostile to religion. I just can't swallow that.

So what is the alternative? A new Freedom Party that strikes at the roots of our problems, rather than just flailing away at the leaves.

First the Freedom Party must assess what's worth keeping:

1) The Constitution: After Y2k, there may be a cry to reject the Constitution as inadequate for the brave new world. Actually, many of the ills that plague us are because our own government has burst its constitutional fetters. The Freedom Party must fight any and all attempts to abandon the Constitution. It must take us back to the seminal concepts that motivated the Founders—that government is, as Jefferson observed, a singularly dangerous beast and must be chained (by the Constitution), and that the Constitution assumes that we will be, in Adams's words, "a moral and religious people."

The Constitution also clearly spells out the very limited powers granted to the federal government, and specifically reserves to the states any other powers. Federal laws and regulations must be required to pass through that constitutional filter *before* they can be implemented.

2) Free markets: As I have said, where there are no free markets, there is no free anything. Our government must become the protector of entrepreneurs, corporate shareholders, property owners, and business, as well as the weak and helpless. Opportunity must be placed ahead of security, while private charity, personal and institutional, must be encouraged and honored.

The Platform

The Freedom Party must radically change the direction and philosophy of government.

1) The Freedom Party must create a system of sound money. Because the backed-by-nothing-but-paper cybermoney is likely to be a part of the wreckage left in the wake of the Y2k tsunami, this could be the opportunity of a lifetime to start over with a new monetary system, as we did at Bretton Woods right after World War II. It may become politically feasible to set up a gold-backed, sound-money system in the wreckage of the old system. There are several possibilities:

- We can, by statute, create a gold-backed currency by requiring that the Treasury maintain a specified gold reserve and redeem paper money for gold.

- We can allow banks to issue currency backed by gold reserves. The Swiss do it that way and have the world's most stable currency. Each Swiss bank has a gold reserve equal to 40 percent of its currency behind its money, and the money is fully convertible into gold upon demand. In fact, if you have a Swiss bank account, your money can be denominated in gold or in any currency you choose.

A gold standard disciplines the money-creation process and serves as an impediment to those who for years have been able to buy votes without the restraint of a gold standard by starting the "printing press"—meaning the money-creation process, no matter what form it takes.

A gold standard would promote price stability, create a predictable background for business decisions, and destroy inflationary expectations for a few generations—at least until our painful lessons are forgotten.

There may be even better free market–based ways to do it that can be devised by wiser men than I.

2) A Freedom Party administration must put the shattered government agencies out of their misery. We can start with the most useless ones: Commerce, Energy, Education, and all of the giveaway agencies. We must take all welfare out of the hands of the federal government. The states can decide how charitable they wish to be with your money. We must offer generous tax benefits for private charitable contributions.

Then we go to work on the more dangerous and intrusive Watchbirds.

Moreover, we must wipe out, by constitutional amendment if necessary, the

Though we may feel helpless in the face of the threats to our society, we must be vigilant about stemming the tide of these problems.

present distorted "separation of church and state" policies of the federal government. Most people think "separation of church and state" is in the Constitution, but those words are nowhere in that document. The Constitution says only that "Congress shall make no law respecting an establishment of religion, or prohibiting the free exercise thereof." That's all. Nothing about excommunicating God from the federal government, schools, and all the rest.

The federal government should have a benign and cooperative attitude toward the charitable and educational activities of churches, without endorsing any particular church or theology. A lot of good could get done that is now prevented by the current church-state policy. We mustn't let a handful of militant antireligion atheists drive God out of government with specious legal arguments.

On the other hand, we must not create a theocracy. No one should be compelled to practice a particular religion or any religion at all or be made a second-class citizen if he doesn't believe in God or belong to the right church. The constitutional fiat that prohibits any religious test for public office must be meticulously honored.

3) The Freedom Party must restructure our education system from the top down. We can start with lopping off the head—the Department of Education. It was created by the Democrats as a political payoff to the National Education Association, the teachers' union that is in reality the single biggest impediment to the education of our children and a major constituency of the Democratic party.

Like all unions, the teachers' unions have evolved into a power mechanism for protecting and promoting the financial self-interest of its members. They have fought teacher-testing and evaluation of their performance based on the tested academic performance of their students. This has protected and institutionalized poor teaching and unfit teachers. The federal government should get out of the education business entirely and place control where it belongs—in the states, which should then pass the responsibility down to even smaller governmental units.

I defy anyone to prove to me that the federal government has educated a single child. It has only drained off tax money for bureaucratic payrolls that might have never left your local school district. In many places our schools are in an advanced state of collapse, exposing our children to physical, moral, and intellectual peril. Our children attend increasingly violent schools and may be exposed to drugs, alcohol, and sex. The prevailing peer pressure, more often than not, is opposed to everything their parents have taught them.

In the classroom our children are too often taught phony history, socialist economics and government theories, and the beauties of "diversity," which usually means homosexuality and unmarried sex. We are moving rapidly in the direction of the Swedish, value-free model.

There are a number of steps the Freedom Party can take to clean up this deteriorating system.

To begin, we must eliminate "tenure" so we can fire incompetent teachers. Teachers must be required to pass periodic state or local tests for competency in the subjects they teach. And for Heaven's sake, don't leave the testing or certification to the federal government.

We have to change the teacher qualification standards and no longer require a teachers' college certificate, only a degree in the teacher's subject, or alternatively, a professional history of competence in private industry. Most schools of education devote at least two-thirds of their required curriculum to teaching teachers socially trendy fads that are of no earthly value to giving the children the survival skills and knowledge the world demands of them, rather than teaching them how to effectively convey honest, fact-based knowledge or real skills to their students.

Too often, schools of education teach teachers how to teach their students to accept deviant sexual practices as mere "alternative life styles," or they promote radical, man-hating feminism and phony ethnic history to give minority children an unearned false sense of "self-esteem" unrelated to achievement or merit.

We also must dramatically increase teacher income to attract better, more competent people, but we cannot reward mediocrity. Amazingly, three-fourths of all teachers come from the lower one-fourth of their college classes. There is one simple reason: the upper three-fourths can get better paying jobs. Teachers should be well rewarded, talented professionals. Our smartest and best people should teach our children, and we should pay them accordingly.

John Silber, chancellor of Boston University and chairman of the Massachusetts Board of Education, has a terrific idea—make the first $30,000 of teachers' salaries *tax-exempt*! This would be an average take-home pay raise of about $9,000—*provided* they pass a demanding test to demonstrate mastery of their subject matter. As it is now, in many states teachers who are certified by a teachers' college or who have a degree in education can teach anything and everything.

This test should be designed by a panel of eminent teachers and scholars who are *not* part of the public-education establishment, and administered by the local school boards as part of their certification requirements.

I would add one additional requirement—that qualifying teachers must also be judged every year by the academic performance of their students, as measured not by grades (which the teachers control), but by tested mastery of the subject.

We must appeal to teachers' self-interest; let them choose. If they don't agree to personal competency testing in their subject or objective evaluations of their teaching skills, no tax exemption. If we increase the take-home pay of competent teachers by $9,000, whether they tutor over the Internet or teach in traditional classrooms, we will attract higher-quality teachers.

Moreover, computers can be more consistent teachers than humans because they are relentlessly and infinitely patient and logical teachers. Several companies have produced brilliant, academically impeccable CD-ROMs that teach effectively and test comprehensively (see the Appendix).

New Internet technologies will soon take us beyond the Internet as we now know it. There is no reason why public education cannot integrate education on the home computer with public-school education. There are enough databases and organized courses on the Internet now to create not only complete K–12 courses, but also college courses. Utah and Colorado are pioneering this concept.

The available technologies enable parents to homeschool their children, or even to supplement their children's public school education with work on home computers, thus freeing parents to choose the educational model they feel is best for their children.

4) *The Freedom Party must filter all legislation* through a constitutional-impact filter, based on how it affects freedom. Perhaps a Freedom Impact Statement should be required. Nearly every existing government regulatory structure should be nuked. If that is not politically doable, half a loaf being better than none (maybe), we should at least take the judicial function out of regulatory agencies and create a separate hearing agency under the court system that is not answerable to the agencies that bring administrative hearings. This will reestablish the separation-of-powers concept that is crucial to the Constitution that the Founders created as a reaction to King George.

5) *Here is a truly diabolical idea:* Move elections to the first Saturday after April 15 so people go to the polls hopping mad about the taxes they pay. I think our elections would have an entirely different result, which leads me to another diabolical idea.

6) *The Voluntary Tax Increase for the Rich:* The government does need money to support a standing military, pay for the time of our president, legislators, judges, customs, and immigration, and regulate interstate commerce. So where should it get the money?

We must pull up by the roots our present income-tax Godzilla—which is an even-bigger flop than the movie, and wreaks much more havoc. Y2k might do this for us. In its place, we must create either a flat tax of no greater than 10 percent or a national sales tax—but not both.

Because the public acceptance of legislation is almost directly related to what it is called, we can sell this idea by calling the flat tax "the voluntary tax increase for the rich." Rich people generally pay low rates because the sheer complexity of the IRS code and regulations creates loopholes and opportunities that can be exploited by expensive accountants and lawyers.

So rather than getting rid of the present tax structure, if it has survived at all, we must allow people to *choose* every year either to pay their taxes under the present structure or to pay a flat tax of 10 percent on *all* income—no deductions, exemptions, shelters, nothing.

If you choose the flat tax, you wouldn't have to prove any deductions; you wouldn't have to hire an army of accountants and attorneys; you wouldn't have to save all your receipts. If you are audited, you would only have to prove you had reported all your income. You could file your tax return on a postcard after an hour of work.

I'm willing to bet that most prosperous people would opt for a higher total flat-tax bill just to get rid of audits, record keeping, accounting, and tax preparers and advisors—a massive hidden tax that costs Americans hundreds of billions of dollars. Then most of the IRS employees could get real jobs.

Try that on for size—the Voluntary Tax Increase for the Rich.

A Fresh Start for America

A catastrophic Y2k event would be a great opportunity. It would clean out the encrusted layers of laws, regulations, and bureaucracy and give us a shot at a fresh start. If we don't grasp the moment and make these structural changes, the pain of the Y2k crisis will have all been in vain. What a waste!

Chapter Thirteen

Do Thy Patient No Harm

The Hippocratic oath which every doctor takes says, "Above all, do thy patient no harm." I have taken great pains to lay out a program that will not hurt you even if events do not turn out as badly as they theoretically could.

You can always eat your food storage, and gold and silver are at historic lows as I write these words, with very little downside risk. The Y2k repair companies whose stocks I have recommended will benefit from being part of the Y2k solution, and there is no question that the Y2k repair work must be done.

Reaffirming that virtue and sexual fidelity will be a part of your life has no downside. Setting up a family organization and preparing a personal history can only add to the sum total of your family's happiness. A new Freedom Party would be needed even if there was no Y2k crisis, and creating a political movement to stand against government intrusions on our freedom is a positive thing, since many of the solutions—or the salvage operation if necessary—can only be implemented politically.

My overriding objective has been to help you and yours have a safer, happier life, whatever the outcome.

Of course, there are those who think it is written in stone that Y2k is the end of the world as we know it, and they are quitting their jobs, burning their bridges behind them, and building small armed fortresses in the mountains. They may turn out to be wiser than I, but I have tried to be a calm voice of reason rather than a scream in the night. Because uprooting your family and heading for the hills is not an option for most of you, and certainly not for all of America, I have tried to propose solutions that you can implement close to home, near community and family support systems and friends.

My message is not fear, but knowledge and preparation as an antidote to fear.

In 1979, while on tour promoting my book *How to Prosper During the Coming Bad Years*, I was on a morning TV show when the host introduced me by saying, "Today we're going to study Psycho-ceramics. I have with me a crackpot from Utah." The host then asked me, "You're the leader of the end-of-the-world, head-for-the-hills survivalist crowd, aren't you?"

"No, I'm not," I responded. "I think they are crazy."

"I can prove it. You moved to Utah, didn't you?"

"Well, this may surprise you, but we have flush toilets in Utah. Of course, we don't have electricity, so we have to watch TV by candlelight."

A year later I came back to the same show, and this time the same host introduced me as "one of America's most distinguished financial analysts"! It seems he had read the book, bought silver, and tripled his money. And he hadn't headed for the hills.

Perhaps your most important protection in hard times is your state of mind.

The media will probably label this a "doom and gloom" book, and just the prospect of a Y2k crisis will scare the wits out of some people. My views of the sexual revolution, moreover, may only trigger guilt, resentment, and hostility in some people, not repentance.

But that's not my intended message. My message is not fear, but knowledge and preparation as an *antidote* to fear. I hope I have nevertheless caused enough concern to motivate people to make some prudent preparations.

It may seem like faint comfort, but hard times may be a blessing in disguise. Many of us feel that life could not go on without our cars, central heating and air conditioning, instant information at our fingertips, social safety nets, medical miracles, movies and TV, and billions of dollars available for discretionary consumer spending. Though we may have forgotten, these things were not "normal" until quite recently—and they're *still* not normal for the vast majority of people on the planet today who are not as fortunate as we.

Our ancestors lived, laughed, cried, loved, and persisted—and flourished—without these things. If you read history, biography, and scripture, you will find that our wealth and luxury give us no more personal happiness today than there was in other eras—perhaps less.

If we find that our lives have changed forever, even in a worst-case scenario, will happiness end?

Adversity has its uses. Sometimes it humbles us into increased spiritual awareness; there are, after all, no atheists in foxholes. If it reunites our families in a common cause, we will certainly be happier.

Happiness does not come from outside ourselves. It always flows from the inside out. It comes from a clear conscience before God and the world. It comes from loving and being loved and being part of something we care about. It comes from being of service. It comes from surmounting insurmountable obstacles or reaching out-of-reach objectives.

It is especially sweet when you recover from adversity and loss.

There have been traumatic and painful events in my life: the death of a toddler because I did not cover our pool; a 1968 business bankruptcy; big business setbacks caused by arrogance-driven bad judgment, which cost me my ten-acre estate and my beloved restored one-hundred-year-old school that I had converted into an office building.

There was a time years ago when my actions cost me the respect of my wife and children until they could accept over time that my contrition and change were genuine. The common denominator of happiness or unhappiness was not money. It was in repenting and striving and achieving and rebuilding. And the real happiness was not in getting there, but in the journey.

Perhaps the most satisfying moment in my life was the day I wrote the $12,000 check that closed the books on my 1968 bankruptcy. It had taken me twelve years, but the moral decision to pay off that half-million dollars in debts—from which I had been discharged by the bankruptcy court—was the best spiritual and business decision I ever made. I knew I could not pay the debt off with a part-time job or out of my personal income. I had to get rich. That decision led to the *Ruff Times* and more prosperity than I had ever dreamed of. But that wasn't the greatest blessing that flowed from that decision. Kay and the children were, and are, proud of me for doing the right thing, even when it was not legally required. I earned their respect.

And with that came a sense of accomplishment that has to be experienced to be understood. It wasn't the success that really mattered, but the struggle that profoundly influenced me and molded me.

Best of all, I am no longer afraid of adversity or failure. I have been there, done that, and it holds no fears for me.

Money is my profession. I have had hundreds of thousands of subscribers and millions of readers, and have met and talked to thousands of them over almost a quarter of a century. I have observed that happiness does not seem to depend on your balance sheet. Happiness seems to be equally distributed among the rich and the poor, and that seems to hold true in the eighty-nine countries I have visited.

I know some super-rich people that I wouldn't change places with for all the gold at the Fed. I know some poor families who find glowing happiness in their mutual love, and even in their struggles. At times I would have traded with them even-up.

I think God wants us to be happy, and it grieves Him when we look for happiness in the wrong places. So take this book as a glorious challenge, and create a home and family where happiness is the common currency, where love rules, and where we rise to challenges with faith and enthusiasm. This will bless your lives, even if the world doesn't change much.

Now let's close the circle and review and summarize.

Diagnosis and Prognosis

Several dangerous events will intersect on or before the beginning of the year 2000.

1) The long economic boom and the bull market in stocks have generated grossly excessive stock valuations, making it an extremely vulnerable, overinflated bubble just looking for an excuse to burst. And there are plenty of excuses in the making, even without Y2k.

2) Our banking and monetary systems have always been smoke and mirrors, but they worked as long as there was confidence, because "money is an idea backed by confidence." Y2k may be a confidence-shattering event, causing a mass movement into cash, and there isn't enough currency printed to meet more than a modest increase in demand.

3) Y2k may be a final kick in the groin to an economy that is already down and hurting. It threatens the infrastructure that delivers to us the services that a modern society must have to continue in business, such as electric power, air-traffic control, railroads, safe water, emergency services (police, fire), etc. Because millions of Americans have become dependent on government money and services, their interruption has almost unthinkable consequences for those millions, especially in the big cities. And the federal government has zero chance of repairing all its systems in time. Interruptions of any of these benefits for even relatively brief periods will cause suffering, fear, and anger, giving rise to civil disorders in areas near large government-dependent populations.

We know there will be a crash effort to repair the mainframe programs and replace or reprogram the embedded chips before the inflexible deadline, but we don't know how many or just which ones will either be repaired or remain functional. We don't know how many embedded chips will be at risk or need to be replaced. But we do know there is a critical shortage of qualified programmers and engineers, and many of them are fleeing government service, either for greener pastures with private industry or to get their families away from the large urban centers where they work.

4) *You can plan on at least a recession before Y2k,* if only because one is long overdue.

5) *The government may not be able to enforce* and administer the tax code, or pay refunds for many months. It may not be able to write the usual fifty million government checks or deliver food stamps or veterans benefits.

6) *The viability of foreign markets is in serious doubt,* because the rest of the world is in worse Y2k shape than we are. And, as Alan Greenspan told Congress, the whole system of international payments is "at risk" because of Y2k.

7) *As this is written, America is in the middle of* a moral and political crisis which I hope will be resolved before you read these words. There is no good outcome. Either we will be in the middle of a paralyzing impeachment crisis with an impotent president limping to the end of his term, or we will be changing horses in the middle of a stream that could better be described as a Class 5 rapids, with world crises all over the place, and despots and terrorists aching to take advantage of our weakness and distraction.

8) *We are caught in a growing family and economic crisis* caused by the sexual revolution, a trend that shows no signs of reversing.

Our children are under a relentless assault by evil and conspiring men. It is no overstatement to describe it as a tidal wave of evil, and moral sandbags are needed to protect us against the filthy flood pouring out of our TVs, our stereos, our PCs, and the neighborhood Cineplex. Our forty-second president is a living reproach to those who wish to fight against this tide, as are those who choose to defend this undefendable man.

I have tried to propose solutions that you can implement close to home, near community and family support systems and friends.

9) *Freedom has been under assault* from our own government for decades, with no political opposition to the trend from either party. In fact, the problem receives no attention outside of a few fringe characters like me.

Prescription

Assuming you have accepted one of my Y2k scenarios, we now come to the question that inevitably comes to mind: How do you handle your debts and allocate your limited cash resources, especially if you don't have enough money to do everything I have recommended?

Of course, if you are in hock up to the hilt, you have no option but to hope that a cybernetic Alzheimer's epidemic erases all memory of your debts, but that is far from a sure thing—and of dubious morality.

Here is a list of priorities, arranged in order of importance, for managing your finances. It's a lot easier if you have a little financial maneuvering room, but if your resources are limited, start at the top and work down.

1) *Panic-proof your family* by accumulating a food-storage program and other consumable necessities. This is most certainly your first priority; don't even start on the rest of the list until you have

done that. Include water, blankets, and warm clothes if you live where there are cold winters (remember, the millennium rollover is in the middle of winter).

2) Get rid of all high-interest consumer debt. Pay off all charge accounts and credit cards. Do not incur any more debt, unless that is the only way you can accumulate a food-storage program. Curtail your spending and start saving money. You don't have much time to get ready. Then if the Millennium Bomb is a dud, you will at least be on sounder financial footing than you were before.

3) Get liquid and stay liquid. Start withdrawing cash in small increments from your bank. Beat the crowd that will probably be there later. If some spark sets off a panic, cash will be king, along with gold, for some indefinite time.

By November 1999 try to have enough cash stashed away to meet all your monthly payments, including your mortgage, for at least six months.

There is a time to sow and a time to reap—and a time to store your seed crop until spring.

4) Start buying silver coins. Start with pre-1965 silver dimes, then quarters, then halves. If you can afford it, buy junk silver by the bag from the vendors recommended in the Appendix. Accumulate up to $3,000 worth (current value) for each family member.

5) After securing your core holdings, buy gold and silver coins as an investment for the bulk of your estate.

6) Preserve your wealth and purchasing power so you can take advantage of the inevitable opportunities after the worst is behind us and almost everything will be on the bargain table. Get out of the stock market immediately, except for T-bonds and defensive stocks like utilities, at least for now. This is not because of Y2k, but because we are probably in a bear market now. Then be prepared to dump even your utility stocks and your T-bonds as a prudent defensive measure as Y2k approaches.

7) If you are near retirement age, don't retire yet. Keep up your cash flow as long as you can, and put away as much of it as possible. Your Social Security check may be at risk.

8) If possible, pay off your mortgage. This is not a financial decision; it is a security decision. As a practical matter, you should either be mortgage-free or have your home mortgaged to the hilt. If you are mortgage-free, you will not have to worry about a place to live, even in a worst case. If you have only a small mortgage, you become a more attractive foreclosure target if your cash flow is cut off and you have nothing with which to make your payments. A bank would rather write off a small loan to foreclose on a home with a big equity than a big loan with a small equity.

9) Learn how to take advantage of the opportunities such volatility always offers. Learn to short the market as explained in Chapter 10, or put at least some of your money in a mutual fund that shorts the market, like Rydex Ursa.

10) Make hard copies of all important documents—passports, birth certificates, loan and mortgage payments, tax returns, CDs and other securities (if you still have any), titles to any property (cars, boats, real estate, etc.).

11) Relocate to a smaller community at least fifty miles away from the big urban centers, even if it means a longer commute. Don't create an isolated retreat in the mountains away from friends, neighbors, and community support. If you own investment real estate in a big city, sell it. If you have rental properties in smaller towns or cities, keep them, especially homes or apartments. I expect a boom in small-town real estate, probably starting sometime in 1999.

Preparing Your Family and America for a Brave New World

As I wrote this last section, I asked myself, what factors would be most critical in a Y2k crisis and beyond? The answer was obvious: the family and the nation.

Strengthening the Family

First you must organize and strengthen your family's lifeboats to ride the waves of the stormy sea ahead. Our crises are as much spiritual as they are technical and financial. We must restore the American family to its former unquestioned preeminence in our civilization, and this effort begins in each individual home.

Of course, you must start with the tangibles—food, water, safety, etc.—since it will be next to impossible to do anything constructive if the home front is not secured. It's hard to remember you are draining the swamp if you are up to your hips in alligators. After those urgent matters are tended to, it will be easier to turn our attention to things that are really more important in the grand scheme of things:

1) Reenthrone God in your home. Begin a calculated program to make Him an ever-present and welcome visitor. Find a church that preaches the gospel of individual redemption and traditional family values, rather than the trendy social gospel *du jour*.

If religious faith is not part of your life, at least start systematically teaching fundamental moral and ethical values. In my opinion, that's a poor second, but it's a lot better than nothing.

2) Set up an extended-family organization for mutual support and for passing your family traditions and values to your children and grandchildren.

3) Prepare family and personal histories, and teach your family about America's traumatic and miraculous birth.

4) Teach family members about Y2k, and urge them to prepare themselves.

5) Be sure your home computers are Y2k compliant, and begin to exploit the computer's vast potential as a tutor for your children, while installing the programs that will protect them from the filth that is so prevalent on the Internet.

Renewing America

Now, after your home and family are secure, you can turn your attention to renewing America. This is a huge project that, paradoxically, will be much easier if the government is in cybernetic ruins. We need a dose of old-fashioned patriotism and political activism by a mass movement of informed and motivated people who have survived the turn of the millennium with their wealth and morale and principles intact.

America is closer to God's plan of free will for man than any nation the world has ever seen. She is great because of her principles and the freedom and opportunity she offers. We must not let our nation die by its own hand, strangled by bureaucracy, laws, and regulations. We must not sell our freedom birthright for the mess of pottage of benefits offered by Washington.

Appendix

Recommended Books

Y2k

You can review and order each of these books at the web site for Time Bomb 2000:

The Millennium Bug: How to Survive the Coming Chaos, by Michael S. Hyatt. $24.95. A great book! Available at most bookstores, and at 888-219-4747. <http://www.michaelhyatt.com>

The Year 2000 Computer Crisis: An Investor's Survival Guide, by Tony Keyes. $29.95. How to invest in a Y2k world. Available at most bookstores. <http://www.y2kinvestor.com>

A Survival Guide for the Year 2000 Problem, by Jim Lord. $29.97. How to protect yourself, your family, your home, your assets, your job, and your personal safety from the effects of Y2k. Available at 888-925-2555. <http://www.survivey2k.com>

Computer Crisis 2000, by Michael Fletcher. $12.95. Invaluable for those who are self-employed or have a home business. Available at 613-692-0752.

Time Bomb 2000: What the Year 2000 Computer Crisis Means to You!, by Edward and Jennifer Yourdon. $19.95. An exceptional book from a legendary software giant. Must have. Available at most bookstores.

The Year 2000 Software Problem: Quantifying the Costs and Assessing the Consequences, by Capers Jones. $29.95. Available at most bookstores.

Survival and Technology

Boy Scout Manual. Great reference material on basic survival skills. Available from any local store that sells Boy Scout supplies.

Making the Best of Basics: Family Preparedness Handbook, by James Talmage Stevens. $19.95. This is the best-selling book ever on basic storage programs for everyday necessities. Available in most bookstores, and at 888-925-2555.

Don't Get Caught with Your Pantry Down, by James Talmage Stevens. $29.95. Includes the most complete directory of preparedness vendors. Available in most bookstores, and at 888-925-2555.

Info Power III, by Matthew Lesko. $29.95. Available in the reference section at any good bookstore.

Advisory Newsletters and Political Publications

The *Ruff Times*. P.O. Box 887, Springville, UT 84663; 800-773-7833, 801-489-8681. <http://www.rufftimes.com>

Richard Russell's Dow Theory Letters. One of my favorites, written by a wise old pro. An excellent source of market information. P.O. Box 1759, La Jolla, CA 92038.

Human Events. A must-read for politically concerned conservatives. Published by Eagle Publishing, One Massachusetts Avenue, NW, Washington, DC 20001; 800-787-7557, 888-467-4448.

Gold Stock Mining Report, by Bob Bishop, P.O. Box 1217, Lafayette, CA 94549. 925-284-1165.

Remnant Review, by Gary North. Y2k's reigning pessimist, but a cornucopia of Y2k information. Published by Agora Publishing, Inc., 410-234-0691. <http://www.garynorth.com>

The *Y2k Investor*, by Tony Keyes. One of the pioneers of the Y2k "movement." 703-893-8808. <http://www.y2kinvestor.com>

Year 2000 Survival Newsletter, by Jim Lord. 888-925-2555. <http://www.survivey2k.com>

The *McAlvany Intelligence Advisor*, by Don McAlvany. 800-528-0559. <http://www.mcalvany.com>

Forecasts & Strategies, by Mark Skousen. Published by Phillips Publishing, Inc., 301-340-7788.

Gold Newsletter, by Jim Blanchard, 2400 Jefferson Highway, Suite 600, Jefferson, LA 70121; 800-877-8847.

U.S. & World Early Warning Report, by Richard Maybury. 800-509-5400.

Strategic Investment, by James Dale Davidson and Lord William Rees-Mogg. Published by Agora Publishing, Inc., 410-234-0515. <http://www.agoraworldwide.com>

World Wide Web Sites

<http://www.rufftimes.com>: The *Ruff Times* newsletter.

<http://www.survivey2k.com>: Jim Lord's web site featuring his book, newsletter, speaking schedule, and other Y2k-oriented materials.

<http://www.y2kinvestor.com>: Tony Keyes's web site.

<http://www.year2000.com>: Peter deJager's Year 2000 Information Center. A must-read! This is where it all started. The press-clippings section is particularly useful.

<http://www.y2ktimebomb.com>: Westergaard Year 2000. Great collection of Y2k experts who write weekly columns. Terrific archive of Y2k articles.

<http://www.year2000.com/articles/nfarticles.html>: One-stop shopping for all of the Y2k articles appearing in the daily press around the world.

<http://www.garynorth.com>: The leading Y2k doom-and-gloomer. A superb resource because of the incredible collection of links to definitive Y2k information.

<http://www.senate.gov/~bennett/y2k.html>: The Senate Special Committee on the Y2k Technology Problem. Senator Robert Bennett (R-UT), Chairman.

<http://www.y2kinvestor.com/links.htm>: One of the most extensive collections of Y2k-related links, categorized by subject.

<http://www.y2klinks.com>: Excellent resource for a wide variety of Y2k-related links.

<http://www.itworks.be/bookmark/year2000/index.html>: United Kingdom–based site with a European bent. A terrific site.

<http://www.comlinks.com>: Lots of good general Y2k information and a hefty archive.

<http://www.economist.com>: *The Economist* magazine.

<http://www.washtimes.com>: The web site for the *Washington Times*.

<http://ourworld.compuserve.com/homepages/Dreyer_infonet/politics.htm>: The Conservative Politics Network.

<http://www.drudgereport.com>: Site of the infamous journalist Matt Drudge.

<http://www.marketpartners.com>: The American Bankers Association's exclusive provider of Y2k information, products, and resources for its membership.

<http://www.spr.com/html/year_2000_problem.htm>: Expert metrics on why this problem will be so terribly costly and hugely disruptive.

<http://www.y2kjournal.com>: Site for the *Year 2000 Journal*, which contains mostly technical information.

<http://www.implement.co.uk/milweb1.htm>: *Millennium Watch*, the official newsletter of the United Kingdom's government and Taskforce 2000.

<http://www.comlinks.com>: *ComLinks* magazine. Alan Simpson's site. Especially useful collection of articles on the legal implications of Y2k.

<http://www.itpolicy.gsa.gov>: General Services Administration (GSA). Good kickoff point of U.S. government sites.

<http://www.gao.gov>: The General Accounting Office (GAO) web site. Downloadable archive of reports on the status of Y2k in various government agencies.

<http://www.itaa.org>: Information Technology Association of America (ITAA). A major trade association that has been very active on the Y2k scene. Maintains an extensive Y2k calendar, listing conferences available nationwide.

<http://www.mitre.org>: The MITRE Corporation. A federally funded research and development center. Particularly good material on the impact of Y2k on personal computers with links to vendors offering repair software.

<http://www.y2kwomen.com>: Karen Anderson's site devoted to Y2k issues for women and families. Lots of good preparedness advice.

<http://www.millennia-bcs.com>: Paloma O'Riley's Cassandra project, a grassroots, community preparedness organization. Best Internet collection on this subject.

<http://www.webcom.com/infinet>: The Montana Market Place web site is loaded with emergency essential products and information.

Precious Metals Dealers

Investment Rarities, Inc., 7850 Metro Parkway, Minneapolis, MN 55425; 800-328-1860, 612-853-0700. Friends for twenty-three years. <www.investmentrarities.com>

Liberty Mint, 651 Columbia Lane, Provo, UT 84604; 800-877-6468, 801-373-9300. I am a minority shareholder. <www.libertymint.com>

Also recommended:

Camino Coin, 851 Burlway Rd #202, Burlingame, CA 94010; 800-348-8001, 650-348-3000. Very dependable and competitive.

Gold Mining Stockbrokers

Rick Rule (800-477-7853).

National Securities (800-532-7574).

Mining Stocks

Seniors: Newmont Mining and Newmont Gold (about to merge); Barrick Gold Corp. (ABX/NYSE); Euro-Nevada (EN/T); and Goldfields of South Africa (GDFDY), Rick Rule's favorite.

Junior producers: Aurizon Mines (ARZ), Manhattan Mining (MAN/TE), Western Copper (WTC/TSE), and Viceroy Resources (VOY).

Exploration companies: Madison Resources (MNP/V), my favorite; Manhattan (MAN/TSE); Rio Narcea (RNG/T); Miramar (MAE/T).

Emerging producers: Greenstone Resources (GRE), Iamgold Corp (IMG), Metallica Resources (MR), Rio Narcea Gold Mines, Ltd. (RNG).

Tiny producer: Ariel Resources (AU).

Other exploration companies: Golden Star (GSC), Solomon Resources (SRB), Nevsun Resources (MSI), and Channel Resources (CHU).

Mutual Funds

Rydex Ursa Fund (800-820-0888) for bear markets.

Benham Gold Equity Index Fund (800-472-3389).

U.S. Gold Shares (800-873-8637).

Invesco Gold (800-525-8085).

Food Storage

Martens Health and Survival (800-824-7861).
Preparedness Plus (800-588-5412).

Vitamins, Minerals, and Protein

Meleleuca: Tim Ruff (888-846-7833). He is my son, but I have no financial interest.

Neo Life: Norvel and Joann Martens (800-824-7861). I've done business with them for twenty-five years.

Usana: John Carstensen (800-481-4900). I especially like their Vitamin C.

Quality Educational Software

Many so-called Educational Software programs are really "Edutainment"—5 percent education and 95 percent entertainment.

You can buy *Pride's Guide to Educational Software* at your local bookstore. Author Mary Pride details nearly every title.

Here is a quick reference to some of the best choices in each curriculum category:

- *Math Curriculum*

  Tomorrow's Promise Math, by Jostens Learning

  Lifetime Library Math & Algebra, by Learning, Inc.

- *Math Drill*

  Professor Finkle's Times Table Factory, by Sing & Learn Software

  Quarter Mile Math, by Barnum Software

- *Preschool Math and Reading*

  Rusty and Rosy Read with Me, by the Waterford Institute

  Professor Finkle's Math Mania, by Sing & Learn Software

- *Reading and Language Arts*

  Tomorrow's Promise Reading & Language Arts, by Jostens Learning

  Plato Personal Pilot, by TRO Learning

- *Science*

  Tomorrow's Promise Science, by Jostens Learning

  Adi's Science, by Sierra

- *Spelling*

  Tomorrow's Promise Spelling, by Jostens Learning

  Language Tune-Up Kit, by JWOR Enterprises

- *Test Preparation*

  Ace That Test, by TRO Learning

- *Typing*

  Typing Tutor 7, by Davidson & Associates, Inc.

You may be able to find some of these programs at your local computer store. For more information contact educational software consultant Vicki Chick at 800-487-9449. She is a seasoned home-schooler.

Homeschooling Information

Home School Legal Defense Association
P.O. Box 3000
Purcellville, VA 20314
Tel: 540-338-5600
Fax: 540-338-1952

About the Author

(Just so you know me!)

I am sixty-eight years old and have been married to a celestial lady, Kay, for forty-three years. We have thirteen children—nine homemade and four adopted—and forty-eight grandchildren, and we have endured the accidental death of one child. We have also raised eighteen foster children, mostly teenagers.

I have been publishing the *Ruff Times*, an international financial and political newsletter, since 1975.

I am opinionated and outspoken, and sometimes controversial. I have been fighting an extra thirty-five pounds tooth and nail for all my adult life—unfortunately, mostly with tooth.

I love fishing, BYU football, and the Utah Jazz, and our family's spiritual life is the centerpiece of my life. I am addicted to jokes (good and bad) and believe that personal peace of mind, rooted in a clear conscience and a working relationship with God, is the most important thing in life.

As I contemplate an event-filled life, I remember a neighborhood barbecue when we played a game where we had to recount things we had done that we thought nobody else there had. That fun trip down Memory Lane started my memory running wild. This information should at least give you a flavor of the man whose advice you are considering taking:

- I traded one spool of eight-pound test monofilament fishing line to a chief of a village in the Amazon jungle in return for two monkey-skull necklaces, a blow gun and darts, a bow and arrows, and an Anaconda snake skin. And, after consulting with Kay, I respectfully declined the chief's offer of a night with one of his wives in return for a second spool.

- I've walked through the dramatic story of the death of Rasputin, the Mad Monk, right on the actual murder scene in a restored palace in Leningrad.

- I've interviewed (with Jack Anderson) President Vaclav Havel of Czechoslovakia in Prague Palace while he was wearing Nike shoes and a UCLA Bruins sweatshirt.

- I've visited the Forbidden City and the Great Wall in China, Machu Pichu, the Imperial Palace in Bangkok, and wild-game preserves in Kenya and South Africa; snorkeled on the Great Barrier Reef and watched great sea turtles lay their eggs and their baby turtles hatch; cruised or floated the Nile, the Amazon, the Danube, the Mississippi, the Columbia, the Potomac, the Kenai, the Truckee, the Klamath, the Sacramento, the Baltic, the Mediterranean, the Caribbean, the China Sea, the Sea of Japan, the Gulf of California, the Alaska Passage, and assorted Alaskan rivers.

- Ralph Nader and I held a joint press conference in the U.S. Capitol Building—and actually agreed on something.

- I visited with George Bush in the Oval Office.

- I've caught every major North American freshwater game fish (except a muskie), an 85-pound halibut, a world-record African pompano (with Kay's help), and a 125-pound sturgeon on 20-pound test line.

- Ollie North, my Washington staff, and I persuaded Ronald Reagan to send Stinger missiles to the Afghan Freedom Fighters, which bogged down the Soviet army in Afghanistan for six years, which led to Soviet bankruptcy, which led to Gorbachev withdrawing Russian financial and military support from Eastern Europe, Cuba, and Nicaragua, which led to a breakout of freedom, which led to the crash of the Iron Curtain.

- I had a modest fifteen-year career as an aspiring opera and musical-theater singer.

- I have sung solos with the Mormon Tabernacle Choir, the Philadelphia orchestra, the National Symphony, and on the *Ed Sullivan Show*.

- I performed, conducted, or directed hundreds of performances of Gilbert and Sullivan operas and am currently the general manager of the Utah Lyric Opera Society.

- I had my own national TV talk show and radio commentary in more than three hundred markets.

- I was called a liar in an angry speech on the floor of Congress by Congressman Neal of South Carolina.

- I was a church choir director at age sixteen.

- I was denounced by Pravda, Tass, and Soviet-controlled radio Kabul as a "radical reactionary."

- I once refused a phone call from an angry President Ronald Reagan. He swore at me, then sent me an unsolicited, personally autographed portrait as a peace offering.

- A ruffled Jimmy Carter succeeded in knocking fifty stations off my radio syndicate by threatening them with license-renewal trouble.

- My wife Kay and I have been through thick and thin (I used to be thin) for forty-three years, probably because we have one thing in common: we're both in love with the same man—me!

- We masterminded the successful write-in campaign that elected Congressman Ron Packard of Orange County, California.

- I broke up an orphanage run by American pedophiles in Bangkok, which resulted in jailing them and caused an international incident between ABC-TV, me, and the Thai government. The Ruff Foundation now supports the children (and can use your financial help).

- I have been on *Donahue, Good Morning America, Today, Merv Griffin, Dinah Shore, Oprah, Regis and Kathie Lee, Crossfire, PBS Late Night, Nightline, Char-*

lie Rose, *McNeil-Lehrer*, *Wall Street Week*, and hundreds of local radio and TV talk shows.

- My book *How to Prosper During the Coming Bad Years* topped the best-seller lists for two years and was the biggest-selling financial book in history.

- I learned to play racquetball at age forty-nine (I'm slow, but crafty), despite being a nonathlete all my life.

- I made an emergency landing in my single-engine aircraft with oil all over my windshield, obscuring my vision and forcing me to lean out the side window to see where I was going.

- I had two serious death threats, one from the pedophiles I was after in Bangkok, and the other from a sleazy competitor who was later murdered in Belize by unknown assailants.

- We brought an $8.4 billion government bailout of the big banks to a screeching halt for six months.

- I had dinner with Chiang Kai-shek and Madame Chiang; the secretary to the king of Denmark; and President Synghman Rhee, the father of modern Korea.

- I sang the national anthem at the White House numerous times as a soloist for the Air Force Band and Singing Sergeants.

- I sold 100,000 copies of an album, *Howard Ruff Sings*, with the Osmond brothers and the BYU Philharmonic and A Capella Choir as my backup groups.

- I read aloud the Apostle Paul's sermon in the restored amphitheater at Ephesus on the Turkish coast, from the exact spot where he stood when he incurred the wrath of the silversmiths who sold statues of the Goddess Diana. They ran Paul out of town (Acts 19:22–41). They ignored me.

- I caught a piranha in the Amazon and ate it (poetic justice?).

- I once traveled nine thousand miles from Bangkok to attend a Utah Jazz game.

- I've owned nine airplanes and logged 3,500 hours as "pilot in command."

- I was forced into bankruptcy in 1968 by a newspaper strike, then paid off $500,000 (plus interest) in debts from which I had been legally discharged. (It took me twelve years.)

- Evelyn Wood personally taught me to read three thousand words per minute, and I then developed the marketing and advertising that made her famous.

- I founded a Washington lobby and a PAC.

- I built my own trout lake in my front yard.

- I was roasted (for fun) by Lorne Greene of *Bonanza* and Chuck Conners of *The Rifleman*.

- I cruised the Mediterranean with Art Linkletter.

- I ate a mud crab and a morton bay bug in Australia, and squid cooked in its own ink over rice in Uruguay.

- I took over Madame Tussaud's Wax Works in London one night for a private party for my subscribers.

- Kay and I flew to Ireland just to spend a weekend in a castle with Elizabeth Taylor. Unfortunately, she didn't show, so we spent a weekend in a castle in Ireland without Elizabeth Taylor.

- I have a major role in the movie *Rockwell*, released on video. One unenlightened critic called my performance as a corrupt federal judge "not much of a stretch."

- I've written and sold more than three million words.

Whenever I think I've accomplished a lot, I just remind myself that when Mozart was my age... he'd been dead for more than thirty years!

I intend to at least double this list by retirement in twenty-two years at age ninety.

Acknowledgments

A ny book is the product of many helpful hands. I would like to express my gratitude to the *Ruff Times* staff. Without their help, I probably would have never finished this project. Joann Allen, my assistant for eighteen years, typed part of it, helped with the research, and copied and faxed her little heart out. Anthony Ramon, my son and general manager, saw that I had all the tools to do the job. Annette Whitefield, our office manager, spent countless hours fixing my balky and perverse computers. Robert Noble, my research assistant, did most of the research on the "Power to the President" chapter and supplied many of the numbers in several chapters.

The staff at Regnery was stupendous: Jeff Carneal, president of Eagle Publishing (and my former personal assistant, before he grew up); Jed Donahue, my boy-genius editor; and Richard Vigilante, who made some invaluable recommendations about the organization of the book.

I am also grateful for Y2k experts who gave me an eye-opening education on the subject: Jim Lord, who first brought Y2k to my attention; Tony Keyes, who worked with me on how to invest in Y2k; and Michael Hyatt, whose book, *The Millennium Bug*, gave me some very powerful insights. My sons, Eric and David Ruff, and my son-in-law, Lars Rasmussen, either challenged my work, which made me think things through, or fixed my computer when it got nasty with me.

Last of all, Kay, my wife, tolerated with infinite patience the thousands of hours when I ignored her while I sat hunched over my computer keyboard, as this grew from a project to an obsession.

Index

Adams, John, 7
Adultery, 123–124
Advertising
  investment opportunities, 186
Advisory newsletters, 240–241
Airlines
  investment risks, 185
  Y2k crisis, 60–61
American Eagle coins, 168–169
American history
  importance to families, 212
Apparel
  investment risks, 185
Asia
  economic crisis, 31–32
  Y2k compliance, 63
Aurizon Mines, 192
Austrian Philharmonic bullion coin, 173
Author's biography, 249–255
Automobile industry
  investment risks, 185–186
  Y2k crisis, 78

Bank notes, 26
Bankruptcy
  author's experience, 15–16, 229–230

Banks
  bank failures, 26
  bank notes, 26
  cybermoney, 22, 27–30
  fractional-reserve banking system, 26
  savings and loan associations, 92–93
  Y2k crisis, 29–30, 50–51
Barrick Gold, 192
Barter system, 23–24, 161
B complex vitamins, 155–156
"Bear raids," 198
Benham Gold Equity Index fund, 194
Bennett, Robert, 55–56, 73
Berkeley, Alfred R., III, 51–52
BGR Precious Metals, 194
Bishop, Bob, 192
Blacks
  illegitimacy rates, 8, 126
Book recommendations, 239–240
Bradbury, Ray, 83
Brokers
  Y2k crisis, 51–52
Bronfenbrenner, Urie, 119, 127
Building industry
  investment risks, 185

Bullion coins, 176
Bullion Reserve, 170
Bush, George
 state of emergency declaration, 76
Business Week, 54
Byte, 48

CACI International, Inc., 187
Canadian Maple Leaf, 173
Certification of teachers, 223–224
China
 economic crisis, 32
Churches
 family security and, 207, 209–210
 separation of church and state policies, 221–222
Civil servants, 87
Clinton, Bill
 budget deficit, 106
 potential Y2k action, 79–80
 sex scandals, 8, 121, 124
 state of emergency declaration, 76
 Y2k commission, 40–41
Clinton, Hillary, 205
Computers. *See also* Internet; Year 2000 computer crisis
 cybermoney, 22, 27–30
 educational CD-ROMs, 213, 245–246
 investment opportunities, 187
 pornography, 213–214
 testing for Y2k compliance, 70
Congressional Record, 96–97
Constitution
 assessment of, 219
Construction industry
 investment risks, 185
Contrubis, John, 75–76
Coronas, 173
Cowles, Rick, 55
Credit cards
 paying off, 234
Crime, 126–127

Cuban Missile Crisis, 137–138
Cybermoney, 22, 27–30
Cyber Patrol, 214

Data recording functions, 46
Data services
 investment opportunities, 187
Date functions, 45
Date-programmable devices, 48
Davidson, James Dale, 186
Dehydrated foods, 147–149
Democrats
 failures of, 219
 formation of the National Education Association, 222
Depression
 Y2k crisis predictions, 36
Dividends, 199–201
Documents
 copying, 235
Dodd, Christopher, 54, 73
Downticks, 197
Dutch Guilder, 173

Economy. *See also* Money
 adapting to market volatility, 20–21
 Asian economic crisis, 31–32
 potential problems from Y2k crisis, 3–6, 36
 recession, 31
 stock market predictions, 30–31
Education
 options, 213
 recommended software, 245–247
 restructuring, 222–225
 teacher certification, 223–224
 using Internet technologies, 224
Electric power industry
 Y2k crisis, 53–56
Embedded chips, 38–39, 43, 44–48
Emergency food storage. *See* Food-storage programs
Energy self-sufficiency, 157

Entitlement programs
inflation and, 6
Environmental Protection Agency,
100–101
Euro, 63
Euro-Nevada, 192
Europe
Y2k compliance, 63
Executive orders, 75–81

FAA. *See* Federal Aviation Administration
Families
author's family, 14–15
education options, 213
erosion of the family, 10
government programs as replacement for family, 205–208
importance of, 72, 123
relocating to a smaller community,
68–69, 235
sexual revolution and, 118–120
social purpose, 8
strengthening the family, 236–237
suggestions for family success,
209–216
Swedish laws and family structure,
207–209
Family histories, 211–212
Family Research Council, 125–126
Famines, 139
Farmers
effect of Y2k crisis, 142
FDA. *See* Food and Drug Administration
Federal Aviation Administration
Y2k crisis, 60–61
Federal Emergency Management
Agency, 78
Federal Register, 75–76, 96–97
Federal Reserve
available currency, 34
Federal Trade Commission, 101

Fiat money, 24
FICA taxes, 106–108
Financial Management Services, 114
Fiscal years
computer problems, 62
Fishing
for food supply, 158–159
Flat tax proposal, 225–226
Fletcher, David, 61
Food and Drug Administration, 88,
99–100, 151
Food-storage programs
B complex vitamins, 155–156
canned foods, 150–151
commercial programs, 149
cost of, 147
distinguished from hoarding,
144–146
do-it-yourself programs, 148
frozen foods, 150–151
importance of, 135–143
information sources, 245
nutritional problems, 149–150
nutritional supplements, 149–151
providing protein, 153–154
recommendations for, 150–154,
156
shelf life of foods, 147, 150
sugar and honey, 154–155
where to store food, 147
Fractional-reserve banking system,
26
Freedom Impact Statement, 225
Freedom Party
assessment of the Constitution, 219
education system restructuring,
222–225
free market protection, 220
government agency reform, 221–222
legislation filtering, 225
monetary system, 220–221
platform for, 220–226
tax reform, 225–226

Free markets
protection of, 220
Freeze-dried foods, 147–149
French Rooster, 173
FTC. *See* Federal Trade Commission

Gent, Michael, 54
Global Resource Investments, 192
Gold
avoiding scams, 174–177
functions, 161
gold coins, 171–173
gold mining stockbrokers, 244
gold/silver ratio, 166
the gold standard, 162, 220–221
monetary history, 24–27
mutual funds, 193–194
precious metals dealers, 243–244
price cycles, 164–165
stockpiling, 162–163
stocks, 191–193, 244–245
world gold market, 163
Gold and Silver Report, 170
Goldfields of South Africa, 192
Gold Mining Stock Report, 192
Good-until-canceled orders, 199
Gore, Al
potential Y2k action, 79, 80
Government agencies. *See also specific
agency by name*
distrust of, 94–95
Federal Register, 75–76, 96–97
government programs as replacement for family, 205–208
growth of government power, 97–98
importance of renewing America,
217–218, 237
principles of government, 98–99
recommendations for the Freedom
Party, 221–222
regulation by, 84–94
Y2k crisis, 56–60
Great Britain
Y2k compliance, 63

Greenspan, Alan, 42
GTC orders. *See* Good-until-canceled
orders
Gun ownership, 158–159

Hartline, Robert H., 92–94
Hatch, Orrin, 208
High-level management systems,
47–48
Hispanics
illegitimacy rates, 8
Home School Legal Defense Associ-
ation, 213, 247
Homestate Group Year-2000 Fund,
188
Homosexuals, 128–129
Honey, 155
Horizons, 187
Horn, Steve, 58, 73
*How to Prosper During the Coming
Bad Years*, 9, 115
Hunting
for food supply, 158–159
Hyatt, Michael S., 28

Illegitimacy rates, 8, 126
Inflation
Y2k predictions, 5–6
Interest rates
stock market and, 180
Internal Revenue Service. *See also* Taxes
author's experience, 89
estate-planning, 211
Y2k crisis, 59
International issues
Asian economic crisis, 31–32
famines, 139
world gold market, 163
Y2k crisis, 33, 63–64
Internet. *See also* Computers
education technologies, 224
recommended web sites, 241–243
Invesco Gold, 194
Investment Advisor's Act of 1948, 90

Investment Rarities, 174
Investments. *See also* Gold; Silver
 interest rates, 180
 opportunities during Y2k crisis,
  182–183, 186–188
 pre-Y2k opportunities, 179–182
 risks during Y2k crisis, 183–186
 short selling, 194–202
 stock market, 30–31, 180
 stop-loss orders, 189–190, 196, 199
IRA coins, 169
IRS. *See* Internal Revenue Service
It Takes a Village, 205

Japan
 economic crisis, 31–32
*Jim Lord's Year 2000 Survival
 Newsletter*, 44
Jones, Capers, 57–58
Junk silver, 167

Kangaroo Nuggets, 173
Katzen, Sally, 58
Keane, Inc., 187
Keyes, Tony, 183–188
Krugerrands, 173–174

Legal issues
 government regulatory agencies,
  86–89
 Y2k crisis, 52–53
Leveraged contracts, 176–177
Libertarians
 failures of, 219
Liberty Mint, 17, 169, 174
Life stories
 importance to families, 211–212
Limit orders, 198–199
Linkletter, Art, 15
Lord, Jim, 41, 44–48

Madison Resources, 192
Mainframe-computer programs
 fixing the Y2k problem, 49

Maintenance tracking functions,
 46–47
Making the Best of Basics, 70–71, 149
Manhattan exploration company, 192
Manhattan Mining, 192
Margin calls, 196, 198
Market orders, 198–199
McAlvany Advisor, 54–55
Medication supplies, 159
Meleleuca, 154
Microcomputers, 37–39
Millennial Trade Units, 169
Millennium Bug. *See* Year 2000 com-
 puter crisis
The Millennium Bug, 28
Mining stocks, 244–245
Miramar, 192
Money. *See also* Gold; Silver
 bank notes, 26
 cybermoney, 22, 27–30
 Federal Reserve's available supply, 34
 fiat money, 24
 fractional-reserve banking system, 26
 new monetary system recommen-
  dations, 220–221
 paper-money system, 25–27
 purpose of money, 23–24
 the true nature of money, 22–23
Morality. *See* Sexual revolution
Mortgages
 paying off, 235
Mr. X, 192
Mutual funds
 gold, 193–194
 information sources, 245
 short selling, 201–202
 Y2k mutual fund, 188

National Association of Securities
 Dealers, 51–52
National debt, 106
National Education Association, 222
National emergencies, 75–78
National Securities, 192

Neo-Life Company, 154
NERC. *See* North American Electric
    Reliability Council
Net Nanny, 214
Newmont Gold, 192
Newmont Mining, 192
Newsweek, 39–40
The 99 problem, 62
Nixon, Richard, 27, 162
North American Electric Reliability
    Council, 54
Nuclear Regulatory Agency
    Y2k crisis, 53
Numismatic coins, 176
Nutritional supplements, 149–151,
    153–154, 245

Office of Management and Budget, 58

Paper-money system, 25–27
Penthouse, 129
Pesos, 173
Playboy, 129–130
Political publications, 240–241
Ponzi fraud, 109
Pornography, 129–130, 213–214
Powdered milk, 153
Precious metals dealers, 243–244
Presidential power, 75–81
Protein supplements, 153–154
Public schools. *See* Education
Puritan work ethic, 117–118

Railroads
    investment risks, 185
    Y2k crisis, 56
Reagan, Ronald
    executive order, 77
Recession, 31
Reformers, 206
Regulatory agencies. *See also* Gov-
    ernment agencies; *specific agency by
    name*

Religion
    family security and, 207, 209–210
    separation of church and state poli-
        cies, 221–222
Repair companies
    investment opportunities, 187–188
Republicans
    failures of, 219
Rio Narcea, 192
Role models, 129
Roman empire, 3–4
Roosevelt, Franklin D., 27, 76
Rosenthal, Dan, 170
Rossotti, Charles, 59
Ruffco, 174–175
Ruff Hou$e, 92–94
Ruff Times, 7, 17–19, 71, 90, 192
Rule, Rick, 192, 194
Rydex Ursa fund, 201–202

Satellites, 47
Savings and loan associations, 92–93
Scarcity premiums, 167
Schools. *See* Education
Securities and Exchange Commis-
    sion, 90–92
Self-sufficiency. *See also* Food-storage
    programs
    energy, 157
    hunting and fishing, 158–159
    medications, 159
    stockpiling items, 158
    water storage, 158
Senate Special Committee on the
    Y2k Technology Problem, 54, 55
Sexual revolution
    children living in unmarried family
        units, 124–126
    consensus of society, 118
    economic aspect of, 121–124,
        130–131
    homosexuals, 128–129
    importance of male role models, 129

Sexual revolution *(continued)*
  pornography, 129–130
  public reaction to Clinton sex scandals, 121
  as threat to family support structure, 118–120, 125
  TV talk show reaction, 115–116
Short selling
  borrowing stock, 196–197
  concept, 195
  dividends, 199–201
  placing an order, 198–199
  shorting on margin, 196
  stop-loss orders, 199
  strategies, 200–202
  uptick rule, 197–198
Silber, John, 223–224
Silver
  American Eagle coins, 168–169
  buying on margin, 169–170
  gold/silver ratio, 166
  Millennial Trade Units, 169
  monetary history, 24–25
  price cycles, 164–165
  scarcity premiums, 167
  silver coins, 166–168
  stockpiling, 162–163
Single-parent families, 8–9
Single-purpose systems, 47
Smith Barney, 52
Social Security Administration
  depletion of funds, 108–111, 108–114
  FICA taxes, 106–108
  trust fund, 104–105
  Y2k crisis, 60, 113–114
Society
  coming changes, 22
  erosion of the family, 10
State programs
  Y2k crisis, 60
States of emergency, 76–77
Stevens, James Talmage, 70–71, 149

Stock market
  bear raids, 198
  dividends, 199–201
  gold stocks, 191–193
  interest rates and, 180
  mining stocks, 244–245
  opportunities during Y2k crisis, 186–188
  predictions, 30–31
  pre-Y2k opportunities, 180–182
  risks during Y2k crisis, 183–186
  short selling, 194–202
  stock splits, 199–200
  stop-loss orders, 189–190, 196, 199
  uptick rule, 197–198
Stock splits, 199–200
Stop-loss orders, 189–190, 196, 199
Strategic Investment Newsletter, 186
Sugar, 154–155
Survival Guide for the Year 2000 Problem, 44
Sweden
  family structure, 207–209
Swiss Francs, 173

TAVA Technologies, 187–188
Taxes. *See also* Internal Revenue Service
  flat tax proposal, 225–226
T-bonds
  investment opportunities, 180–182
Teachers' union, 222
Tenure
  for teachers, 223
Time Bomb 2000: What the Year 2000 Computer Crisis Means to You!, 57
Time/duration functions, 45–46
Tocqueville, Alexis de, 85
Transportation. *See* Airlines; Railroads
Tytler, Alexander Fraser, 122

Uptick rule, 197–198
U.S. Bureau of the Census, 124

U.S. Department of Agriculture, 100–101
U.S. Department of Education, 222
U.S. Department of Health and Human Services, 206
U.S. Gold Eagle, 173–174
U.S. Gold Shares, 194
U.S. News and World Report, 37, 54
U.S. Treasury Department
  web site, 106
  Y2k crisis, 182–183
Usana, 154
Utilities
  stock opportunities, 180–182
  Y2k crisis, 53–56

Value system. *See* Crime; Families; Sexual revolution
Vancouver Exchange, 191
Viceroy Resources, 192
Vitamin B complex, 155–156

Wachter, Michael, 113
Wareforce, 188
Water storage, 158
Water systems
  Y2k crisis, 61–62
Web sites, 241–243
Welfare, 122, 126
Western Copper, 192
Whites
  illegitimacy rates, 8, 126
Wood-burning stoves, 157

Year 2000 computer crisis
  action steps, 68–71, 81–82, 233–237
  airlines, 60–61
  avoiding panic, 227–229
  banking system, 50–51
  brokers, 51–52
  cause of, 36–37, 41–44
  cybermoney and, 27, 29–30
  electric power grid, 53–56

Year 2000 computer crisis *(continued)*
  embedded chips, 38–39, 43, 44–48
  executive orders, 77–81
  fixing the problem, 49–50
  food supply and, 135–143
  government agencies, 56–60
  international compliance, 33, 63–64
  investment opportunities and risks, 182–188
  litigation predictions, 52–53
  microcomputers, 37–39
  the 99 problem, 62
  potential economic results of, 3–5, 35–36, 64–68
  predicted effects of, 39–40, 64–68, 231–233
  railroads, 56
  recommended books, 239–240
  repair companies, 187–188
  state programs, 60
  testing home computers, 70
  water systems, 61–62
The Year 2000 Software Problem: Quantifying the Costs and Assessing the Consequences, 57
The Y2k Advisor, 183
The Y2k Investor, 183
Yourdon, Ed, 57

Zero-plus ticks, 197–198
ZMAX, 188